NOTEBOOKS

1960-1977

Athol Fugard

NOTEBOOKS

1960-1977

THEATRE COMMUNICATIONS GROUP

1984

Notebooks: 1960–1977 is published by Theatre Communications Group, Inc., 355 Lexington Ave., New York, NY 10017.

TCG gratefully acknowledges public funds from the National Endowment for the Arts and the New York State Council on the Arts in addition to the generous support of the following foundations and corporations: Alcoa Foundation; ARCO Foundation; AT&T Foundation; Beatrice Foundation; Citibank; Common Wealth Fund; Consolidated Edison Company of New York; Eleanor Naylor Dana Charitable Trust; Dayton Hudson Foundation; Exxon Corporation; Ford Foundation; James Irvine Foundation; Jerome Foundation; Andrew W. Mellon Foundation; Metropolitan Life Foundation; National Broadcasting Company; New York Times Company Foundation; Pew Charitable Trusts; Philip Morris Companies; Reed Foundation; Scherman Foundation; Shell Oil Company Foundation; Shubert Foundation; Lila Wallace-Reader's Digest Fund.

Published by arrangement with Alfred A. Knopf, Inc.

Library of Congress Cataloging in Publication Data
Fugard, Athol.
Notebooks 1960–1977.
1. Fugard, Athol—Diaries. 2. Dramatists, South
African—20th century—Biography. I. Title.
PR9369.3.F8Z47   1984   828[B]   83–49025
ISBN 1–55936–012–7

Cover photo by Mary Benson

Cover design by The Sarabande Press

First paperback edition: October 1990

Contents

Introduction

Athol Harold Lannigan Fugard was born on 11 June 1932 in the Karroo village of Middelburg. His English-speaking father was of Irish/Polish descent and his mother was a Potgieter. 'I suppose,' he says, 'that it's in my response to all her stories about the Potgieters of Knoffelvlei that I recognise my bastardised identity — an Afrikaner writing in English. It is certainly to her that I owe my sense that South Africa does also, just occasionally, give me the opportunity to love and laugh at the Afrikaner in the truly celebratory sense of those two words.'

The family moved to Port Elizabeth in 1935. There his mother ran a boarding house and, later, the tearoom in St. George's Park. After studying motor mechanics at the Technical College, Fugard went to the University of Cape Town to study philosophy and social anthropology, but in 1953 he dropped out and hitch-hiked up Africa. Joining a ship in Port Said, he travelled the world as a merchant seaman.

Returning to Cape Town in 1956, he got a job writing news bulletins for the South African Broadcasting Corporation. Meanwhile he was courting Sheila Meiring, an actress, and together they started an experimental theatre group, writing much of the material for Sunday-night performances at the Labia theatre. After marrying, they moved to Johannesburg. 'There,' says Fugard, 'we were introduced to Sophiatown and, coming out of my excited response to that world was the idea for a play, *No-Good Friday,* for a group of black actors. The group included writers like Bloke Modisane, Lewis Nkosi, Can Themba and Nat Nakasa, and one splendid actor, Zakes Mokae.'

At first the only job Fugard could find was clerk of the Native Commissioner's court in Fordsburg — the Pass Laws court: 'I knew that the system was evil but until then, just how systematically evil, no. That was my revelation.' But after production of his first play, and then of *Nongogo* — both of which he directed — he was given his first paying job in theatre as a stage manager in the National Theatre Organisation.

During 1959 the Fugards went to Europe in search of theatrical experience. 'We were in London and absolutely broke when

I put down my first notes for a play involving two brothers.' It was 1960 and those notes, the basis for *The Blood Knot*, were the beginning of these notebooks. With the news of Sharpeville, he determined to return to South Africa. Notes sketchily made during the voyage home would become a novel, *Tsotsi*, only uncovered and published many years later.

Of the notebooks Fugard says, 'From the start, as far as possible I made it a point to exclude "self" and the content was incidents, ideas, sentences overheard. They became a habit, serving many purposes — at one level a constant literary exercise which I hoped would lead to greater accuracy in expression. Without them my thinking and feeling would be confused, blurred. I never quite understand the chemistry of my relationship with them. Sometimes it was compulsive, at others I wrote nothing. They reflect a certain reality in terms of the South African experience but although I have lived through very major political crises, these are not reflected. And though I never consciously used the notebooks as a playwright, everything is reflected there — my plays come from life and from encounters with actual people. But I found that as soon as I got deeply involved with writing a play, I either forgot the notebooks completely or had no need of them.

'The sense I have of myself is that of a "regional" writer with the themes, textures, acts of celebration, of defiance and outrage that go with the South African experience. These are the only things I have been able to write about.'

Fugard used brief extracts from the notebooks in introductions to his published plays. He was then encouraged to consider publishing a wider selection, and in 1979 asked me to edit the original notebooks. A year later the South African Research Program at Yale University provided fellowships which enabled us jointly to prepare the collection for publication.

London 1982   Mary Benson

1960

London. Notes for a play
Korsten in Port Elizabeth: up the road past the big motor assembly
and rubber factories, turn right down a dirt road, pot-holed, full of
stones. Donkeys wandering loose. Chinese and Indian grocery shops.
Down this road until you come to the lake — the dumping ground
for waste products from the factories — a terrible smell. On the far
side — like a scab on the hill rising from the water — is Korsten location: a collection of shanties, pondoks and mud huts. No streets, no
numbers. A world where anything goes — any race, any creed. When
the wind blows in the wrong direction, the inhabitants of Korsten
live with the stink of the lake.

In one of these shacks at Berry's Corner are the two brothers
Morris and Zachariah.

Morris is a light-skinned coloured who has found out that to ignore
the temptations to use his lightness, is the easiest way to live. It has
not made life better, but it has made it simple. He is a coloured and
that is that. He must suffer for it, but rather that than live with fear
and uncertainty. He has some education, can write and read — and
the latter is his escape from life. He reads avidly and as a result has
picked up a sort of education. He is calm, controlled, rational. A man
of few words unless he gets talking about something that interests
him.

In contrast there is his brother, Zach. The contrast is, to begin with,
physical. Zach is a dark-skinned coloured, almost an African. The
contrast is also in the character. Zach has no education — has made
no attempt to acquire any, will never have any. Morris is a man who
has discovered the subtleties to colour — rather than the mental torture of 'trying for white' he has chosen the crude, physical hardships
of being a coloured, but Zach can never be anything else, he is black
and that is that. There was no choice for him — his one reality is the
brutality of a dark skin, which allows of no subtleties. This has made
him direct, straight, resentful. He has no control. In a moment he can
be both happy and laugh loud, or hate completely to the point of
violence.

Morris, if anything, hates himself.

Zach hates the world that has decided his blackness must be pun-
ished.

9

Morris works as a clerk in a hides-and-skins warehouse. Zach is a waiter.

Their relationship as brothers: Zach is confused. At this year in his life he has seen enough to have inside him the seeds of suspicion and envy. The question — Why? It was the same mother! The same father! He is emotional — and goes to the other extreme. While Morris has real love and pity for Zach. Once Zach went away — after a fight as boys — and when he came back there were lines on his face, age, that moved Morris deeply.

The blood tie linking them has chained them up. They are dead or dying because of it.

Zach might have been content to live, as he had been born, a coloured. But his brother is almost white. This is what unbalances him. Morris knows it. Morris has invented the game of writing to newspapers.

Morris, because of his *personal problem,* ignores the white world, and allows himself to feel nothing. Zach thinks about it resentfully. He can never have it.

The night comes when Zach wants a woman. The letter is written. She is a white woman, Ethel. Morris wants to drop the idea but Zach insists. Morris doesn't even want to know about meeting her. It is masochism and revenge that makes Zach insist that he must. Zach could in the beginning, and eventually does, envy Morris the lightness of his skin.

Morris meets her and grows to love her. His conflict emerges — blood responsibility to Zach plus the new life, offered by the woman. With this development in the 2nd half is Zach's increasing absorption in the affair.

Morris brings home to him the gifts, the photographs, etc. given him by the woman.

Morris destroys the illusion when it becomes too much for him — 'She couldn't look at you!'

The situation — the imprisonment in a blood tie — cannot continue after the appearance of Ethel: things have been brought to the surface — Zach's hate and envy, Morris's crippling sense of responsibility. To continue would mean death — spiritual or physical. The guillotine must fall — cutting off something.

Morris is the better equipped mentally for this last fight — also, weakened by thought and sympathy. Zach has the physical strength and impetus of hate. Zach wins.

December

Departure from Southampton to the Cape.

The ship's brass-band playing patriotic British music. Nostalgia and a flood of sentiment. Sheila in tears — myself too, but suppressed. Indulged this mood, savoured the bittersweet of our leaving. The last tug that had followed us to the harbour was turning away, our ship was slipping, alone, into the ocean. Gulls, black and sinister, hung overhead, like spiders waiting in the web of spars and cables. The lights, remote now. The sea, cold and quick. A strong wind tearing down one side of the ship. A pale full moon, sailing abreast of us through storm clouds.

The moment was charged with an ominous presentiment of a dark future — and we were sailing to the Cape and sunshine!

The evening on deck. Biting cold. Wind and spray. I let the wind into my hair and through my nostrils and mouth into the furthermost crannies of my skull. Gone were the cobwebs of Europe and the past twelve months. I felt awakened — renewed — in life I again see the dimension, the big dimension. The 'big conception' of my youth. The spars were singing. God! How could I forget so much. Life is big, its possibilities infinite.

Joburg to Orlando train. Tsotsis.[1] Bicycle spoke — death.

The idea for a story — criminal: completely shrouded in darkness. At a moment — a stab of light and pain. This followed, developed, in the span of a short time leads to the full Christian experience after a meeting with a priest in an empty church.

The end — a life saved. (A useless life saved? Old man?) Held and refusing to let go. Carried, cherished — dying with it? Love.

His dark shroud expressed in nihilism, anarchy. Hate.

'Nothing is precious. Nothing is worth keeping. Destruction.' And then to find something precious. Shoe-box baby.

Beauty to be effaced or made ugly. Fear of the unknown. In beauty a mystery that stirs and moves him — this is the danger. And hence, the violence.

Confrontation with the priest in the church. Knife in one hand, he pulls down and desecrates a crucifix. There is anger and fury, a sense of impotence against the change taking place. The priest immobile at the altar — the enigma.

Beauty — an old face, leaves in the mud, the dust flying off a mine dump, laughter, tears.

His fear of being 'moved' — a realisation.

The kennel in the backyard where he hides from the police.

11

The yellow bitch, rat-faced, gives birth to her pups a few feet from his face. He can't move, chases her away. He must watch.

Madondo was his name — a long time ago. A name dimly remembered.

Finally, the value — life = love is found and clung to, guarded, cherished (the old man). After all the doubt.

Uncertainty = unknown. Maybe? Why? *Why not?*[2]

Cape Town: Landed just before Christmas.

Sea Point — 11 p.m. Cool clear night, the crowds withdrawn to the cafés and their flats. Walk along the beach front, passing the children's playground. Four coloured nursemaids on the swings, singing. Large African woman on the roundabout, turning and turning around, around. She sat quite still, a disconsolate figure in a maid's white apron and cap.

Story (contd) — The kid is leader of a gang. Four members including him.

The 'change' as a positive force, outside of himself. Resisted.

One of the members and the victim — chosen because he knew with unfailing accuracy where the heart was — his bicycle spoke never missed.

The puppies born dead. Life ugly.

Hiding as a young boy from the police. Someone kicked the yellow chained-up bitch, it crawled as far as it could go, towards him in the shelter, then lay down and gave birth to death.

No-one came to remove them because everyone was taken away in the removals, and he didn't dare leave because through the day he heard the harsh voices of policemen.

The baby in the shoe-box: it was small, and black, and older than anything he had ever seen in his life. Its face, lined and wrinkled. Left by a young girl, in a shoe-box in the ruined house where he had crawled, wounded.

The first night it rained — summer thunderstorm. So they had water and that kept them alive until the next day.

Sequence: (1) Killing on train.
(2) Shebeen — gang fight or police.
(3) Ruin — baby and the memory = light.

Looking for milk for the baby: 'Mama, have you any milk?' Takes her back and forces her to feed the child.

Sophiatown — ruin of one of the buildings.[3]

In the end, rushing to save the child as the bulldozer moves in.

The wall collapses on both. Or alive? — the kid crying.

He got there with a few seconds to spare. But they were few. Time only, as the first crack snaked along the wall and then bulged, time only to throw himself on all fours over the child, so that he took the first weight of falling brick, before he was flattened out, smothering them both.

Christmas eve — on the road from Cape Town — at the Riversdale Petrol Station a truckload of coloured trippers going to Port Elizabeth and a few coloured musicians from the location and the odd carload of whites passing late along the road, all at the café.

Carols and Boere-musiek and 'Heppy-heppy!' 'We're all the same, hey!' and a lot of other Christmas sentiments. It was 1 a.m.

This same petrol station about five years ago when I was waiting, late at night, for a lift. Moths — thousands of them — around the lamp in the room where I sat with the night attendant.

Veld sound — pebbles rubbed together — a small, clean, rounded sound.

Pre-dawn at Knysna. The cocks crowing, calling and answering each other in all quarters of the town. Breeze from the sea moving through the big oaks in the main street. Stars reflected on wet corrugated iron roofs.

Dawn on the road. First it was a black silhouette having no depth, running beside us, unfolding and changing as shapes loomed, humped against the paling sky.

At a moment there was depth and difference — the cold shades that lie between black and smoke-grey, and the depth of the koppie unhurried on the horizon and the impatience of tree and house and rock and river, rushing past.

Then, taking a bend in the road, facing east now, light and colour, the sore red of the soil where the road had cut through the groin of a hill.

Port Elizabeth: Back in the Bird Street flat.

Dependence — Dad. Nothing left in his life — the limits of it shrunk to his corporeal possession of the world. Twenty-four hours a day of nothing.

With his cards, playing patience. Glenda:[4] 'You play patience a lot, don't you, Dad!' Dad: 'Yes. Anything to pass the time, darling. Anything at all.'

13

Dependence. Relationship with my mother.

Hate — Love. Where is my life? What is left — tell me. What is left?

And myself, charming away the pain, the truth of the pain, the impatience, the revolt, with words, mouthing clichés about 'You've got so far' etc., 'right thinking', 'courage'. Hiding from the fact, the reality behind verbiage.

Story (contd) — The Kid. Boston — clever and a coward — he could read. Die Aap — strength. Butcher — sadist.

Cripple in Mom's café in St. George's Park — twisted, shrivelled legs. Pulled himself along by his hands — wearing leather gloves. On his head an umbrella — small, two-foot diameter — attached by a circle of thin metal rods to a band round his forehead. Earns his living pulling out weeds in the park nursery.

1961

January

Story (contd) — The reality of what you recognise and admit to exist. Conscious = present — drifting impulse, motive and purpose. Sub-conscious = deeper morality.

The even darker regions where the images live.

Tsotsi — progression is an admission of an ever deeper dimension to his living.

Tsotsi — a freedom (1) to choose his victim. (2) Not to have a victim.

The mimosa thorn at Kirkwood. Yellow bloom, green foliage and white Christed thorns. The dead bush — grey and the thorn still white — even whiter — bleached the colour of death and bones in a desert.

On one of Oupa's farms, the Hendricks family, bywoners. The tree — green conifer, sort of cypress but larger, with more bulk. The tops always moving in the breeze. Inside large spaces of coolness and darkness where the patient agonies of growth had left labyrinthine ways of dry wood and bark. The life of the tree — ants along the branches, birds — sudden killers swift to the grass below, or doves at noon.

And in this shade three generations of Hendrickses had sat out through the recurrent droughts of the valley. As the shade moved with the day across the earth, they followed, keeping in it because in that sun the galvanised iron house was as hot as hell. With sighs and red eyes, patiently they sat there, waiting for rain.

Cry of the bittern — slow, sorrowful warble.

The silence of trees in a breathless, blazing noon.

The swift — most aerial of all birds. Gathers all its food and nesting materials flying. Drinks by skimming low over still ponds. They mate in mid-air. Sometimes spend a whole night in the air. Never set foot on the ground.

The ant commends itself to study by man.[1] Measured by the dispassionate standards of survival, the most successful of nature's inventions. Most numerous of all land animals, both in numbers of indivi-

15

duals and species. It has occupied the whole surface of the earth between the margins of eternal frost.

Oldest of living families dates back more than 65 million years. Social organisation reached the present state of perfection 50 million years ago. Man by contrast is a dubious experiment in evolution that has barely got under way.

The behaviour pattern of the ant — written in its genes.

Man's tragedy — written in his genes.

Dr M.'s[2] outburst: 'I believe myself to be better than any nigger. . . . Do you know that there is such a thing as kaffir-stink? . . . Those bastards — dagga and drink. What they need is a fist in their face.'

At Kirkwood this evening, travelling the three miles to the village in a soft gentle rain, we passed five men (Africans) walking through the night. Sacks on their shoulders. Two of them carried a big box — coffin?

Oupa[3] at Hillside: sitting alone on the stoep in darkness. The rain, occasionally the lights of a passing car as it swung around the bend in the road near the river, touching the tall palms in the garden. The air moist, a moment of serenity. He was thinking of the past — the long, chequered, ancient past. 'I have buried three wives:'[4]

He had forgotten the face of the first one, and the second was only dimly remembered. 'The last years weren't romantic, you know. It was more companionship.' The third, dead only a few months, was remembered not so much as the woman he had known but as an image of loyal, fertile, faithful Womanhood. In all the years, through all the epics of drought, there had been a wife beside him in bed, at table. 'I have buried three wives.'

They were three sisters.

In his conversation there were long pauses — he would break off as one word reminded him of another, and that of a third and so on until an image, a face, an incident from the past, rose up, and in the end he finished the sentence he had started.

He spoke about the family of wagtails in the garden — one family, all generations of them for fifteen years.

And Pietertjie, the coloured boy, son of Effie the cook, who now slept outside his door. There in the dark the difference between the man, awake in bed, and the younger one — the much younger one — drowsy on the floor, the difference between bed and floor, white and coloured, between eighty-two years and nineteen, would disappear and sometimes in the long silent hours, the old man would talk about

16

the land, the valley he loved, the orchard and the fruit, and the other would listen and say, 'Ja, baas', and feel and understand that love, and from that the old man would pass on to faces and places Pietertjie had never known until Pietertjie drifted off to sleep and the old man found himself talking to himself.

Then the dreams, half-dream half-reality, a greater reality than he had ever known because the soft winds outside moved clean and cool through his mind as well, where the dust was also settling: a part of the valley now, of the earth itself, that he had watered with his sweat and cursed in the months of drought, and the roof of his skull — because the bones showed clear through the flesh — was as wide as the heavens outside and as mysterious to read.

And a thought that occupied him increasingly in the hours alone, in the darkness on the stoep, even in bed, was when he had started preparing for death.

Because he was prepared.

His hands were dead from holding the crutches. 'I let things fall, you know.'

The tremendous satisfaction and pride of Mom that she had got beyond God as an old man with a white beard sitting on a cloud in the sky. 'God is in you. He is in me. We are all God — if you know what I mean.'

'I was walking up Bird Street and I thought I must ask Athol what he thinks about God.'

Mom, Dad — the tremendous disfigurement of their bodies, by time, age, life, living.

She drags her feet now as if reluctant to take up and waste in petty movement some of the remaining, numbered steps.

T. — African National Congress politician in New Brighton Township. Physically tall, bearded, gentle eyes, delicate hands with long fingers. Tuberculous. Sensitive about it — will not mention or discuss. Deteriorating because he no longer eats regularly, grabbing food wherever he finds it. Sleeping wherever he finds himself. Works at a leather tannery. His mother very sick in her one-roomed dwelling.

Met him at H.'s flat. He was very tired and had only come out of politeness. It was the time of the bus boycott. 'I must get back. There is a group I walk in with every morning. We leave at 5.30.'

Possibly because of his tiredness — tired now for many years — his physical exhaustion, he was falling quicker than he would have normally into group attitudes — 'The whites', 'We blacks' — with an

17

effort dissociating the few from the group label. 'My people' said with deep love.

H. – in connection with not being able to create overseas: 'Being in South Africa is like a bad marriage and leaving the country, the divorce. I mean, why should I paint that house, this scene, that tree . . . it had no meaning to me.'

The existence of purpose leads on to meaning.

In the flat at night, the sounds of Mom and Dad asleep. Sudden groan, whimpers like a dog with bad dreams, wheezing each time they drew in a laboured breath. In the distance a dog was baying. At moments in my feverish turnings in bed, fighting for sleep, I could no longer separate the baying from the wheezing – the two sounds spinning together.

A sound like a yawn, suddenly very wide, drawn out, tapering away into a sigh. A quality to it of groaning, lament, complaint. The bed creaked as a body turned and for a few moments my ears, deafened by the silence, would hear nothing until they sharpened again and I caught the sound of breathing.

From my bed I could see a door in the opposite wall. In the half-light filtering in from the street lamps outside, in the long whispering silence that began when the lights were switched off and they began to roll in their beds, searching for sleep, that door, particularly at moments when I was caught between dream and reality, half-awake but powerless to stop the anarchy of my senses and thoughts, at such moments the door was sinister, it loomed very large. And the fear of that moment was the opening of the door, a subtle terror that played like a ghost with relics of my childhood. What would there be behind it? Nothing? A face more hideous than anything I had ever seen? Some monstrous deformity? Once a gust of wind opened it just a crack so that I could see the dark gloom behind it. My heart stopped, I stopped breathing and waited . . . What if God came walking through there, if the door swung open and God walked in?

February
Discussing death, burial, cremation over dinner. A common fear – that a person will return to life after burial and find himself in a coffin. My mother: 'Let me lie there for a week – that you must promise me. Make sure I'm dead. I will do the same for Daddy.' Talking about pros and cons of cremation, she said of my Dad: 'No, there's no funny business there. He just wants to go to his grave quietly. He's happy with his grave.'

18

Told the story of my Oom Hennie who wouldn't get cold. His arms and joints loose (no *rigor mortis*), the skin warm and cheeks flushed. 'I wasn't going to bury him like that! I told Mr Jones the undertaker, you can't put that man into his grave! So the doctor came, and he told me, Mrs Fugard, he said, your brother is dead. But his *nerves* are still living. His heart collapsed but he wanted to live. His body is full of life. So I said, Please, doctor, I'm not burying him like that! He said, But there's an injection I can give him. He was right! When I went back in the afternoon Hennie was cold and stiff.'

'Don't the nails, hair and beard grow fractionally after death?'

Lunchtime in the café with Mom and Aunt Kitty — discussed sweepstakes — the eternal prospect of a lot of money suddenly. Then spoke about finding money — story of my Dad, the 'wonderful thing' that happened to him one day: he found four shiny half-crowns in the park. So excited he was out of breath when he got back to tell Mom. 'The happiest day of his life.'

Mom telling about the time she got off the Newton Park bus and saw silver coins lying on the ground. 'It's the most wonderful feeling you ever had. Just money where you look — just money. You pick up here and you see one there — just money!'

Mom re Kitty — 'Sy's nie greedy nie, but she likes a lot.'

The laboured erratic rhythm of trains shunting in the night. They come in cycles of three or four — broad powerful thrusts of sound, and then a few very quick and short. Clouds of steam drifting through the arc of yellow lights in the yard. Whistles.

Mom joined us in our room tonight after supper for a chat about 'the old days'. A marvellous fund of stories about her family, the Potgieters, at Middelburg, Cape. The family had a small Cash Store (basic groceries). One day when Mom ran the shop, a coloured woman travelling by donkey-cart with her husband, had given birth to a baby at the side of the road and she went to help. 'There was no one. Nothing. No clothes for the baby. Just rags.'

She collected cast-offs from the whites in Middelburg and gave them to the woman. When she went back in the morning to see how they were, they had gone, baby and all.

A story about Aunt Kitty in particular evoked the dusty heat and lazy afternoons of life in a Karroo dorp at the height of summer. Kitty was serving in the store, hoping for the sale of three-pence worth of sugar or a penny-worth of pruim twak. A travelling salesman arrived there at a time when the only things moving in the street were

19

the shadows of the bluegum trees. Mom remembered him very clearly as a man who 'liked jokes of the practical kind'. He entered the shop to find Aunt Kitty (back to him) totally engrossed in something in front of her on the counter. He sneaked up behind her, hoping to give her a 'really good fright' — and saw what she was doing. In front of her on the counter was a gluepot — she had the brush between her teeth while between the index finger and thumb of each hand was a struggling fly. Kitty was painting their backsides with glue then she very carefully brought them together and settled down to wait for the glue to dry.

Mom couldn't remember the results of Aunt Kitty's experiment.

Mom borrowed one of Dad's rusty blades to trim her bunions. Mom: re decimalisation, she spoke of 'Dismals'.

Summerstrand beach — African man and young boy in donkey-cart, after collecting dry wood from the bush to sell in the location, the old man let the boy play by the sea while he collected driftwood.

Sandpipers, grey and white — their busy legs moving like a straight line across the shifting sand. Bluebottles — blue threads, sting. The heads of dead sharks left by fishermen — eyes picked out by the birds. Dead cormorant. Dead penguin — gulls fighting like cats around the grey corpses. Crabs scuttling away in their borrowed shells, fighting the incoming tide to get back into the water. Waves would knock them over and carry them up the sands and they would scuttle back again.

On the way to Cape Reciefe lighthouse — the deserted hovel made of driftwood and corrugated iron. No sign of life. Just the black, savage dog on the white sands.

Boys and golden girls with wet, rats-tail hair, drifting through the park, going home after a night at the swimming-bath. They were loud and, like squirrels, played with pine-cones. Then fell silent, drifting under the yellow light of streetlamps, the light shining on their hair — drifting home to sleep.

What was today? Today was the smell of bread in the leather schoolbag, and flies against a window and tadpoles in the water.

Tramp: As long as you have a mythical home it's all right.

Frogs a ripple of sound in the distance. It came floating to me in the wind moving up the valley. Sometimes it was near, very loud, quivering, and then as the wind veered, or dropped away for a moment, the sound receded until it was barely audible.

Two lorries: milk lorry, painted white, the milk white, the driver white, three Africans in white overalls. Coal lorry, black and grimy, the load it carried, the three men who delivered the coal. The two lorries passed each other in the street.

Two coloured men came to the door. Trying to get to flat No. 4. 'That way,' I said. 'Thank you, baas. Thank you, my baas. We were frightened, you see. We just couldn't walk in there, could we baas? It's not our place.' This was said for my benefit. They were collecting 'empties' to be resold to bottle stores. Their shoes were worn away so much at the heel, their feet were almost out. The sack they carried was almost new. A feeling of two men, hungry and thirsty, deciding: 'Empties. Here, man. Let's try Empties!' 'Okay, Dolf, okay.' 'Empties!' 'Ja. What do we do?' 'A sack, man. That's all.'
    Their first time on a job done only intermittently, the rare moment of a resolution: 'I must do something. I'm going to earn my living today.'

A bird was chucking about round pebbles of sound, rubbing them together in the tree, occasionally throwing one harder than the others so that it broke into sharp fragments. A fountain of sound, bubbling its round pebbly way through the early morning.

Three days of rain and low skies and then the halcyon day — the light that strikes you a thunderous blow between the eyes, the startling existential individuality of every living and dead thing like stones and weeds and birds on a lamppost, and a woman dusting her carpets on a balcony two storeys up. Trees stood along the side of the street like shaggy old men. I wanted to shake their hands and ask their names.
    The tops of trees had swum away into the blue depths of the sky. As if the world was forging its sounds that moment and for the first time. Birds in the tree. The man whistling while he swept the stoep, each syllable distinct and the grammar of the whole clear in its construction of life and living.

Strange little house in the valley. Two roomed. One half of it painted, tidy, the stoep waxed red, curtains in the windows, the windows themselves neatly painted. Even the piece of chimney painted on its side. The other side derelict, abandoned, as untidy as the other was

21

tidy. The house was set off the main Valley Road, under a cliff.

Baakens River in the valley. Now a trickle of water in a narrow cement canal. Occasionally still comes down in flood. There had been good rains a few days previously. Coloured children were catching tadpoles. Behind them was Mangolds Iron Foundry.

J. van R.: as a young barefooted Afrikaner boy on the Free State farm, was fascinated by the Bushmen paintings in a cave in the hills on the farm. J.: 'I can understand how people are fascinated by them, especially children. They are fantastic and beautiful − and so old. For me they hadn't been painted by people. It was a holy place. Spiritual, you know.'

His hands locked together as he spoke or struggled after the right words. One felt he did that to his hands, one holding the other, as if for fear they would do wrong or evil.

'I am an artist. I know I've done nothing yet, but I'm an artist.'

He modelled beautifully in clay.

One eye had its lid low, giving his face a shy look, as if something was hidden. On his chin and lips sometimes an ineffectual fuzz of hair. Flat body, loose-boned.

The Afrikaner who went to the township to the house of the African leader and apologised for the cruelty of his people, the pain they had caused.

His wife, Lettie − her wedding ring a stone which he found in the Vaal River and had mounted. An example of the sensitivity and beauty in him, even at that time when he had been a member of the Ossewa Brandwag[5] before his 'change' when he was 'converted' by the MRA ten years later.

The wild, violent crews of the garbage lorries. His image of childhood which stays with him through life. His first impression of the black man, his final.

Dice game in the light of a lamp in the Donkin Reserve, About six young coloureds ten-fifteen years. An African man had joined them − about thirty. Either he was losing or they were cheating but he said something. They picked up their money quickly and walked away − 'Nee Oom, ons speel nie soo nie.'[6] He got angry, started swearing. They laughed and called him names, 'Kaffer! Swartgat!' Once he tried to chase them but they were too quick. He had a tremendous battle with his pride and tried consciously, very obviously, just to walk away.

Party at the flat of a Catholic woman, B.

Solly, bespectacled quiet-spoken leftist. Something of defeat and tiredness — a man in his fifties, a Jew. 'I tell you what I believe now. What they [blacks] want they must get for themselves. They must just take it, and forget about the whites, or waiting for them to change.'

Opposed in this opinion by Piet B., red-faced, big-handed Afrikaner. 'We must stand together, man. Together. Together we take the world. They want us. Hell, Solly, when I take my bus out Cadles way at five o'clock, I see them. I see them walking with their backs straight, walking home [the bus strike]. It's the people, Solly. ". . . And they shall inherit the earth." '

His passion was English poetry, and he quoted endlessly, relevantly and with feeling. The words sonorous and precise in his Afrikaans mouth. Byron, Shakespeare, Keats, Shelley. 'We come to bury Solly, Not to praise him.' 'Oh, the time when I was young and green in judgment.'

Piet B. had been born on the farm Riverside in the Alexandria district. Only son — one sister. 'My people were god-fearing. We kneeled at night and our workers kneeled with us and prayed. There was no difference, man. I was brought up to respect and believe in the Christian principles. My friends were the picannins on the farm. Race relations did not exist for me.'

He tells the story of Soya, an African childhood friend. He returned with T.B. and died in the Settlers' Hospital, Grahamstown. They were both young men. The hospital authorities phoned and told him to collect the body. 'I wanted to bury him in a Christian manner — "Lord, let not this dust . . . " etc. I was building a dairy. So I tore down the roof to get wood for the coffin. When we buried him they said, "Inkosi, speak." I looked at the coffin. All I could say was, "There lies a good man", and then walked away into the veld and had a bloody good cry.'

Piet is today a bus driver. He has lost most of his money in fighting court cases in the struggle for freedom, in helping Africans, and in an election campaign. He stood as the Coloured Representative, proposed by S.A.C.P.O.[7]

This parliamentary constituency was at that time the largest in the world — Bredasdorp in the Cape to Harding in Natal and Calvinia in N.W. Cape. Incident that hurt him most was when he addressed the Korsten meeting, 'Broers en susters' and they laughed at him. 'Hell man, that hurt! No mortal sling doth pain as deep as injustice.'

D., brilliantly well-read (Piet is not a real intellectual — it is more humanity with him) followed him around on his tour organising opposition. His attitude was that if a coloured could not represent the coloureds they would rather have no representative at all.

A Government stooge they both despised eventually got in.

D. and Piet were friends but D. thought that Piet, in coming so close to the truth and then compromising it, was more dangerous than the Government stooge who was obviously a fraud.

The wildest, most beautiful of all animals, the Martial Eagle, Lammervanger. Enormous black talons. The legs splayed wide apart. Flat head: unblinking, yellow, utterly fearless eyes.

Mom spoke of the draining board being cockrotted. Frits for fridge.

Sheila in her pregnancy. We have been married nearly five years now and suddenly it seems I can see the change that those years have made in her, very clearly. Why now? The silence of pregnancy as if she was posing for life to see the effect it has had on her. Presenting herself.

In those five years, the shy, uncertain, inward girl — then green and secretive — had opened up. She is now open, with all of her ghosts laid, almost unafraid and giving back as much as she is receiving. Of all experience I think this 'giving' has been the most profound in its effect on her.

She went to London looking for a 'new personality', not knowing that it was still being formed. Now, returned home, she says, 'It is like an old coat that no longer fits me.' The new personality is there.

If a baby was not coming I am almost sure she would have turned to something as positive to express her commitment to life.

The baby will give her more living room. Her total involvement: in life, carrying life.

H. spoke about the conflict a white man has in South Africa — between his libido, the compelling sex images that demand satisfaction, and his moral conscience, his sense of responsibility towards others, the need to change the world. The first, in some ways, the product of the white society of which he is a part, is irrational and has no connection with the second, i.e. his moral responsibility to his black brothers. 'I sit in a "white" café, admiring breasts and legs, and outside on the pavement are hungry African children.'

He also said: 'South Africa is a damned mixture of old and new. Of African youth and vitality and European age and loss of interest.'

24

Future: 'Either going to end up old, without ever having been really young — you know — nothing before, nothing in between, no middle years. Or else we, this country, will really be young, like nothing has been in the world for a goddam long time. There is a good chance of the former though. I've met most of the up-and-coming non-white leaders and I'm telling you that some of them are small and restricted.'

March
Park Constable. Sallow-faced, morbid slab of a man. Scabby sores on hands and face. Always slinking among the trees as if hiding and waiting for a misdemeanour such as cycling through the park, dog not on leash. His speciality was catching young coloured lovers. One case — the young girl cried, 'Please let me go, baas. I won't do it again, I promise, baasie.' But he handed them over to the police.

Another time, the old coloured woman who had stolen an armful of the best dahlias. He felt she was too old but Mr Prosser, Park Superintendent, said, 'Take her down, moer her and learn her a lesson.' She was sentenced to £5 or one month. She asked the Magistrate to put her on 'outside' work but he explained there was no outside work for women. She must sit it out.

Sam Semela[8] — Basuto — with the family fifteen years. Meeting him again when he visited Mom set off string of memories.

The kite which he produced for me one day during those early years when Mom ran the Jubilee Hotel and he was a waiter there. He had made it himself: brown paper, its ribs fashioned from thin strips of tomato-box plank which he had smoothed down, a paste of flour and water for glue. I was surprised and bewildered that he had made it for me.

I vaguely recall shyly 'haunting' the servants' quarters in the well of the hotel — cold, cement-grey world — the pungent mystery of the dark little rooms — a world I didn't understand. Frightened to enter any of the rooms. Sam, broad-faced, broader based — he smelled of woodsmoke. The 'kaffir smell' of South Africa is the smell of poverty — woodsmoke and sweat.

Later, when he worked for her at the Park café, Mom gave him the sack: '. . . he became careless. He came late for work. His work went to hell. He didn't seem to care no more.' I was about thirteen and served behind the counter while he waited on table.

Realise now he was the most significant — the only — friend of my boyhood years. On terrible windy days when no-one came to swim or walk in the park, we would sit together and talk. Or I was reading — Introductions to Eastern Philosophy or Plato and Socrates — and when I had finished he would take the book back to New Brighton.

Can't remember now what precipitated it, but one day there was a rare quarrel between Sam and myself. In a truculent silence we closed the café, Sam set off home to New Brighton on foot and I followed a few minutes later on my bike. I saw him walking ahead of me and, coming out of a spasm of acute loneliness, as I rode up behind him I called his name, he turned in mid-stride to look back and, as I cycled past, I spat in his face. Don't suppose I will ever deal with the shame that overwhelmed me the second after I had done that.

Now he is thin. We had a long talk. He told about the old woman ('Ma') whom he and his wife have taken in to look after their house while he goes to work — he teaches ballroom dancing. 'Ma' insists on behaving like a domestic — making Sam feel guilty and embarrassed. She brings him an early morning cup of coffee. Sam: 'No, Ma, you mustn't, man.' Ma: 'I must.' Sam: 'Look, Ma, if I want it, I can make it.' Ma: 'No, I must.'

Occasionally, when she is doing something, Sam feels like a cup of tea but is too embarrassed to ask her, and daren't make one for himself. Similarly, with his washing. After three days or a week away in other towns, giving dancing lessons, he comes back with under-clothes that are very dirty. He is too shy to give them out to be washed so washes them himself. When Ma sees this she goes and complains to Sam's wife that he doesn't trust her, that it's all wrong for him to do the washing.

Of tsotsis, he said: 'They grab a old man, stick him with a knife and ransack him. And so he must go to hospital and his kids is starving with hungry.' Of others: 'He's got some little moneys. So he is facing starvation for the weekend.'

Of township snobs, he says there are the educational ones: 'If you haven't been to the big school, like Fort Hare, what you say isn't true.' And the money ones: 'If you aren't selling shops or got a business or a big car, man, you're nothing.'

Sam's incredible theory about the likeness of those 'with the true seed of love'. Starts with Plato and Socrates — they were round. 'Man is being shrinking all the time. An Abe Lincoln, him too, taller, but that's because man is shrinking.' Basically, those with the true seed of love look the same — 'It's in the eyes.'

He spoke admiringly of one man, a black lawyer in East London, an educated man — university background — who was utterly without snobbery, looking down on no-one — any man, educated or igno-

26

rant, rich or poor, was another *man* to him, another human being, to be respected, taken seriously, to be talked to, listened to.

'They'[9] won't allow Sam any longer to earn a living as a dancing teacher. 'You must get a job!' One of his fellow teachers was forced to work at Fraser's Quarries.

Robson Gala from Tsomo in the Transkei: working at Don Pedro Jetty, Port Elizabeth as stevedore. One of the buckets with which they were offloading a ship (coal or grain) fell on his foot, virtually severing off the big and second toes. He put plaster around the toes — but because the blood still flowed copiously one of the white railway clerks had torn off a few bills-of-lading forms from a pad and he had folded them around his foot. They then took him to Bird Street and off-loaded him outside the surgery of the railway doctor. That was where I found him. It was lunchtime and he was sitting on the pavement. Surgery hours were from 2.30 to 3.30. A number of inquisitive white people stopped from time to time and asked what was wrong. One young woman was particularly keen to know if the toes were completely off.

His foot was black with coal dust. Where the blood had congealed the paper was as good as glued to his foot. He hobbled around carrying his shoe.

Dazed by the shock and pain. Didn't seem to hear me at times, and when he did had a hard time understanding me or making himself understood. I gave him two aspirins. He threw them into his tea, stirred it up then drank it.

Small quiet man, about twenty-five.

Basket-makers of Korsten location. Little ragged khaki boys in the streets of Port Elizabeth with bundles of baskets.

Their settlement organised on completely communal lines.

Peter and Joseph. They asked for a drink of water. Shoes (a pair of my Mom's): 'No good. It's for a she.' Another second-hand garment I offered, they rejected because the other boys would laugh at them.

Korsten is about five miles from the city centre. They *walked* to and from it each day.

Port Elizabeth day: windy, very white. High cloud, wispy like smoke or cottonwool teased out until you can see through it. No colour was definite. Green of trees or grey distance, walls and men walking away and paper in the streets, all seemed the same through the smoky haze.

27

Port Elizabeth coast — vegetation: green with gold mixed in, other patches very dark green. Black-green some of the bushes, reflecting the sun — metallic and painful to see, each leaf like the shiny back of a black beetle. Every sense in league to overpower you with heat. Sound of cicada's intense sibilance — clouds of this sound. Your skin feels the relentless blaze of the sun. Smell acrid, heady vapours steaming in the bush. Sky an intense blue. Birds — small white hawks, swallows, doves, hoepoe, shrike and drongo. Cape Canaries. The incredibly lucid, pellucid light of clean windswept air. Along the coast a slight haze of white spray.

The play *Nonquase* at the Crispin Hall, Port Elizabeth. Playwright and producer: George Pemba.

Started an hour late. 'Speaking aids' kept urging the waiting audience: 'Hello-Hello-Hello. Please be quiet!' A later announcement in the course of the play was: 'Please clap louder!' — the audience responded with a round of strong applause.

The caretaker attendant of the hall, an old, fine-boned, bearded man, small, who sat in a chair beside the stage smoking with a fancy cigarette-holder. Once he walked past with an armful of toilet-rolls as if every member of the audience was going to have a crap before the night was out.

The curtain didn't meet the floor of the stage — a six-inch gap through which we could see the performers' feet.

The chaos of the ticket-selling and seating plan in the lobby — system so involved that while the public built up in a vast congested crowd in the lobby, spilling out over the step outside, impatient and garrulous, the actual flow into the auditorium was a mere trickle.

During the long wait those who had been fortunate enough to get through and to their seats, read the evening paper, ate apples, shouted at friends. No programme. It was provided by M.C., a fat man in a suit who walked onto the stage and told the public what they were going to see: 'It is a gripping play. The beautiful maiden Nonquase ... written by our local man of words, the painter Mr George Pemba.' He disappeared and then the play started. Not a light went off in the auditorium. The curtain opened on an empty stage.

During the performance the audience laughed, talked, shouted interjections, clapped a good remark, were highly amused at the highest moments of tragedy.

Speaking aid: 'There will now be a ten-minute interval' (half-an-hour). Cool drinks sold. Someone had forgotten the opener so the tops were bitten off with white, strong teeth.

Play resumed without an announcement. Sale of cool drinks went on. People crossed in front of the stage without the least embarrassment. A man went around collecting empty bottles.

At the end of the play the M.C., the playwright/producer and another poet appeared on stage. The M.C. called on the poet (describing him as a man whose latest work had been prescribed for matric) to express a 'Vote of confidence in the play'.

Singing of the National Anthem: *Nkosi Sikelel' iAfrika*. Then all the seats in auditorium were cleared away, a piano was pushed onto the stage and a dance began. It was 11.30 p.m.

Later thought: In the beer-drinking scene the 'prop' for the beer was a large double-size Cobra Wax Polish tin. An unconscious but superb Brechtian touch. With this difference not just the 'person' revealed behind the mask, but 'New Brighton' behind the stage. It was 'the people' doing a play.

Autumn in P.E. comes as a slightly chilly windswept day. A few grey grey ones, a few clear ones — and with the latter, when the sun sets the yellow, lime-washed buildings glow with an orangy bright, reflected light.

Tonight a clear silent evening. A cricket starts up and in its short, leaping chirp the suggestion of a panting — the same rhythm as if the earth was tired. Like a sound of the stars. Distant throb of the surf.

Evening dew heard in a pendulous drip-drip-drip from a gutter. Not so much drops of water as the settling of the night, the darkness, in a thin film on the roof and this seeping to the gutter, dribbling along until it reached the crack and there forming, pendulous, then falling onto the stones below with a 'blat!' The darkness dripping.

A street lamp hidden from view by a bush with huge velvety leaves. The edge of the leaves refracting the light in a serrated thread of silver like a strand of a cobweb in silhouette against a black sky. So clear and precise that I could have traced the line with a pencil.

Some light in the kaffirboom tree — pieces of silverfoil. Moth sailing into the light and then out. Bats flurrying past, silently, in the darkness.

Two sounds: car door slamming and a woman laughing then a few syllables of scorn. For the rest, silence.

May
Dad's pain: fluttering, throbbing . . . soft as a dove. Pussy paws kneading away at the tender part. Occasionally a claw slipped out and caught the nerve and plucked from his consciousness a sharp raw note.

Caressing his pain, crying out, alone in the dark, in the silent sleeping house. In the other bed, Mom, sleeping. In the other room, also sleeping, Sheila — the young woman with child — and myself.

The face of a man, a fine face, the face of a noble man, but when he opened his mouth in the dark, the whimper and whine of a child came out, utterly without protest or anger, a final, total resignation, asking only to sound his suffering. 'Hai hai hai — aina! Jeeeses. Oh God this is terrible. Ho — ho — ho — s-s-s-s — shooo . . . eeeeee — ha! Jeeesus Christ! huh! huh! huh! huh!'

The face — the mask — the mien — hiding nothing I thought, a vacuous mind poring over comic books in its easier moments. The habit of suffering, the inward wait and watch for pain. The lesson of a life. He knows it — the way other people know pets — the anatomy of pain, the secret places where it plays — the chest, toenails, stump, cramp in the good leg. This and the habit of dependence; the habit of humiliation; of loneliness. A man withdrawn — marooned, finally, on the last unassailable island of the individual — pain.

One night the aspirins didn't help; driven to desperation he took two pills prescribed by the doctor for high blood pressure, in the hope — the raw red hope — of relief . . . vomited, nausea.

The pill — in the dark between his trembling fingertips — so small, round: visions of mighty pain-killing properties, of relief, of sleep, like the others in their beds. He never took them with water or swallowed them. They went onto his tongue and lay there until they crushed apart and soaked away with his spit. No awareness of bad taste, bitter quinine, the sharp sourness of aspirin — pain had annihilated the other senses.

. . . I listened for a long time, each jangle of pain playing on my nerves. Gradually my eyes grew heavy. He was still moaning. I drifted off to sleep through the fog of his pain.

Tonight, after two weeks of pain, of sleepless nights, of crying and whining in the dark, of vainly imploring Jeeesus and God, Dad broke down and sobbed like a child. Tears and flat spit bubbled his lips. We searched around for pills, for nerve pain specific, and dosed him with the lot. He pulled himself together for a few minutes then, just before I left, he called to me, 'Come here, my boy' — started to say something, then floundered and drowned in another flood of tears. Eventually, he managed to say what he wanted: 'Don't let them do anything to my leg. Don't let them take it off!'

Behind the bland withdrawn expression what terrors moved! Behind the midnight agony . . . That a cripple might lose his remaining

30

leg — his final vestige of independence, of manhood, would go.

There was pain, no doubt. But in the dark, lying in wait for the next spasm, his mind had magnified and built up his fear. It was not just the pain any more that made him cry — it was his terror as well. Earlier he had suggested this: 'It's always terrible in the dark,' I'd said, 'no matter how slight the pain.' 'My God, yes, chum. Your thoughts race past . . . '

Also his obsessive concern with the district nurse who was to come and change the dressing of the small cut between the toes.

Idea — African leaders banished by the Government to some lonely desolate, drought-stricken outpost.

The lies and half-truths that I have spread about Dad — alcoholic, fought in the war, etc. The truth — humility, resignation to suffering.

A character who deliberately propagates and establishes a public image compounded of cowardice, weakness, dependence of another man who was the exact opposite. But done, not out of hate, but in submission to the inevitability of his (the other man's — Dad's) fate — and, finally, love.

He was misunderstood: the silence taken for vacuity, the groans at night for weakness, the one leg for dependence.

Dad in hospital. Semi-private four bed ward. One bed empty, waiting. An evening visit. Two other patients — robust, balding, middle-aged type and an elderly, decrepit Afrikaner, collapsed in a chair, dying of cancer. Visited by his wife (dressed in black), daughter and son-in-law. Brought him a one-gallon flask of his favourite soup. His visitors left early. Suddenly, in a silence, the old man spoke up. In slurred, sepulchral tones, he gave the prospects and position of his children and their spouses. How much each one was earning, how much they were likely to earn — this was very important. He knew the exact figures. His closing remark: 'Of course they don't think of us (meaning him and his wife) but thank God I had the foresight to provide a little.' The robust balding type tried to talk to him in reply — an obvious gesture of goodwill, using the voice reserved for children. But the old man didn't hear him. He hadn't spoken to anyone for that matter. 'He's deaf' the robust man said aloud, to cover his embarrassment.

Dad's ward: the empty bed had been filled by a case from George. Lean dried-up elderly Afrikaner. Complexion almost blue. Blood transfusions. Asleep, his mouth (no teeth) was puckered like a deep wound that had never quite healed. Heavily drugged when I first saw him; stirred occasionally and groaned with pain, 'Ooh God! Ooh God! My voete my voete my voete – my bors!'[10] Voice as harsh and dry as a thornbush in a drought.

One evening he looked a little better – blue in his skin faded to a more promising sallow hue. He surprised us all by suddenly addressing the woman of the other old man (flasks of soup, coffee and a melktert every night) and asking about buttermilk. He almost seemed logical and aware of the circumstances but the delirium asserted itself eventually in a confusion of time and place. He seemed to think he was on his farm: 'the boy' should have brought him his buttermilk. Wasn't it Thursday? Everybody in the ward was either embarrassed or smiled with pity and condescension.

He lapsed into silence. Then started talking again. This time about his youth when he was sixteen years old on his father's farm, supervising work in a potato field. One of the coloured labourers broke off work, having decided he had had enough. A 'special sort of man' – a *difficult* one. Proud. The son of a coloured woman and a Jewish smous. He – with all the strength of his sixteen years – had piled into the coloured man and kept him down on the ground until his father came and gave the labourer a hiding and sent him back to work.

But he turned out a good 'boy'. Years later, as old men, whenever the white man was in town and went to the hotel for spots, and the coloured man saw him, he could come up and ask, ' "Gee daar tickey vir 'n dop, baas." En as ek dit hê – dan gee ek.'[11]

Two images: (1) the coloured man – ultimate degradation, after the pride of his youth. (2) The white man – his loneliness. It wasn't his wife or children or parents he remembered, but the coloured labourer who ended up begging tickeys for a dop. Was there an awareness of the degradation – which was his as well? A common bond.

His name is Barnard.

Barnard – his outing was a visit to the sea, armed with two bottles of beer and a pack of lemon cream biscuits.

The beach beyond Summerstand – tide receding left behind a sheet of shallows among the rocks, wind-rippled and, standing in it, as if they had forgotten about their wings, two gulls. Immobility. Occasionally they took a few steps. Once, one actually remembered his wings but all he thought to do was hold them outstretched, like useless arms, while he hopped a few feet forward and then again tucked them behind his back and was quite still. It was a subtle but deep contrast. Beyond the flat, thin pool in which they stood, the restless chuffing sea.

As though those birds had fallen physically into the stillness (the silence) which their flight — those broad unhurried unflurried curves — seems almost to be touching; but always circling it, skimming it.

Mrs M. and her circle of friends: their vivid, emotionally charged pasts and their tenuous relationship with the present.

Mrs M. and her divorce; Mrs F. — her sex-life; Mrs S. and her homosexual husband; Mrs P. — frigid, her inventions and depressively violent husband.

All of them in little rooms, or one-roomed flats, meeting for tea — talking, working out their grudges and grievances; criticising the present generation. Around them a country on the brink of revolution and violence[12] — the fear touches them (hawkers at the door) but they do not get involved. The gossip (spite). Then they retire to their rooms, brew their lonely pots of tea, dip a biscuit, listen to the wireless, work out the crosswords. On to sleep. Neglect and decay.

The view of the sea, and gulls, and sunsets — a ravishing, violent beauty every evening outside Mrs M.'s. window.

Sheila and birth of Lisa Maria
At about twelve o'clock p.m. the sister suggested that I go home, feeling that my presence was keeping Sheila awake and making things more difficult for her. I went to tell Sheila — found her in the dark, crying. The sister had also told her that I should go. Sheila asked me to stay, somewhere, close at hand. The waiting-room. I promised I would and left my car-keys beside her to prove that I would not go.

I spent two hours in the cold comfortless waiting-room. After an hour two other men brought in their wives and I had company. One was a lean athletic young man — about twenty-one. Pretended indifference. His first child. Seemed totally unaware of what lay before his wife. Referred everything to himself: he was hungry; it was his basket-ball game that had been interrupted; he had timed the pains; he didn't mind what it was — boy or girl — they're all the same. The other was man who had already fathered two children. Working-class — fitter and turner. Seemed conscious of the travail of the woman — humbly, wryly and with thanks: 'Thank God I'm not a woman.' The glow of expectancy was not there, he'd already been through the mill — if anything, a touch of disappointment. The baby was being born to uncertain times; at his factory a lot of men had been laid off; he himself, one of the lucky ones, had been put on short time. Only mention of the impending Republic came from him — with almost savage satisfaction he said: 'Anyway, it's those very ones what voted for the Republic has been laid off!'

I had been working on a poem before they arrived — with them present it became impossible. The strange vacant silence I had found myself in, alone, was shattered.

At two o'clock one of the nurses came and asked me would I like to sit with my wife. (Sheila had asked.) I was profuse: 'I would appreciate it very much. I would be very grateful. How is she?' etc.

They had moved Sheila out of the labour ward and into the delivery room. (Short of beds.) She was sitting up on the table, resting on her arms. They made me put on a mask and gown. When I had left her earlier, the pains had been coming regularly, but were still only moderate; now it was a totally different situation: the pains were savage, reducing her to vain cries and swearing and a terrible writhing of the body. The effect was shattering. I felt useless, guilty, frightened; grabbing her arms every time a spasm began and, together with her, fighting them down. There was a chair so I sat down opposite her — and in this manner we passed five terrible hours.

Once I fainted — the usual feelings: giddiness, everything getting remote; Sheila forgetting her agony temporarily but her voice coming from a long way away. The next thing I knew is that I was on the floor, Sheila was ringing for a nurse, and asking me frightenedly what had happened. She wanted them to give me Sal Volatile but fortunately no-one heard the bell.

Every hour we rang and a nurse came and we said Sheila felt like bearing down — pushing — so the sister came, I went out, and they made a rectal examination. No. The cervix was not yet sufficiently dilated.

Meantime, Sheila was getting more and more doped and tired. She had already been without sleep for forty hours and had her third injection of pethedine. So by four o'clock she was keeling over from exhaustion between each pain. Then I started counting during each contraction; Sheila breathing laboriously with each count. She said it helped. Nurses were surprised whenever they came in and caught us at it. At first I only counted to twenty, and by then the pain was gone. Later though I was going up to forty. And every hour another rectal examination, a hopeful wait outside in the corridor until: No. Cervix not yet dilated enough.

Sheila — heavy-eyed; snatches of uncontrolled delirious talk —

looking up abruptly: 'What was I saying?' She had nothing on except a half-length monkey jacket, tied with loops behind, a sheet round her legs which was spattered with patches of pink blood, a sanitary napkin between her legs. Occasionally the exhaustion became too much and she flopped down on the delivery table. Within a few seconds, was fast asleep until, 'Here it comes! Help me up. O God! Help me up!' 'One — two — three . . . ' This was the worst. She was unable to prepare herself mentally for the next contraction. They caught her unawares and before she knew it she was in the middle of another grinding, tearing pain.

There were no tears. Not once did she cry. The only tears had been when she was still in the labour ward and they asked me to leave. In the delivery room her protest, her pain was voiced in a series of yelps, throttled cries and the one recurrent statement: 'I can't carry on. I just can't.' Face flushed, eyes bleary, every so often seeing me, thanking me for being there, kissing my neck when her head rested on my shoulder.

At seven o'clock, because there had not yet been any progress, she was wheeled back into the labour ward. I sat by her bedside. She drank a cup of tea. I ate the porridge on her breakfast tray. The surroundings were more comfortable. I was free of the embarrassment of mask and gown, but the pains were worse and more frequent. I too began to get tired, and together with Sheila dropped off to sleep between each contraction. I awoke with a start every time — 'Count, Athol!' or 'Another pain' or 'Here it comes!' — and, as if it was a deeply ingrained reflex, grabbed her hard and started counting before I even knew where I was.

The new day was bright, hard, comfortless sunlight in the windows. Her lips and teeth coated with dried spit. Her breath foul-smelling. Every time a nurse came in (half-hourly examinations), I had to leave. Once I had to leave the labour ward four times in succession with hardly a minute's rest between — pacing up and down outside.

Finally, at about eleven o'clock a.m. (Saturday, May 27), the staff nurse came out after a rectal examination and said, when she passed me, 'I think she's ready now.' They wheeled her into the delivery ward, a staff nurse told me to wait in the waiting-room; but as there were other people there I walked up and down the street outside the hospital.

I heard the incredible chatter of weaver birds in a tree — their nests hanging from branches, one freshly made, the grass still green. I saw poinsettias in bloom, a woman in a red dress, a red motor-car, and decided red was the colour of pain. Suddenly, miraculously almost, it was a new day, the sun bright, sky blue, everything beautiful — a day separated by fatigue, despair and now hope, from the cold comfortless sunlight that had filled the window of the labour ward where Sheila had been in pain.

A young man came out of the hospital, eating an orange. Hadn't split it into quarters, it wasn't even properly peeled. He ate it with a strange animality. Good-looking, dark, almost Italian complexion — physically a beautiful male. He gave me a smile: 'The marching brigade, hey.' 'Yes, she's inside.' It turned out his had been born seven weeks ago, but with a harelip, for which they had operated today. Fear, disappointment, anger, pain and doubt as to his capacity to love, lurked in his eyes. 'They say if he grows a scar you won't hardly see it.' Ate his orange. 'Them that's been like that makes up for it they say. They say they got brain. Isn't that so?' It was a deformity, his eyes said it. He was hurt and knew in feeling this, that he in his turn was hurting — his wife, his child, himself.

I went back to the waiting-room. It was now deserted so I sat down. I had dozed off when at about 12.30 a nurse was suddenly beside me, smiling: 'I am proud to tell you you are the father of a lovely daughter.' Lovely daughter: for the first time I felt the mantle of parenthood. Lovely daughter — the sound of the words themselves was an experience without precedent in my life.

I had to wait a few more minutes outside the delivery room, and then, after the trolley filled with bloody swabs and basins of water had been wheeled out, I was allowed in.

My God! Sheila! She was lying face flushed but alert and intelligent to everything, on the table, and beside her the baby wrapped up in a blanket. I had heard a cry while waiting outside. Now it was quiet, grunting like a pig, spit bubbles ballooning out and bursting on its lip. There were rusty stains of blood in the blanket; Lisa's head was also covered with what looked like rusty dandruff. Sheila, flushed, untidy and a little bit uncertain, was aware of the disappointment in me that it was not a boy. 'We can have another. I won't mind. There's nothing to it really.' The agony of the past twelve hours had been washed out of her mind. There was pride too, in her self, in the child. A tentative pride, like a child given a toy, which she wants, but by a stranger, and uncertain to take it up and play. But she was beautiful and loved me, and I loved her. The baby was carried away to be washed; Sheila was given a tray of tea and toast which she ate, and I went home to sleep. Then, and last night, and again tonight, sleep is not easy. For a few terrifying moments I see her again, as she was when the pains were coming, and with a violent vengeance.

Sheila, suffering, vulnerable, fragile — and the terror of something going wrong looms up real and urgent before me, regardless of the fact that now it is past, and she has survived, and nothing at all went wrong. It is like a terrible nightmare and I need the constant assurance that I have woken up.

Tonight for the second time I have seen her since the birth. She was beautiful, and calm, and apart from a new awe-inspiring depth to the blueness of her eyes, almost unmarked by the experience of her travail.

Lisa Maria is growing on me, as I expected. I can hardly remember now that I wanted a boy. The disappointment of finding myself the father of a daughter seems absurd, and something of which I am ashamed and want to forget.

Childbirth, a woman in labour, has become one of those thoughts, images, experiences, which I will only be able to approach with reverence, like Christ on the Cross. Levity, humour or smart irreverence, are unbecoming, besmirching, ignorant. That strikes me — the ignorance which men (and some women too) have of the experience, showering it with banalities, clichés, crude humour and sighs and up-turned eyes — as if that was a virtue on our part: to be tolerant and patient!

Random images: The nurses in their green delivery room aprons and white masks. The moments of confusion (so it seemed), haste, hurried activity, doors opening, slamming, nurses running, a stretcher wheeled in the delivery room — and then the cry of a baby, the same activity but quietly now, relaxed — the job done — the baby bawling away in the room where it was bathed.

Two other thoughts: Sheila's reference to 'Hell's Hour' (I'd read about it — but now I knew what they meant) when I joined her in the delivery room at 2 a.m. when the pains were really savage. And being glad for the mask they had given me to wear because behind it I was smiling. The strange elation that lit my fear and terror; elated at knowing 'this was it' — 'this means the baby is coming'. The elation wasn't long-lasting. Then there was just fatigue, dulling the recurrent terror of her pains.

June
A comparison: Lisa Maria's arrival on May 27 and, last night, 'The Birth of a Republic'.

Found the second happening quite by accident. The usual walk at eleven — full moon, heavy dew and then back in bed, in the dark, smoking a pipe, when a bell began to toll midnight. The birthcries of

37

the Republic: an engine whistle down in the marshalling yards (the driver kept it going for at least three minutes), sporadic blowing of hooters in the distance. People seemed to wake up to the fact that South Africa was now a Republic in fits and starts. At about 12.30 someone drove the length of Bird Street with his hooter blaring all the time. The celebration was even more dreary than the hooter blowing and bell chiming that sees in the New Year. By 12.45 it was all over — just the moon; the bright streets, the dew tapping in a roof gutter outside; the crickets.

This morning on the radio I caught a snatch of the inaugural ceremony of the State President. A Dutch Reformed Church minister, in deep, exaggerated fervour, was thanking God for giving us a Republic and a Staats President. When the commentator announced that the ceremony had 'now reached the most solemn moment of all' — I turned off.

Slowly accepting Lisa's cry as a normal sound of my life. At first it terrified me, bringing on fits of desperation, insomnia, lying awake waiting for it; that made my nights hell again. I had heard too much, in too short a space of time — Dad, Sheila in labour, Mom, and then Lisa — now I am beginning to forget again.

The tea-party for the Meirings — four generations: Oupa, Doctor, Sheila, Lisa. Lisa being passed around. Crowded noisy, smoke-filled room. Oupa, benign satisfaction (another one! Five grandchildren, five great-grandchildren). Doctor M. and his second wife — frustrated desire to love and acknowledge her; his suspicion of women, loneliness, clumsiness; Mrs M. childless; Mom, like Oupa; Sheila; myself. Lisa as if she tangibly felt it all, behaved worse than she had since coming home — crying, fretful, colic.

Now two weeks and four days old.

Tonight Mom put out a hand to touch Lisa's chin and I saw that the last joint of the index finger was badly crooked — as happens with rheumatism. The last hand I remember as having that was her own mother: grey unwanted old woman, poking about the dark corners of houses, waiting patiently with a pathetic little black bag, in between the endless shuttling from one relative to another. She died in the Fort England Mental Home, Grahamstown.

Mom and her mania for putting shoots and seeds and plants into old tins. One of them gave her trouble and somebody suggested that there might be a mole inside, 'it could have got in with the soil.'

Mom fetched a vicious broad-bladed butcher's cleaver and plunged it into the soil several times — 'I'll kill it!'

Tonight Petros, the little basket boy from Korsten, came round to the flat again and rapped loudly on our window. He has been coming regularly — mostly around lunchtime — and Sheila and I have always given him something to eat — orange and a few biscuits, a few sweets. Less frequently he has come to the door in the late afternoon (already dark — it's winter now), and asked for a sixpence for bus fare. These I gather are the days when he has not managed to sell a basket, and has therefore no money for his fare.

Giving money has been hard. We don't have much, and most times what Sheila does have in her bag comes from my Mom. I have tried to stop him asking for money — giving him a stupid talk about not having much ourselves — but a few days later he is back again and I weaken. Once or twice my Mom has been present — we invariably had an argument about him.

Today he came first at lunchtime. He was not alone. His companion (his 'brother' Willie) was so small he made Petros look big. If Petros is about ten years old, Willie must have been five. What — *what* do I remember of him? The incredible 'smallness' — fragility of thin matchstick legs sticking out of the khaki shorts, wide white eyes, brave but bewildered. Petros picking him up over the small wall that cuts off the one side of the stoep outside our window. He was too small to climb over *that*. The trust he so obviously had in Petros, following, knowing nothing of what was happening or about the bearded white man who gave him an orange, a biscuit and a scone.

Tonight, shortly after it grew dark, the knock at our stoep door. I knew who it was. I first pretended not to hear it. Then a second time, and louder. I went with the first words of a stern reprimand on the tip of my tongue. Tonight there would be no sixpences.

Petros and little Willie. (I remember something else — the way Willie's eyes jumped around, all over my person, from my hands to my face, trying to find the source of the next miracle.) 'What is it Petros?' — hard, severe. Petros pointed, 'Hy is klein.'[13]

That was all. Because he was, and he had to be helped over the wall, and it was at least five miles back to Korsten, and it was already dark, and winter.

'You want sixpence. All right, Petros, all right. I'll give it. All right, I'll give it.'

'Hy is klein' — what does that reveal? Petros wasn't begging for himself. There was need, and there was me, so he pointed, believing, at least hoping, that I would understand. The unimportant things like bus fare, food, water, yawning wide in a child's eyes.

It was a distance of five miles from Korsten, where his people did their basket-weaving, to the city so it meant that much of a walk every morning except on Sundays. Unless he was able to sell a basket in the city, it meant that much of a walk back in the evenings as well. Sixpence, the bus fare, is a lot of money when you haven't got it; when all you've got is baskets which nobody wants; when you're small, and black, and can hardly speak the white man's language.

So most of the mornings and the evenings of his tenth year, Petros walked the five miles between the city and Korsten. They weren't a bad five miles . . . except — Sydenham — gangs of white boys. Passing bus queues on his way back in the evening. Dogs. The technique of selling to a white man — watching eyes.

October
Dad's death.
Mom referred to Dad's carcass.

'Daddy, why are you chanting like a Jew?'
'Don't be silly. It's Persian.'
'That doesn't sound like Persian songs, Daddy!'
'You want to know what it is? My pain. I'm making my pain sound nice.'
He sang that until he died.

He dipped his crutches and rowed into the shallows, where he waited. Death effaced a gentle gesture. His hand floating between the white sheets and his lips, pursed on a cigarette. His eyes, blinking with sleep, focused on the ceiling. I came to the death bed, eyes wet with love, looking back and laughing at pleasures only hours old.

Afrikaner women in mourning — Mom, Katie, Ann, Lenie, Mrs Swart — sitting around, monumental, black.

Dad with his shock of silver hair as bright as they were sombre.

The coloureds who took off their hats when the hearse passed. Petros, the little Korsten basket boy who Dad had chased from the flat, watched the procession from a pavement.

Dad's crutches. Dad's story — the man who ended up feeling unimportant.

People must be loved. That is the really crucifying experience in the short time we have as human beings — that intimacy which breaks through our defensive isolation and shows the capacity — if need be

40

no more than that — just an awareness of the potential — of someone else's suffering.

The Bird Street flat:
Retrospect — pain, musty cupboards, mouldy leather.

Two rooms — the large folding doors separating them. In one room my father (dying) and my mother. In the other, Sheila (pregnant) and myself — writing *The Blood Knot*.

The departures and arrivals. My father to hospital, there to die. Sheila to hospital, to give birth. Returning with Lisa.

Also a door to our room. Watching the world from it — starlings, sunshine on white walls, rain. Visitors to the door — Petros, the basket boy from Korsten.

Of course also the front door but I am (in retrospect) oblivious to it. Sheila answered the knocks, said no to the hawkers, turned away the Salvation Army collectors. The traffic between myself and the world was through the glass double-door of our room opening on to the stoep. Symbolically, it was through these doors that late at night I went for my walk around the park, and through them that I returned to the room.

The room — my life, its privacy, its contact with other lives, its moments of peace, inadequacy.

Only one perspective for the act of love — from within.

1962

January
Johannesburg — Braes o' Berea[1] — abuses, obscene slanging match between two women in annexe next-door. 'Ou poes', 'you mongrel bitch', 'fucking ou hoer'. The one, big, burly aggressive, had beaten up the other — black eye, broken lips. Late at night. Inevitably a small crowd had collected and stood round watching, like statues — absolutely motionless. The woman who had been beaten up turned to them and in between berating the other one, appealed, 'Please call the police!' No one moved.

'You rotten old bitch. I want my bloody money. You fucking old shit. It's my room. Call the police for me! Phone them, tell them to come. I'll show her.' No one moved.

There was one other person in the scene, a young girl, Frieda. Hiding behind a low wall. She was the daughter of the woman who wanted the police. Just occasionally her mother remembered her: 'Where is Frieda? Frieda! She's my daughter. *My* daughter!'

Also involved, but peripherally, was an old Studebaker convertible — artificial leopard skin upholstery — with a load of swarthy unemployed young men, Duckies. It cruised round the block and every time it passed the two women the young men called to them — but indistinctly.

On New Year's morning, another woman outside Braes o' Berea bruised from a fight with her husband on New Year's eve, now temporarily reconciled (that uneasy truce!) in the light of a new day and a New Year — carrying her baby, wearing a pair of men's shoes. The old car they got into.

The Liberal Party braaivleis after the last night of first run of *The Blood Knot.* Zakes[2] and I the guests of honour. Private house crowded with blacks and whites — hypocrisy, shallowness. Blacks holding out limp hands and calling you comrade while their eyes spoke the truth.

The couple due to appear in a few days' time on an immorality charge. She — round baby face. They were caught when she was in bed, he sitting beside her. I found myself wedged in a corner, holding a brandy, when he, drunk came up. Then she appeared and he intro-

duced her as 'the girl I was caught with' — but the affair had been going on for well over a year. Her shyness, her excitement — the nervous inconstancy of her eyes almost feverish. He was pestering a girl,
trying to make a pass at anything that was white and she joked about
it: 'What I like about him, he always tells me he's going to make a
pass at something else' — quick sharp laugh.

Dorkay House[3] — in one of the empty rooms on first floor. Floor
tiles loose in large ulcerous patches. On one bench, flautist and his
doll, petting mildly. Drummer and saxophonist drifted in and out.
Flautist had a bottle of brandy and one cup — he poured out tots
and passed them around.

Ferreira - caretaker of warehouse where the National Theatre Organisation kept scenery — once a warder of Pretoria Central prison.
Terrifying experience of the death chamber where he worked. Mass
hanging of Africans.

The man who wouldn't be weighed and measured — so to spite
him the hangman gave him a fall that tore his head off.

Scrubbing the bodies afterwards. Squeezing them into coffins.
Ferreira was convinced of the moral degradation of the death penalty
and capital punishment.

April

Eastern Cape — drive to Kirkwood. Autumn. Good rains, veld green.
Swarms of butterflies and on the telephone wires, resting or darting
repeatedly across the road, catching them, swallows or swifts.

In the valley, the veld carpeted with small yellow flowers. Also
patches of the pink flower — 'Seeroog'. Coming back, sun already set,
hundreds of snow-white egrets, roosting in trees on the banks of the
Sundays River. A large flock wheeling about the river bed — dry but
for a few stagnant pools — as we shot across the bridge.

Butterflies — soft orange with underside of wings pale green,
white and, rarer, dark bitter-chocolate brown with intense luminous
colours — blue, green, red — in spots.

A last image: quite dark except for the pale wash of the twilight
nether-light on the farthest horizon. Squat, sprawling farm-houses
crouched low into the bosom of the earth in a grudging surrender to
the darkness.

Car accident near Swartkops. African cyclist knocked down. Dead
or alive (the silence of shock or pain?)? A few cars had stopped and
whites were standing around in the garish glare of the headlamps. He
lay stretched out on his back, under a blanket, staring at the sky.

The great vindication of capitalism in the west — free enterprise. 'Anybody if he's got it in him can be rich.' Rich? And what can be said for the rich man — or the men who do not get rich?

The fight for human dignity by Kyo Gisors, the communist leader in *Man's Estate* (Malraux). 'No human being can live meaningfully and with dignity if he works twelve hours a day and does not know why he is doing it.' — or words to that effect.

Camus's *The Outsider* — and the old woman in the home. The paradox of starting to live when life is over.

The extreme viciousness of old age. An observation to Sheila: 'When they are that age and the child is as old as us, or is at least adult, it's no longer love, or respect, or the seeing of people as individuals, the clear contours of personality, that govern relationship. We fumble around in the debris of guilts, bad consciences, and hunger for revenge that a lifetime of bad living has cluttered around us.'

There is a startling parallel — resemblance — between Sheila and the Outsider: that same indifference to hypocritical, shallow, superficial demands of society. A living outside — a withdrawal. In retrospect I see that I have always been aware of it, never quite accepted it: at times deliberately intervened to correct (in reality, twist into something more convenient) the 'public image' Sheila created of herself. Very silly, superficial of me. There is a rock-bottom morality, a compassion.

The six months with Sheila in Bird Street last year, waiting for Lisa to be born, writing *The Blood Knot*.

I return to it again and again in thought as material for a prose-work. The superficial problem — the structure, in terms of writing. On the surface — just six months, a routine, a string of incidents. Yet that, I know, is not the reality, particularly on rereading pages in my notebook from that period.

Two thoughts occur: Firstly, Lisa's birth as, in reality, the climax of that period. An affirmation. A breakthrough of Life, in (mine) a life through retrospection, and introspection, cluttered with the debris of thirty years of cowardice, brief courage, blindness, deafness — all brought back vividly by memory of those six months. Secondly: that period as one of those quiet, almost slumbering periods, when the living body mends what damage has been done, and prepares the pattern for the next years. This is definitely true. There was a before and an after (the present, the now) and they are fundamentally different: and what is more, the 'after' was prepared in those six months.

The fascination of this thought being that the great 'happening' was hidden from all except my eye; the task to explore this process buried as it is in the deepest, inward levels of my living.

Visit with Maggie to Harold Strachan at local jail.[4] A long wait outside the locked double doors. Africans and coloureds lined up like a platoon of school cadets, waiting to visit relatives inside. Carrying parcels of food, tins of fish etc. Let in, eight at a time.

Eventually Maggie and I were admitted and, after signing our names in the visitor's book, shown to the visiting cell where Harold was waiting. Small room; two barred-off sections with gap between. Harold in one, Maggie and I in the other. Only furniture was one rather battered chair in the visitors' section. Harold and I squatted on the floor. One policeman present. Had to ask his permission to slide a few sweets along the floor to Harold.

More than anything else one was conscious of, and embarrassed by, the indignity.

Trial to start in about three weeks. Harold is impatient — has already been in for four months.

No false optimism or clutching at drowning hopes in Maggie: 'First there was talk about the death penalty; then twelve years; now they mention five years.'

Four-months-old baby.

First visit with Sheila and Lisa to Van Staaden River mouth. On the drive there, and coming, an idea: a young boy in one of the fascinating Cape Road corrugated-iron Poor White houses. Eventually ends up a bus-conductor in Port Elizabeth.

Walked off along the beach. Seemingly endless stretch of wide virgin sand, sloping down from ridge of very high dunes crowned with bushes — behind them a maze of wild, intractable, pockets of bush. Dead silence except for the distant surf and an occasional liquid note from a bird. Spoor of buck.

Returning to Sheila and Lisa, found the latter playing in the sand — face, hands, legs covered with it. Unbelievable innocence of her smile under the pink floppy bonnet. Only ten months old and yet already there is a sharply defined (to my eyes) contrast between her character in the simple setting of that beach, and the complicated quick-silver reactions that constitute her, in a room, in the presence of people. More simply: the naive, innocent (even in adults — myself) responses when confronted with the great elements: sea, veld, sky. A directness, frankness. Opposing this: all we are, seem to be, try to be, pretended to be, among fellow creatures.

Yesterday at the café — the swimming bath manager, six-foot tall, strapping, suntanned extrovert type, interrupted our tea: 'Come and see what tried to get in for a swim! Come!'

He led me out to the front and pointed down the path to the retreating back of a small boy. Barefoot, khaki trousers and carrying a towel. Mop of brown curly hair.

'He's a coloured!' said the manager. 'Told me a lie, said he went to Marist Brothers. You lie, I said. Yes, he said, I go to the South End School. He's a coloured, man, I know his mother.'

A nice, clear example of sheer unconscious brutality of the South Africa I know. Just one question: What? What did that little kid say, or ask, or reply to himself? How did he fit that rejection into the tentative pattern of his living? What is that pattern?

Visit to Mrs Ashbury in Cora Terrace. She had seen *Blood Knot* twice down here, written to me expressing appreciation, then asked if we would come around one evening. It started off grimly: 'I hope you won't mind, but this is going to be a *Blood Knot* night.' Sat in the lounge, drinking and eating peanuts. Horrifying consciousness on her part of my presence, as the Writer, the Artist. I made some remark. 'That's the trouble, you see, you're an artist.' (I had disagreed with her husband.) Also: 'It must be fascinating to write a play. I've always wanted to.' Her husband — big well-built man, slow lumbering movement and speech. Sharp initial antagonism until he discovered that I was prepared to talk about the things that interested him: smoking — giving it up — he had, seven years ago; how many a day; motorcars; photography.

Tentative nibble at politics. We all agreed that you have to give the other man a chance. Paralysing generalities.

My mother, because of her asthma, has located the Achilles' heel of the human being in the lungs (lunks). Particularly noticeable in terms of Lisa and everything she puts in her mouth — a piece of paper, a feather, a piece of a screw. The worst imaginable fate though is a 'Cat's hair on the lung.' The night the ginger cat walked in from outside, Lisa was attracted to it, my mother was rigid with horror, waiting tense for the calamity — a hair on the lung.

My mother's technique — used every time she is given a chance or when she feels she knows best and therefore must be obeyed — is to try to panic the other person into doing what she wants: when I gave

Lisa a piggy-back ride, Mom thrust out her jaw, clenched her fingers and screamed, 'Her back! You'll break her back!'

E., discussing sabotage trials, made the point that all the recent attempts at sabotage were amateurish in execution and planning, that the wrong people were planting the bombs. Sheila elaborated on it later: 'After reading Malraux's *Human Estate* you know one thing for certain, there is a type that throws the bomb. A definite, specific breed.' In Malraux, Chen, the terrorist.

E. listed the mistakes — the clumsiness, the lack of secrecy in plans for sabotage. The most glaring idiocy was that after planting and setting off bombs at the Brickmakers Kloof electricity sub-station, the saboteurs ran *up* the hill, and were of course caught. Downhill would have been faster and taken them into the dark maze of the valley, with some chance of escape.

This one, inconceivably stupid mistake — and as a result they face a possible ten years in jail.

Have always seen Lisa's birth with reference to my family, e.g. her birth, my father's death. There is of course a much more 'organic' involvement with Sheila's family, Sheila being the daughter, the real continuity of family — *no*, of life, running from mother to daughter.

The Meiring family, like a mobile, and Lisa's arrival a new displacement of weight on the periphery, causing unexpected shifts through the precarious structure.

Sons provide the continuity of a family. Daughters, the continuity of life.

The intellectual concepts, 'ideas', which motivate the white man in South Africa today are of the sort which, when taken to the extreme, or in certain situations, reduce men to barbarism, 'The nationalist has a broad hatred, and a narrow love.' Gide.

The 'character' of the beaches along the coast. Sardinia Bay: broad, virgin stretch of sand and, because we always choose a weekday to visit it, completely deserted. Amsterdam Hoek and St. George's Strand — driftwood and shells. Sea View: rock pool. Went there today. Indescribable beauty of some of the pools with their multi-coloured jumble of stones, seaweed and urchins. Latter particularly — purple, red, white, pink — hard, symmetrical beauty, set down like precious ornaments. Contrast with the anemone pools near Cape

Town which were soft and more like gardens.

I hesitate to put down this thought: that my death be so arranged that I can prepare. Now, thirty years old, feeling at times mortally sick from the corruption and duplicity of my country, I think that given time I could prepare, and find peace, by remembering, re-seeing, the little that I already have seen of life; and relive my dawning astonishment and wonder at the great beauty, complexity and honesty of that vast area of 'living experiences' that have nothing to do with man.

Has any previous age been so self-centred, so conscious of the human shape to the exclusion of all else?

The humility I felt this afternoon, crouched over a rock-pool, watching.

May

Incredible statistic in a newspaper lying on the lavatory floor: ' . . . the total sentences amounted to 2 015 years, and the fines to R3 075.00.' — reviewing of cases tried in the Johannesburg Magistrates' Courts.

Since Wednesday, spent every day at the trial of Harold Strachan, John Jack and Govan Mbeki[5] — charged with sabotage. Went along prepared to note in detail everything: characters, evidence, incidents etc. Instead, a few specifics emerged and then dominated every minute I spent in the courtroom. Everything I heard and saw merely underscored, illustrated these few simple ideas.

I already see now that this moment — this point in my life — is climacteric. Three completely separate influences have converged: my reading for the first time of Dostoevsky's *The Possessed,* Harold's case; and the writing project I have started on. Individually each would in all probability have left me with the same thoughts: taken together, as has happened to me, the imprint is indelible. A moment of my life at which later I might well point back and say, there it started, there I turned.

I know one thing. What I have seen in court has nothing to do with Justice. (Or else Justice is precisely that: Society with its rules closed.) What I saw was Society (not just loosely in the sense of the status quo, but as it will still exist when the balance of power has shifted in this country — I wonder if Harold realises this) avenging, protecting itself. To put it another way: it is the spectacle of society with its hands on the outsider (Camus). The alleged sabotage gave society its chance.

What is the outsider? The man who doesn't subscribe. The man who does not contribute the authority of his consent, to social sanction. Something is — not just jeopardised — but surrendered with that subscription. This is more important for the outsider than the 'common good'. What is it? It is defined by the Christian ethic (or: that which finds its life in the aspiration of the Christian ethic: and is frustrated in 'society') — which can only exist on the basis of complete moral freedom. Society cannot. Society is a compromise of that ethic; and since the ethic cannot be compromised and still exist, society involves its negation.

But even the outsider is 'present' in society. On what basis does he live among the 'subscribers'? A foreigner in a strange land. A man in a foreign country. Looking back — this defines a feeling I have had, among men, so often. The feeling of not 'really' belonging, of being a 'stranger' — even when we 'laughed in the same language'. Particularly this time in the court (and how often I have wanted to be a subscriber — Moravia's *The Conformist*).

A deceit — hypocrisy: this 'outsider' in 'society'? No. Firstly because the authority of 'social sanction' — the common subscription — is no 'greater' or more final than that of the 'outsider' — his inner light.

A paradox? Maybe. Why after all should the nature of man be such that it is compatible — at its highest — with society. Why after all 'meaningful' — why not 'meaningless'. How meaningful is nature at any level — that of the sea-urchins for example. What 'meaning' could be pointed out to me in that blind-deaf cycle of life and death, other than It is Life. It is Good. Which is the outsider in me talking.

The terror of the Law: of the legal machine.

Justice without sensitivity, without humour, without beauty, without irony — and without dignity, or the respect for human dignity. Maybe this is the cause of that 'facelessness' I see in everyone in the court. We have, after all, left life behind, stepped out of it — and it is in life that we live, are influenced and act and react because of those very qualities I find absent in courtroom justice. We are subject to the letter of the law — literally, words on paper.

The strongest, and most disturbing, effect of that courtroom is what I have described to Sheila as the violation of the personal, private image.

49

'The accused then crossed the road . . . ' 'The accused came up to me and said . . . ' 'What did the accused look like?' 'He was agitated, M'Lord.' And all the time the accused is present, hearing his movement, gestures, very words, talked about without any reference to the innermost realities of his being.

Also the freezing at some − in retrospect − irrational moment, the action of your life. In Harold's case, the police photographs of the garage: showing it as he had left it just before his arrest. The bucket half-filled with dirty water; the dirt swept into a corner and not yet carried away.

Certain important actions are recapitulated, re-examined time and time again, e.g. the search of the house. But one gets no further, because after that he was arrested.

An idle, indulged thought: to plead guilty rather than have all the foregoing happen.

Visited the advocate in another case in his chambers in Main Street. He is having a hard time getting started − people regard him as too 'political'. Income this month R 25.00. Found him, feet up on his desk, reading a novel. He's been in practice for about four months and his only real cases have been *pro-deo*.

At his office I met one of the accused in the case, who had spent six months in jail awaiting trial. All three were kept in solitary confinement. The Africans were allowed a little tobacco but no reading matter. 'Even when you tear off a piece of paper for your personal use − you know, the toilet − then you got to prove it to them; you must show them that you taken a piece from the advertisements, otherwise they get suspicious.' The whites were allowed reading matter but, conversely, very little tobacco. So, when the warders weren't around, they traded, using a piece of string to exchange goods. Another commodity the Africans bargained for was bread, which they were not given. Hard, round little loaves, called 'Katte-kop'.

Once you were settled in, however, you could usually organise something with the African warders. In this way, Joe was able to get copies of *New Age* and the local dailies.

Another important person in terms of getting things organised was the 'agter-ryer' − the tough bully singled out by the warder to help him keep the other prisoners in order. Every section had its agter-ryer; awaiting trial, hard-labour, short-sentence, etc.

Agter-ryer and the warder: a mutually dependent relationship − the warder needs the agter-ryer to keep control and get the work done; in return, the agter-ryer is allowed extra tobacco, etc. Sometimes the prisoners find themselves competing — by way of presents, 'lappie' for his boots; big tin of Nugget polish — for the privileged position. One of the functions of the agter-ryer is to help search prisoners and their parcels after visits. Joe told his wife to hide newspapers in the clothes she brought him. While he was being searched by the warder, the agter-ryer would grab the clothes, pretend to search them, and so let the newspapers through.

Being a 'political' made a big difference among the fellow-prisoners. You were treated with respect, and it almost automatically guaranteed the friendship and assistance of the agter-ryer.

White warders? A few, rare exceptions to the general rule of brutality, coarseness, cruelty. 'How did their humanity show itself?' I asked. 'Ja, well, you know, you judges a man by the little things; how he speaks to you; if he says good morning. You know, man, the way he treats you, like another human being.'

Any breach of prison regulations results in being isolated. No food for three days. The half rations for three days, then again no food, etc. Your sustenance on the three days without food is rice-water, the water the rice has been cooked in.

One of the jobs of the agter-ryer is to keep his warder's boots clean — always fussing round wiping off the boots. There is apparently a special way of cleaning those boots so that the toecaps shine like red mirrors.

The size of Joe's cell: eight shoe lengths by six shoe lengths. About four paces.

'You're left to your thoughts, and that's a punishment in itself.'

So my novel (à la Beckett) is no more. Read what I had written to Sheila. Her silence — my own feelings as I progressed from one muddled paragraph to another, were enough. I tore it up.

I don't consider the work wasted. In any case, this business of writing 'prose' because a publisher is interested is fundamentally wrong.

I am a playwright.

So tomorrow — we start again. How many false starts aren't there before one hits on the one beginning that leads through to an end.

But I am hopeful.

One image — has generated an old complex of ideas — Milly's 'cri de coeur' when she finds she's been in her dressing-gown all day. I already have the ending. Came across these notes made in London: *Milly* — divorced three times. Living with Ahlers for about ten years. 'He was nothing when I met him.' She took him in and built up his

51

business, working as his secretary in the factory. It is flourishing and now he is (apparently) no longer interested. He left her once — and came back. Is there another woman?

It is Milly's birthday and he is taking someone else out.

Milly is proud of her past — her ties with a big family.

She lives a lot in her dressing-gown.

Don — intellectual — books, music — knows a lot — knows what is wrong with the world outside. Knows that he is doing nothing.

Shorty — a small man — amateur boxer. Earns his living precariously as a postman. Married Cissy — a child bride. No sex (except maybe for the first night). Keeps silk worms and loves Mario Lanza's singing.

A Jo'burg winter. They sit in the kitchen at night for warmth after their meal. Don writing. Milly reading. Shorty: Mario Lanza and his worms.

Milly, when bedtime comes, is suddenly unnerved by the thought that she is still in her night clothes from last night.

1st Act curtain on the three of them at the table.

2nd Act — still at the table — with a stranger in the fourth chair. Obsession with the empty fourth chair. (Ahlers? Cissy? Man?)

In the second act there is an awareness in each, of someone in the fourth chair. They are frightened!

Play cards.

Yes.

Bridge. Bridge?

Alright.

Who will deal?

(They are frightened because it will mean dealing in the fourth.)

Don does — he hesitates and then deals. The game follows.

In the third act (Did you say something?) they are found as they were in Act I end.[6]

To capture the 'angularity' of action. What do I mean by angularity? The unpremeditated, the sudden, even on the most inconsequential level. But even more: as if at times life, like a jacket a size too small, didn't fit the individual and resulted in stiff, awkward movements.

The last week or so a return of that 'personal shame' caused by remembering myself in attitudes, poses, deceits, incidents from the past. Usually at night when the others are asleep and I am also trying to go to sleep, or in the middle of the night when I wake up and lie half-awake for a long time.

On the other hand, I've realised suddenly that when I go to the barber nowadays, I no longer find myself telling absurd lies ('Out in the bush for a couple of weeks') to explain my long hair. I used to spend all my time, while awaiting my turn, preparing this lie.

I do care less. I'll try to catalogue some of these changes on my birthday next month.

Cinema last night. Two items in newsreels: A display of new bombs and bombing tactics, for the American President. Commentator's final remark, '... hoping that these will never be used in anger.' And: the extermination of a pocket of communist guerrillas in South Vietnam. Last shot of dead commies — again (as in the Sharpeville photos) the strange, lonely postures of Death.

Those games we played as children were our first indoctrination into the morality of our time. Cowboys and Crooks. The good man and the bad man. No question to it: the bad man must die. 'Bang! You're dead.'

'No civilisation is complete that does not make provision for the dumb and defenceless creatures of God's creation.' Queen Victoria.

Yesterday afternoon with Maggie Strachan and her baby, and Julie Shum and little boy, went to a protest meeting (Sabotage Bill) in Korsten. Held in a vacant lot: about 200 people, mostly Africans. In addition to us there were three other whites. A fresh, windy, winter's day. We all sat on the grass and listened to the speakers. Between speeches the Africans were led in 'Freedom' songs by one of the men on the platform. Coloured children from the neighbourhood played about piles of builders' rubble — an official-looking building has just been completed on the adjacent lot. The coloured watchman and a few friends watched the meeting through a window. Drifting through the crowd were men and women selling *New Age,* the *Afrika* pamphlets on Algeria and Angola, and lapel badges.

The Special Branch present in force — about twenty whites and blacks — inside the cars or leaning on the bonnets, taking down the speeches.

No 'incidents'.

One African caught my attention. A big powerfully-built man, 40-50, wearing a balaclava cap, squatting on the ground. Never looked at the speakers. Hard to say even that he 'listened' to, or heard the speeches. Almost as if he really only wanted the sound of those voices; drew his comfort from simply being there, among other Africans. A solid, patient, disturbing image.

At one stage some of the men present went into and about a builder's little corrugated-iron hut to urinate. This brought the watchman out of the building in double-quick time; he set upon them violently — the little hut was apparently his kitchen.

In the evening Sheila and I went to dinner at Julie Shum's house — Maggie's invitation. Also present Joe Jack and Govan Mbeki[7] and their wives.

One woman saw Govan as a Communist and herself as anti-Catholic, anti-Communist 'because the organisations are wrong. Not their ideals. I subscribe to their ideals.' Not really significant — what it all boiled down to was a sort of 'insidism' — a Jingoism wrapped up in woolly philosophical clichés. Responsibility was to one's friends, one's family and nature etc.

What was significant for me in the evening was the moment when she turned her critical powers on *The Blood Knot*. I've waited a long time for the person who would attack the play because Zachariah, the 'African' had all the 'base' emotions and instincts: while Morris was given the fine ones. I'd already met those who saw the play as a defence of the Immorality Act.

I realised, quite simply, my dependence on the one or the few who would see the truth; see what I had written.

A strange elation, and depression at the same time.

June
Returned today from five days in Johannesburg — purpose, to meet John Schlesinger, film director — *A Kind of Loving*.

With him to the Magistrates' Court — the *habitual criminal:* until the very last minute when he was led away to the cells after being sentenced, all we saw of him was his back. He stood with moving and pathetic dignity, stiff and straight, arms at his side. Hair neat, thinning. Brown check suit.

Charge: three counts of theft. He would order food from a restaurant. When it was delivered to his 'office' he would tell the servant (three African women) that the order was incomplete — that he also wanted two Coca Colas '. . . and bring change for £5.' A few simple manoeuvres and he had the change. In two of the three counts, the order was for two teas and four sandwiches. In the third count he added a slice of fruit cake. Total sum involved — just over R26.00.

A long list of previous convictions — all of them petty. Nevertheless he had already been sentenced in the past to a total of fifty-five years. His first crime, as a juvenile, dated back to 1923.

Witnesses: the three cafe proprietors and the three servants. After each witness had given evidence the Magistrate would ask him if he wished to question the witness or say anything. A slight hesitation, then in an even, unemotional voice: 'There is nothing I can say my Lord.' Time and time again, and right at the end just before sentence was passed, that one phrase: 'There is nothing I can say my Lord.'

The Magistrate — because of previous convictions: 'There is nothing for me but to declare you a habitual criminal.'

There were no spectators.

A few points: 1923. I hadn't been born yet. The second World War was still sixteen years away. 1923 and the first knot in this one insignificant, unimportant thread of living had been tied. The Magistrate said there were ninety previous convictions. This one life spinning out its petty length until those final three petty crimes and then, ostensibly, the silly but long bickering between himself and society was over. An Habitual Criminal. No drama. No High Point. This life is turning one of the last corners because of R 26.

My father.
Again — as with Harold Strachan — Society defending itself. And again thoughts about, an awareness of the 'outside' position.
Again — the Christian ethic and Society.

John Schlesinger, when I came out with a clumsy faltering expression of some of these thoughts, thought I was talking about Penal Reform.

With John Schlesinger, Ian and Don to Rustenburg, to show John Tribal Life. The Reserve. An old almost derelict communal hall with two small offices on either side of the entrance. One with a few old *Contact*[8] posters on the wall, a table and broken chairs, was the local Liberal Party office. In the other, the 'Right Reverend ... ' operated as a shoemaker and barber. I asked him about his 'church' — it was the same as the Pentecostal. How many members in his congregation — not too many locally, but in the Belgian Congo, he had 291. Aristocratic features, bearded. He was putting a heel on a lady's shoe as he spoke to us.

So my birthday has come and is now past and there is no catalogue of the changes. The effort is too great. At that level — the level of the fool, the man with five elbows knocking all the glasses off the table — I have never been a major problem to myself. So I am learning how to minimise the self-inflicted humiliations. Well and good. But I can't waste time writing about it. It's not an important, not even a good story.

Reading Camus's *The Rebel.*
Fascinated — yet I can find no concern or involvement with the issues he raises. Rather, let me qualify: a disinterestedness when he writes about the God-Man relationship. How is it that 'God' remains the most artificial word and thought in my life? Can I in all honesty translate my attitude into the words: I don't know whether he is or isn't. The small 'h' came off my pen without thought. It is a good example of what I think and feel in this respect.

I cannot get vehement about something that leaves me indifferent. God's fate at the hands of modern thinkers leaves me indifferent. Let me put it this way: I have felt no need — for Him — for an affirmation of Him, or a denial.

Death, the thought of it, of *my* death, holds terrors. And lately, time, and growing old, have started to nag. I look around and I see all of life sharing in these fates and that assuages the pain and worry. When other writers go to such involved and tortured lengths to find answers to these eternal and universal whys — how can I simply look around me (into a rock pool) and say: So be it — and, what is more, it is GOOD?

This acceptance, this resignation (but let me remember, they are acceptance of and resignation to the 'fight') come so easily that I am sure they are superficial and without meaning except as a phase in my growing up — and how long it takes me to grow up.

After more time, when I'm a little closer to death, I suppose I will also start asking the questions and looking for answers.

This thought occurs: Is it possibly my function precisely to accept — and within the framework of that acceptance to rejoice, as I said before, in the 'fight' — the sound and fury of it.

That in essence is what lies at the core of *People Are Living There.*

It is, all of my last paragraph, in my notes. Rereading them I find that what I have done is to catch life on the wing — to bring down a moment of it, a smell, a sound, a cry, always some new facet to the hard, beautiful reality of life. There are so few questions. In fact, I can't think of one.

Lisa. How important she has become! When all around me, including myself, sicken me — I escape into her world. A vicarious second chance at life.

She is now very firmly established on her two legs; dances in front

56

of the radio, especially to fast swinging jazz; and is trying to shape her first words.

At this moment she stands beside me, her head in my lap, whining and tugging at my trousers. She wants to be picked up. I refuse. She hobbles away, whining disconsolately.

Her birth has settled some of the problems, finally. I have a family — for the rest of my life, a home. These two realities will, between them, determine the pattern of 90% of my living.

And then there is also the thought: one day she will evaluate me — as a father, as a man, as a writer. Maybe this thought covers 9 of that remaining 10%. I will keep that remaining 1% for the fool in me. I'll be making an arse of myself up to the moment of my death. What's the bet that I even hash that up.

The best of me she will find in my writing — even to an understanding and compassion for the mistakes I will make as a father.

What is there in the experience of being eighteen years old, and a young girl, that draws me to this theme?

Firstly, the sense of violation. No violation (of the many) affects me so deeply as the violation of a woman as a woman — possibly because the crudity, savagery of the 'entry' is such a carnal, tangibly-felt symbol of all the other types. And usually all of them come at the same time. The body is violated (maybe even the womb), the spirit, the privacy of the individuality.

Virginity and the ruthless, savage reaction when the family finds it is gone because the young daughter is using her mother's Tampax.

The heart has a thousand virginities.

The weak artist — sincere at the moment — but then his loss of interest as his attention shifts to something else — and the young girl left alone.

Last night, just as we were falling asleep, a scream of terror from the little girl (1½ years) in the next flat — then the angry bitter voices of her parents. They were having another fight. This happens regularly — but without any of the comic, 'they're having another go'. The imprecations are too bitter, the violence in their cries (I hate you. I hate my mother. I hate my father. I hate you all.) too real, the terror of the little girl too real, for it ever to be funny from having heard it so often.

So I lay in the dark and strained my ears to catch the sound of their voices and the small cry — and as always happens in these situations, the beating of my heart became almost deafeningly loud and it seemed so easy for it to stop, to fail. An acute sense of horror. I thought of that family, locked together in their two small rooms, in each other's arms, each other's blood, the one bed, hating and loving — and with time hating more and more — twisting, squirming, without success in the iron, implacable hold that their fate has on their lives.

It could not be funny.

Another time I was having a bath when with explosive violence the same thing burst on the other side of the wall. Again, palpitations and horror, and love, as I sat still in the steaming water, listening.

If there is one story set in Bird Street that I would like to write, it is that one. Myself (the writer) with my family — and the family next-door, fighting themselves out to the death.

Then at last it was silent. Deep, untroubled, but not innocent. At about two o'clock I woke with a start — a car was travelling the length of Bird Street, the hooter blowing incessantly. A few belated revellers, snatches of song being sung by slurred, drunken male voices, as the car passed our window. Then it was silent again — but now sleep was out of the question. I prowled around.

I had seen in a film once that you could hear the conversation in an adjoining room by listening with a glass. I did this. I heard nothing.

The trap I had set for the mouse, sprang at about four o'clock.

One night — I almost say inevitably — came the moment when I was present at one of these fights.

There was a knock at the door. Mrs B. stood there panting heavily, red-eyed. 'Please, Mr F . . ., will you call the police?'

'What's he done?'

'Just call the police, please. I can't go on.' Her lips started trembling. 'I can't go on. I've had enough of that bastard.' She was crying now.

'Did he hit you?'

Opening: Sheila reads out the news item that he is to be tried for the murder of his wife. Evening — our conversation and thoughts about it.

Later in bed — my thoughts.

There is no relief — not even at the thought that their hell, the one shape of it that I knew, is ended. Now there is the court-case — and for me that is also terrible when I know the face of the accused, no matter how petty the crime. No, there is no relief.

Rather there is a sense of disappointment, of let-down, because this ending was never my prediction. We used to talk about it — I even mentioned it to him once. But I never felt it would happen. The last image I had of the three of them was so final — I could see nothing beyond it.

I know them — our back streets are crowded with them. Bigoted, selfish, small — these adjectives apply with monotonous aptness to their lives. And yet — what?

Embattled — that one word. I've looked it up. 'Set in battle array'. Old warriors — veterans.

Yes. I know the backstreets. I know the sound of the fight — with a drunk husband, naughty children, no money — and yourself. Finally — that most terrible of all adversaries — yourself, and why? Maybe as Mrs B. said one night: 'For having been born.'

This question: Can I any more work in a theatre which excludes 'Non-Whites' — or includes them only on the basis of special, segregated performances — is becoming increasingly pressing. Made, if that is possible, even more actual by the fact that British Equity is to decide on a resolution which will prevent any British entertainer visiting this country unless the audiences are multi-racial.

I think my answer must be No.

That old argument used to be so comforting; so plausible: 'One person in that segregated, white audience, might be moved to think, and then to change, by what he saw.'

I'm beginning to wonder whether it really works that way. The supposition seems to be that there is a didactic — a teaching-through-feeling element in art.

What I do know is that art can give meaning, can render meaningful areas of experience, and most certainly also enhances. But, teach? Contradict? State the opposite to what you believe and then lead you to accept it?

In other words, can art *change* a man or woman?

No.

That is what life does. Art is no substitute for life. It operates on top of life — rendering experience meaningful, enhancing experience.

Art — meaningfully ordered.

Life — chaotic.

If there is any argument which makes sense to me it is that the plays must be done and the actors seen (even on a segregated basis) not for the sake of the bigoted and prejudiced — *but for the sake of those who do believe in human dignity.* Let us not desert them. For those who *do believe,* Art can impart faith.

But this is an indulgence.

What is going to happen, will happen even though every liberal-thinking white (and black) in this country lose faith.

I am faced, finally, with the monstrous interpretations put on *The Blood Knot* — by those who were (and chose to be) blind and deaf to what was really happening on the stage.

In my case — forgetting for the moment absolutes and extremes — the crux of the matter is that here in South Africa at the moment (Jhb, C.T., P.E., Durban, Pretoria, Pietermaritzburg) there are venues where a play can be presented to mixed audiences. Some of them are barns — but then, Christ Almighty, does one need to point out that a theatre is made by an audience, the actors and the play, and not by soft seats, well-equipped stages, etc!

Operative in the white theatre in this country is every conceivable dignity — audience, producer, actor, 'professional' etc. — except human dignity.

July

The Equity resolution preventing British entertainers from coming to this country unless all performances were for mixed audiences, was carried. Here in South Africa it has been attacked, as expected, by the Afrikaans press, the English press and our theatre managements.

Their arguments are too peeved, stupid and in many cases downright wrong, to repeat. The old story — white South Africa (English-liberal) doesn't mind talking about the injustice of apartheid provided it involves no sacrifices.

If our society is morally bankrupt, the sooner the whites feel this as a reality, the better. But no, they want to condemn the cook and still eat the cake.

For me there is still a problem — an area in which I am feeling my way. Last night I suddenly said to Sheila: 'It's as simple as this. Compromise is the rule for staying alive, for getting from one day to the next. But it will do no more than that. Ultimately there comes a time when you have to make a stand — and then compromise means death. You can only "win" by sticking to your principles.'

Special performance for 'Non-Whites' — then sooner or later also special or certain plays *only.*

I'm not going to eat my cake if it's thrown down on the floor. Special performances are a 'gesture' in that category.

These last few days in Port Elizabeth — bird-watching.

Yesterday afternoon: Amsterdam Hoek. Low tide. Followed a curlew across the sandy bottom of one of the lagoons. A few moments of incredible tranquillity. To start with there was also a flock of plovers, but these eventually flew away leaving only the curlew and myself. No-one and nothing in sight. Not even vegetation as with the incoming tide the sands we were walking across would all be under water. In the distance, ahead, the sea, behind me the Swartkops and factories.

Then the tide started coming in. Suddenly it was there, bubbling, sucking, hissing, creeping across the sand. Birds — gulls, terns, duikers, plovers, curlews, oyster-catchers — came flying in from all directions to the sandbar at the mouth of the river. The moment of peace, gone. In its place, expectancy, urgency, hunger.

How dared I assess Camus's *The Rebel* after reading only about forty pages! The further I get into it the more light does it bring into those dark and obscure corners of my thinking. So great is my impression, now, that I almost want to speak of an 'inward illumination'.

The tone — disillusioned Honesty.

'. . . (real) freedom consists of the inward submission to a value which defies history and its successes.' Violence — 'necessary and inexcusable'.

Tomorrow we leave for Johannesburg — purpose: six months with the Rehearsal Room; four or five productions. These past four months in P.E. have been important. Firstly, I do believe that I have successfully re-orientated myself after all the noise and distractions of the *Blood Knot*. That play is well and truly buried. I now only talk about it when I am drunk and very seldom find myself thinking about it when I am sober. Also I have laid the foundations of the play *People are Living There* which will be finished. Several other important ideas thought out. Also on the credit side is the first draft of Sheila's second novel — she is satisfied with it, though I have not yet read it.

Talking to Sheila last night about my 'jags'.

'It's a way of coming to terms, directly, with the madness and mystery of life. I can put out my hands and grapple with the dark Angel.' Also . . . contempt.

Johannesburg
We have been here three days. A strange period. A depressing se-

quence of incidents despite which I have somehow remained on top.

The vague despair, inertia, distaste that I always have when I think again of working in Dorkay House. No . . . that I have when, having again decided to work there, I find myself wasting time in the grubby little offices and wading through a thousand 'jazzy' greetings with long-lost friends.

August

A heavy snowfall last night. We woke this morning to find Joubert Park as white as a European Christmas.

Joburg — that little piece of it cooped up in the massive blocks of flats all around here, went mad. Snowball fights. First the children, then the infection spread. Bums started throwing snowballs at men in suits, at pretty girls. There were also racial clashes — young white boys versus African messengers and delivery men etc.

September

First rains of spring this evening. Walking home from the rehearsal of *Godot,* a few showers fell. Near the station and then around Noord Street I was conscious of that warm, musky odour that lifts off the tar when it rains after a hot day. The city's sweat.

I told the cast that Vladimir and Estragon must have read the accounts of the Nuremberg trials — or else they were at Sharpeville, or were the first in at Auschwitz. Choose your horror — they know all about it.

J. — age about thirty, very short, a homosexual. First met him about a year ago — talent contest. We needed a compere and Bob remembered the strange little school-teacher who had taught with him. J. tried hard at that — desperate effort to be funny at the mike and plug the sponsor's product, 'Teaspoon Tips Tea'. Then once or twice he turned up drunk — completely unmanageable — so was fired.

Three weeks ago I started rehearsing *Godot.* Corney, David, G. I needed a Lucky. At the third rehearsal G. rolled up with J. — his jaws in a clamp, they'd been broken in a recent fight. He now had a 'good job' as an African salesman with United Tobacco Company. Anyway we started rehearsals. Like the others, he saw into the meaning of *Godot* immediately. For two weeks he was at every rehearsal, and on time. Then came the evening when he did not turn up. G. came with the story that J. had had a fight with one of the directors of the company, being drunk, and had been dismissed. We rehearsed without him. The next night he turned up but, as was to be

62

expected, high as a kite.

He repeated what G. had said, adding only, 'The Director said I was ridiculing him. Can you imagine that, Athol — ridiculing him!'

A feverish wild impatience to start work on *Godot* and, in particular, Lucky's speech. J. started talking about it, jabbering away incoherently about suggestions he had for playing it. Listening carefully, I gradually realised he was talking absolute sense, that what he was saying about the play generally, and Lucky's speech especially, was 'right' — he had his finger on the pulse. *Godot* was all about what had been happening to him for as long as he could remember — a history monotonously in the mood of his employment (hope) and dismissal (despair) by UTC.

So we started the rehearsal. His working clothes were a blue pyjama-top and an old pair of trousers. Second act comes the moment when Pozzo and Lucky go crashing to the floor. Lucky lies still while Pozzo flounders around. When the time came for Lucky to get up again, we found him fast asleep. It was straight from *Godot*. Pozzo: 'When he drops he falls asleep. Up hog!'

Christ Almighty! It is sometimes more than one can take.

Last night A. stayed with us. After taking off his shoes and coat, I eventually managed to get him to the sofa, covered him with blankets, put off the light — and went out onto the balcony before going to bed. Late — 2 a.m. Joubert Park in darkness, a few cars moving about — their lights faint pulses along the nerves of something as drunk and dead as A. As A. . . . it was too vivid, too obvious to miss. The likeness between the city and the man behind me, both sleeping, both stale with the marks, the smell of use and abuse.

Another 'knot' — and as bloody as all the others. A. and the City. And for both of them the time when they must sleep — or if that is too tidy a description of the oblivion — just drop, wherever they are, in their tracks, to awaken the next day and go crawling off for the start of another round. The hunter and the hunted. But an ambiguity — the old one — who is what? Somehow A. — the image of the man — walking the pavements, up and down, this seemed to haunt the city as much as it haunted him. How could any city sleep peacefully when that day he and men like him — the multitude of others — had walked its pavements. Anyway there was no 'sleeping peacefully' for either — as dead, as hard and heavy as they were, and as silent — one could feel, if not see and hear, the nightmares.

The ruin of this man is alternatively boring and terrifying. He nowadays inspires in me an enormous sense of futility, of inadequacy. He does not want to be helped — except in the way of booze to speed his headlong career into oblivion. I have not before seen him so low, physically. The beating he got recently from the police might have done some abiding damage. He talks of pain — but refuses pills. Only booze.

With him I do not move in the realm of common-sense, of balanced judgments, of listening to reasons. The night of his soul is so dark these little candles light nothing except the sweat of his agony.

Yes. That is it. Why then do these 'little candles' work for others? Because they don't move — or else, after an eternity of hesitation, take one little step. He has chosen to run headlong, stumbling over the unseen obstacles: blind to what lies ahead — but *run* — where the rest stand still, or take one step.

The runner in the dark.

As senseless, but inevitable, as a suicide migration. No — not senseless. Not to me. To the staid fools, yes, but not to me.

Let me remember that A., and his 'run in the dark', is not the story of a black man. It is bigger than that. It is as big as the pain and beauty of our mortality — *our.*

October

The 'poor whites' of our back streets. I've been seeing a good few of them — mainly women (mothers) — when visiting Lisa at the Children's Hospital. It is of course a 'free hospital' and, like ourselves, that is why they are there. It is not their natural environment: Nature's protective camouflage which hides them in their crowded, narrow world of rust, flaking paint, dark doorways, brown furniture in dim interiors and crying grubby children — is useless in the white, antiseptic, starched environment of a hospital — so I see them, clearly.

Always, I first think 'how beautiful'. A really living thing always is — a living thing marked, scarred or broken by life even more so, and they are that.

But I can be much more precise: sallow skins, in some of the women bitter half-moons for mouths, primitive bone-structure in the face, an animal alertness (or furtiveness in some) specially in the eyes.

We lived next to them often enough to know or, rather, understand this. Blows — fists and fate — fall quickly and unexpectedly. One must be constantly on the lookout — a drunk husband, a baby playing in the street, a thieving son at your handbag.

And their bodies. Like Ouma. I think of thorn-trees, of things planted and growing in a harsh world, in hard times.

We wait in the bus-shelter. Hot thundery afternoon. They buy ice-creams and eat them hurriedly. The bus comes.

My writing: communication? Expression?

Or a tool, a means of understanding — reconciling the opposites, the paradoxes.

If 'statement' there is, it is of the nature of the non-teleological — 'it is because it is' (Steinbeck: *Sea of Cortez*). An elaboration of these five little words into a hymn of joy.

Flattering response from the press to my *Godot*. Talking about it, the production, Sheila said: 'The mistake most directors make is not to see their function as interpretive — they try to extend the meaning of the play.'

Zakes left last night. By train to Cape Town, then by boat to England. A Great Send-off at the station. He arrived in high spirits and with 'Whitey' and his entourage — they'd come straight from the shebeen where they'd given him a farewell party. We handed over our beers for the Free State — 'It's dry, Dad' — books to read on board ship, Havana cigar, fruit etc. A warm night — but in talking about the English cold at the shebeen, they had already put him into his warmest clothes.

November

Last night, one of the 'miracles', a sublime performance of *Waiting for Godot* at St.George's Hall.

In terms of 'satisfactions', of humility, of feeling that one had made contact with the rare moment of truth in theatre, this production of *Godot* is as important to me as *The Blood Knot*. Yes — above all else — truth — and truth at the level where it is Beauty. The cast were amazing. Corney's delivery of Didi's soliloquy quite astounding.

I really don't know how I did the play in the first instance — I think back to rehearsals and remember nothing. Last night's performance is obviously an even greater mystery — where did it come from?

Again it has been proved: a play is an actor before an audience. We had nothing else. 'The moment of truth' needs nothing more.

Further: the importance of this play (production) lay in what it did to the actors and in what happened on the stage — rather than in what reached the audience and what it did to them — a valid Rehearsal Room consideration.

65

For over a month now, a quiet, productive pattern to my days. Up at seven, I feed Lisa, read the paper, breakfast and then settle down to work. Nothing is allowed to disturb or take me away from my work until 2 p.m. It is hard for me to say how good the new play is — I write easily and am happy with what goes down on paper.

December

Returned yesterday from three weeks in Durban setting up *Sponono*[9] for its world premiere. Opening was apparently a success — ovation — good notices. Nothing happened in those three weeks to change my opinion that it is an indifferent play and that the production was bad. My association with this venture was a mistake. Never again.

Had previously been to Durban for the opening of DATA (Durban Amateur Theatrical Association) and Bob Leshoai and I stayed with Ismail and Fatima Meer.[10] Their house ultra-modern, tastefully furnished but an outside bucket lavatory — '. . . because it's an Indian area' — an apology from Ismail.

DATA is intended as multi-racial but at the moment almost exclusively Indian — its organisers bending backwards to find Africans to participate. Indicative of the desperate Indian conscience on a lot of levels — concern for the future, knowing where the final power lies, political and humanitarian elements tinged with the memory of the anti-Indian riots in 1949.

Ismail and Fatima both teetotallers and non-smokers. Honest and sincere. As a lawyer he had a big practice. Ismail, re Indians in the Free State: 'In the last census there were thirteen. They must be lonely.' 'What do they do?' 'Waiters, I suppose. At hotels.'

He told how, many years ago, Naidoo, one of the leaders of the Natal Indian Congress, went to an inaugural congress of the African National Congress in Bloemfontein location. Word got around among the whites that there was a black man in the location with straight hair. Crowds flocked to see him.

Bob Leshoai talked about the question of leaving the country — apart from his work in theatre he is a school-teacher. I thought of him trying to resolve this problem, getting into the company of some simple illiterate labourer for whom life is as big a hell, but for whom the possibility of getting out does not exist.

There is a group of derelicts up here in Johannesburg who could be turned into a fine play.[11] Most times they spend on the benches in front of the library — tapping passers-by, 'For a bite to eat — I want to eat, sir. Anyone will give me money for drink. But I want to eat.

God bless you, sir.' This Xmas they went around as a group each with a little cardboard box lid full of bootlaces. They stuck together — four of them — a sherry gang.

One was white-haired, smiling faced, English-spoken. (George or Billy). 'An ex-serviceman, lady. God bless you.' Another, Afrikaner — dark, brooding, violent. All of them violently, unbelievably a-social.

No explanations — a valid image — self-sufficient.

Read Beckett's *Malone Dies* over Christmas. Hard to describe what this book, like his *Godot, Krapp* and *Endgame,* did to me. Moved? Horrified? Depressed? Elated? Yes, and excited. I wanted to start writing again the moment I put it down. Beckett's greatness doesn't intimidate me. I don't know how it works — but he makes me want to work. Eveything of his that I have read has done this — I suppose it's because I really understand, emotionally, and this cannot but give me power and energy and faith.

Talking to Sheila about Beckett's humour, I said, 'Smile, and then wipe the blood off your mouth.'

Beckett has for me succeeded in 'making man naked again'. How to be clearer in what I mean? When it rains — the rain falls on the skin of Beckett's characters.

1963

Beckett again: Visiting the Lipmans yesterday I found myself defending him against the charge of despairing futility. Lionel Abrahams[1] was also present and agreed with them that Beckett left him with nothing. I said it was exactly the opposite with me. What then was positive in his writing, they asked. Give an indication of what you find that is positive.

My reply: Love and compassion. But of what? Man's absurd and bruised carnality. We're made of flesh and blood — firstly — how much more there is than that, I don't know. Beckett indicates that he doesn't really know either. But he does know that we are flesh and blood: that the one becomes old, grey and meaningless; the other thin and always red, red. We eat, we defecate. And at the end of it all is this thing — death. Life dies — a compassionate realisation of this paradox.

Alan Lipman agreed that if this was there it made Beckett meaningful for him, but he hadn't seen it.

Had I?

A critical study of Beckett has just been published and I read the review. It was hard to believe the writer under discussion was the same man who has been influencing me so profoundly. The fault may have just been the scholarly jargon in which they discussed him — but it seemed arid, sterile. Central thesis: Beckett's writing is an extension of the Cartesian statement: 'I think, therefore I am.'

In the space of two or three weeks I have again met or been involved with three writers — Alan Paton in Durban; Uys Krige up here in Johannesburg and Benny Bunsee, a young aspiring Indian writer, also in Durban.

A temptation to compare Alan and Uys. When I do I cannot help realising the accuracy of Lionel Abrahams's description of Alan: '. . . an amateur,' (in all fairness to Lionel let it be said that we were talking of S.A. writing and à propos of Alan he said: 'Thank God for amateurs!') This is exactly what Alan is — an amateur. Over and above that there is the man's staggering compassion, rock-bottom sincerity and Christianity — but he is still an amateur. I could not really talk to him about theatre because he knows nothing about the medium. Incredibly naive — a naivety at the level of tools, craftsmanship, of realising what can be done on the stage, of what has been done. Ignorant even of what is possible with his own plays, like *Sponono*.

Very much aware of the above I bumped into Uys the other day and spent a hectic few hours in his company, buying a pair of trousers, drinking coffee and talking, talking. Above everything else I realised I was in the company of a man who could talk to and with me about theatre. (Those embarrassed, empty silences with Paton after I had said something he did not understand!) Uys's remarks about other writers were sharp and accurate, his concerns and problems — structure ('My God, the Greeks — I always go back to the Greeks!') were real and meaningful to me. And of course he is a poet — he knows the values and beauty of words in a living, actual mouth.

If Alan is the amateur, Uys is the professional. If Alan's weakness is naivety, Uys's tends to be pretension. A final comparison — Uys does not measure up to Paton's compassion and Christianity. Paton really loves. He writes because he loves. With Uys it is now a question of 'doing' because he is Uys Krige. Something is gone. A smallness has crept in — a concern with himself and his Image.

And so: Benny Bunsee. Tall, emaciated, somehow smelling and looking of hunger and desperation. Shabby and now also shiny, suede shoes. Beautiful eyes and hands. An old raincoat. Like a ghost in the grey sultry steam of Durban. 'Jesus Christ, man — the world's on fire! It's on fire and will be in ruins and they (the bourgeoisie) are buying houses and insurance policies.' He talks left-wing jargon but confronted with real truth I have never known him to fail in judgement: Beckett, Brecht — and for me very specifically my new play *People Are Living There* — in every case, Benny has seen right through to the heart.

I have told him about Milly — about silence, about protest, about making a noise so that 'they don't forget we're here' — and Benny has unnerved and moved me by knowing exactly what I was talking about. I hope I never needed it — but in any case, he has given me faith about the significance of Milly and that Braamfontein room — rather (yes) given me hope that the significance of those few hours in that kitchen will be seen by others.

A few details: Benny is at the moment without a home and is drifting from friend to friend and quite often sleeping out in the open — in the gardens in front of the City Hall. Trying desperately to find a practical solution to his desperation. A haunted man — in a lush, sickly green world. Violent flowers — heavy rain.

February
Port Elizabeth — returned home after *The Blood Knot* production in London. This morning I played with Lisa while Sheila went into town. In the five weeks I have been away her mind has acquired marvellous agility and another striking development is her eagerness to trust.

Trust. How deep and far extends that trust asked for and given in a small, private moment. Trust me not to harm, hurt, belittle or abuse.

In a hurried note written before I left London, I said to John Berry (director of the production) — 'And now, the most humble and enormous thank you . . .' What is the nature of my debt to that man — how did he move me?

The many moments when he said something about Morris and Zachariah that made me realise how much he understood, how total was his understanding — '. . . those two impoverished, mutilated bastards.' 'Don't you understand,' he said to Ian Bannen, who played Morrie — chopping off the top of his head with his flattened hand — 'something's missing. They're not complete. Who the hell for that matter is? That's what the play's about, man. They *want something.*'

So he understood — and he understood because he loved. An angry, burning, bitter, beautiful love. And I know that he could cry — does, or will, or has.

Just as rare were the moments when suddenly revealed were the bewilderment, the resentment and bitterness accumulated in his forty-five years of living. The bewilderment I feel strongly because I know it — and for John like myself there is the knowledge that without 'love' the rocks will surely get you, you'll be wrecked.

He was, of course, lonely.

Something else he said to Ian Bannen about Morrie: 'There's one question, present if unspoken, behind everything this man does in that room. "What am I?" That question is his life — at all levels. Is he white or is he black? Is he friend or is he enemy? Is he real or is he a dream? And who the fucking hell knows the answers to that lot! Do you, Ian? We are dealing with a search for identity.'

One night in front of the fire — after a good meal, a bottle of wine and some beer — we were talking — a conversation sparked off by the phrase: 'A tree needs water.' Do you believe that, he asked me. I don't know, I said. I know that a tree requires water to live but if you ask me does it *want* water, does it want to live — I must say I

70

don't know. I can't say no — maybe it does.

So then, one by one, the old questions — the whys, hows, whats, whos. We asked them quietly, almost tiredly. And then John suddenly: 'Christ, man! Do you know what this is — this is what Sartre calls anguish. We are in a state of anguish. I've never seen it so clearly.'

It seemed to me that behind everything John said about Morrie was the recognition of his, Morrie's, anguish. And that John was an anguished man. (To what extent did John's experience of McCarthyism in Hollywood enable him to understand what a corrupt society does to individuals?)

Lying thinking in bed last night, I realised — life with its inherent experience of loss, of losing — gives us an experience more profound and mysterious, more challenging, than death itself. Because we must part and far beyond the moment of losing we must live with pain and an emptiness. There's an image — man ending up like a hollow mountain, a collection of empty caverns. And Death? When it is near I'll have the anticipation of loss but when it's happened, never *know* I've lost. It's this *knowing* that draws blood.

In everything there is the hunger for eternity — for it not to end. I have said I love man for his carnality, for his mortality. It is a hard love — a big love — and I must still grow — and I do so reach out now as I will at the very end to the statement, 'it was good'. Yes, I have learnt a little bit about death.

Just read *A raisin in the sun* by Lorraine Hansberry. My initial reaction: two-dimensional. Why do I feel this? The theme, the things concerned with, are big and in their way deep, in fact terrifyingly so — dreaming, aspiring, wanting, the overall concern with human dignity. But the final statement is comfortable — the audience will leave feeling good and this makes me enormously suspicious. Not because making an audience uncomfortable is my aim, but because a man dreaming, or wanting, is the most painfully beautiful thing I know. As for human dignity, here again the final image was comfortable. I remember the woman with her bruises and her baby, in her old shoes on the pavement outside Braes o' Berea on the first day of a new year. I remember the final passionate cry that came to me from the pages of Malraux's *Human Estate,* I remember Vladimir and Estragon. There is pain, and blood, and ecstasy and great beauty in all these memories. They can never make me comfortable.

We must venerate the muck and purify ourselves by crawling

71

deeper into it. There is no rising above it on spiritual wings.

Yes: two-dimensional because the writer was looking into a mirror of convenience — the cosmetic mirror of life. A real work of art is a deep and bottomless pool into which the author urges me: Jump!

March

The wheel has turned. Two years back, about this time, at this same table, I started to write *The Blood Knot*. I realised this last night when I woke in the dark to hear rain dripping from the gutter. My father was dying, my daughter unborn — and I was writing my play into the face of nothing. Full cycle — not quite. It implies a return — and there cannot be — Lisa is too loud and noisy and hungry and demanding not to remind me that time has only one direction. Let me rather say the wave has broken. Waves — the impulse forward — and the wisdom to ride them at the crest.

I have started to think about Milly.
'Is this all we get?' — hurt . . . or outraged?

Words from John Berry's vocabulary:
Relate — 'This moment must relate to the play as a whole.' Or 'You (Zach), must relate to him (Morrie).' The assumption of relevance. The relationship between parts to the whole.

Dramatise. We would take a moment in the play and analyse and break it down until we had reached, consciously, the deepest possible level, the deepest meaning. When this had been done, or rather, found, John would then say: 'Now how do I dramatise this!' — meaning, action or business or whatever else the director can do to suggest, or make clear, or lead the audience to this meaning.

He was always wrestling with my deepest level of meaning — man and man, not just white or black. At one stage he thought that the best dramatisation of this statement would be a moment when, either through lighting, or because Morrie and Zach sat with their backs to the audience — it would be impossible to tell who was Morris and who was Zach.

Another indication of J.B.'s complete empathy with the play concerned the problem of keeping the audience awake and absorbed during the first half. We were always being told that it was too long — that it dragged. Ian Bannen, sensitive to this immediately, tried to solve it with tempo. John's reaction was unequivocal: 'No! It will be slow, and boring — look like it's getting nowhere if you play it fast. You've got to win that audience through character, and the revelation of character. We all know that our story only gets under way after interval. But that is only half of the play. Something just as important, maybe more so, starts with the very first line — the revelation — and that is what we must settle. This means taking time. Play it fast and it will seem slow.'

(This, like the other notes about John, obviously paraphrased but I have not added or taken away from his meaning.)

Remembering these remarks comes at a very opportune moment: slowly I am beginning to think again of *People Are Living There* — and this question of character and revelation applies even more fully to it. Story line? . . . a sequence of trivial events culminating in an abortive birthday party.

Revelation as a dramatic function.

Action?

The final statement in Camus's *The Rebel*. A disturbingly lucid statement of what I have been thinking and feeling so long. Yet a few minutes later I read the breakdown of the Lord's prayer in *The Rack* — and still later in the evening, T.S. Eliot's 'Ash Wednesday' and find a complete empathy with them. In his Journal, Gide says that all his characters are himself. I am all my characters. Too subtle?

'All my character are me.'

'I am all my characters.'

A statement of unity as against a statement of contradiction.

How thin and insecure is that little beach of white sand we call the conscious. I've always known that in my writing it is the dark troubled sea of which I know nothing, save its presence, that carried me. I've always felt that creating was a fearless and a timid, a despairing and a hopeful, launching out into that unknown. With me it has never been so much a question of something to say as of something, or nothing, to find — the 'searchingness' someone called it.

But now, last night, I realised that 'man' is also up against this — in his living from day to day, his dreaming at night, his hunger and his wanting. The old cliché — knowledge is knowing how little we know. How little we really tell the world and ourselves.

'Talking to this book' — as Gide puts it — I'm so aware of the weak sentiment, the self-pity, the 'troubled' romantic images (and bad ones at that). Still — an indulgence. Self-indulgence, self-pity, romanticism will always be there when the subject is myself. Do I pose? I don't think so — but I'm very given to tears.

The idea of the four Johannesburg hobos and their box of shoelaces. Their common obsession: 'Why do they (the public) give?' Watching each other so as to trap one of themselves into an act of giving.

'That was giving. You were giving. By Christ you were.'

Last night I remembered the crippled African I once passed on a walk along the beach to Cape Reciefe. At a deserted rocky spot he was crawling out of the water. He had left his crutch and clothing on the beach and had been splashing around in a narrow, sandy-bottomed channel in the rocks. He sat in the sun wiping himself off with an old rag. The leg had been amputated below the knee. The right leg.

What struck me last night was that I never asked myself how he had got there, being a cripple and without the use of both legs — withered branches of bone with a little flesh. Then I remembered on other occasions passing on the road, donkey-carts piled high with firewood and heading back to the location. The cripple could have come with a friend, or a brother, a father or a son, on one of these — been left on the beach while the other collected wood and then picked up at night for the four to five hour trek back to Korsten.

Sheila.

I talk about my many wants, my many hungers, my many needs — and never has it occurred to me that this must also be the way with her. Even after writing this statement I still do not *realise* its full meaning. I think to myself, she has got Lisa — and she has, I haven't, and behind this thought is the terrifying injunction, 'Be satisfied.' It might well be that with Lisa and myself, Sheila is satisfied. But dare any human being take that for granted in another human being — most of all myself when I have so often and so bitterly attacked society for saying — this is what you need, or rather, this is what you get, Be Satisfied . . .?

It will do me good, do us good, to think more about the inviolate, private lonelinesses that Sheila has.

What I did realise last night was her dependence on me — I am not proud of it. But it is a fact. I was in London and she was here in Bird Street — but here in proxy as it were. For all the mutual love — Ouma is my mother. I have sunk, and learnt to sink, roots into places. Not Sheila. She dropped hers into living earth — myself and now Lisa. That is the extent of my responsibility — something is living in and because of me.

74

With Sheila, Lisa and Mom to visit Kirkwood[2] yesterday. Find myself at last detached and indifferent to that world, its false values and possible judgment of my life. Five hours of . . . what? Nothing. An incessant dribble of talk about nothing — the colour of a certain capsule that was good for her asthma (Mom); a funny picture she saw (Mrs M.); pompous, vindictive outbursts against the Nationalists (Dr M.) etc. etc. and as always moments when everybody whispered in a corner to somebody about somebody. Sickening. Death before the grave has been dug.

In late afternoon we paid the accustomed visit to Oupa at Hillside. Dr M. and I were sitting on one side of the stoep, when he asked about the theme of my new play. I over-simplified it: 'It's tied up with the predicament of my central character — a woman, fifty years old, who after living in sin with a man for fifteen years is suddenly told, "I don't want you any more". So the woman asks: "Is there no justice?" '

Dr M. saw (this I only felt) a tremendous validity in the theme. He talked unbroken for 15 to 20 minutes on the subject — relating it to his own life. To the question: Is there any justice? he said there was only one answer: No! He also saw it raising the eternal question of the longevity of Love. 'Love dies,' he said. 'That first kick, that tremendous kick is a question of today, maybe tomorrow!' Two people in marriage, or any other relationship, stay together, live and share because of mutual understanding, sympathy, respect, habit, gratitude. But Love isn't there at the end.

And then suddenly, as if in saying all this he had been talking about himself, had been revealing too much, he was speaking about his present wife and his divorce, *defensively*. She, the present Mrs M., suited him, the divorce had to be because . . . etc.

In the garden: male and female of the double-collared sunbird. Also large swarms of the swallow-tailed citrus butterfly.

With Sheila on Saturday night to see the film of Arthur Miller's *A View from the Bridge*. Halfway through I was forced to turn to Sheila and whisper: 'It's going off the rails. It's getting lost.' Feelings, and a final disappointment, that almost parallel my reactions on reading *Death of a Salesman*. Afterwards, we talked for a long time about Miller and the 'tragic' in modern playwriting. I can only remember the gist of the main thoughts.

The essence of Tragedy is surely Truth — and the recognition of it — and then, for all this recognition and understanding of where one is going, to *still* choose or be forced to take the path to the final catastrophe. For Eddie in *View from the Bridge* the final tragic crescendo should have started with a moment when he is told, 'You want her (Catherine)', to which he must reply, inwardly or outwardly, 'Yes. Yes! I want her. And if I can't have her, no-one has her.' Knowing what this means; seeing the shadow of a final catastrophe stretched across that way but still choosing to move because something bigger than he can contain is pulling the strings.

I say 'truth' — and that one word encompasses total awareness; light in the darkest quarter of man's soul; inevitability; madness; the collapse of reason; Finality; Morality.

Finality: an important word — a word that I cannot help feel points to the answer to the old, old talking-point: Why has the tragic dimension been lost in modern playwriting, where has it gone? At this moment I cannot help thinking, feeling, that we have lost it because of our confusion on moral issues — our clever uncertainty about right and wrong — and because of our assault on the concept of finality, the end — FINIS. This is certainly true of myself. With God gone, how haven't I struggled to convince myself about 'life after death' — life on this planet, life in rockpools, life anywhere in the universe. But I have had to say to myself — It will go on. Even though I am dust, it will go on. This is a direct assault on finality. Had Macbeth said that to himself — or her — would their stories have ended the same way? I don't think so. For Shakespeare, for Sophocles, Life was a bridge from light to darkness and man had to face the enormous consequence of any act. By making life a circle I have removed consequence. By trying to eliminate 'THE END' I have unwittingly assaulted the tragic dimension.

My 'life after death' — no retribution is involved.

But to return to *A View from the Bridge* — it is Eddie's self-deception, his meaningless 'Give me back my name, Marco!' his refusal to recognise and face the consequences, that block the emergence of a tragic dimension — because the play in the final half certainly points in the right direction.

Another angle on the above: the light of twentieth century knowledge, scientific, that has banished the dark shadow of tragedy. Incompatibilities — tragedy and enlightenment.

First draft of *People Are Living There* — the first half of which I reread today — only leaves me determined to finish it. Can be a meaningful play. I find it easy to involve myself in it — which is enough for me.

Yesterday, for the first time since my return from London, one of those intensely blue and very 'deep' days that I only seem to find here in P.E. Spent the afternoon at Summerstrand — also took my first swim — more of a bath really in a deep pool among the rocks. The tide had only just started to come in and had not yet reached this pool. The water was warm.

Butterflies on the beach. February-March is obviously their month. A strong, provocative image — skipping over the sand and even quite far out on the water. At one stage I waded out quite a good distance on a gradually sloping rock-shelf. Several of them flew up to me, turning away only at the very last minute, which prompted the fancy that they had mistaken me for a tree.

A bright scrap of time dancing unconcerned on the face of eternity.

There is a divine madness — almost an extravagance — in the way they used up the day. Their fragility, delicacy, makes them so mortal I think they must almost be conscious of it — accept it and fly away into the sun — a laugh given colour and wings.

God, how deep is that image in *The Blood Knot*.

Ezra Pound: 'An image is the presentation of a psychological and emotional complex in an instant of time.' To which he adds a remark about the 'sense of liberation, of freedom' that follows. I use the word 'Image' a great deal. Pound's definition explains my meaning completely. I cannot add a word to it.

I am very conscious of the 'Image' in playwriting. My new play was generated by one such image: 'Milly is unnerved at finding herself still in her nightclothes from the previous night.'

April
Our life here in P.E. is remarkably quiet. I shun contact with people and strenuously avoid making friends. Mom is the only 'outsider' we let into our room — and even then her presence is resented at times. For the rest it is my work, the periodic breaks for bird-watching and shell-collecting, music and our books.

It is Good Friday. I read the paper, observe the solemn silence in the street outside — but it all means nothing to me. I am an alien to this Christianity. Too much has been written on to the label 'Christian' for me to tie it around my neck. I would betray my convictions, my beliefs, if I gave it a name which allowed fools to take a pride in it — as if they had a hand in their bitter-making. In any case I still spell god with a small 'g' — and I suppose that settles it. Always a remote issue this — what do I call myself? Even, What am I? It will never be more or less than the sum total of my doing.

Headline in a newspaper on the lavatory floor: EK PRAAT VOOR EK 'N LYK IS.[3]

The troubled state of South Africa at this moment[4] finds its way into my life in a moment of real fear every night just before sleep. I become painfully, terrifyingly aware of the threat of violence to Sheila and Lisa. As terrifying, is the thought that I would be sleeping if it burst in on us from the night. The silence of the night, the imminent oblivion of sleep, are very real terrors.

Reading Eliot on 'Poetry and Drama' has stimulated me to still further refinement of my thoughts on this subject. I find myself impatient with his opinions. He is so ignorant of theatre and its meaning, in a scholarly, assured way. To discuss, as he does, the fate of 'verse' in dramatic writing, is in no way an appreciation of the function of 'poetry' in drama. Beckett is a greater poet in the 'theatre' than he (Eliot) has been or ever will be. Eliot goes on and on about blank-verse as if the poetic imagination in playwriting must drag this ball and chain. That is surely one of Beckett's greatest discoveries — that we can free the poetic imagination of this dead weight. Beckett, as a poet in the theatre, stands in relation to blank-verse as free-verse does to established poetic forms. But as Eliot himself pointed out, 'No verse is free for a real poet.'

Since my return from London I have had nothing but an irritating and, at its best, tolerant awareness of my mother. At worst, she was an intrusion into the silence and privacy I craved. I became very conscious of how 'excluded' she was when Norman and Glenda came down for the Easter weekend. They talked to her about the things she wanted to talk about; fussed over her; took her out. Now they are gone and she is alone with us again.

Then, last night, feeling out-of-sorts, depressed by the incessant bad weather which affects business at the café, she went to bed early. I looked up from the book I was reading as she left the room — a moment of awareness, pain and compassion. A leaden-footed, dragging step, the broad back now bent; the strength and tremendous 'presence' now shapeless: very tired and maybe thinking of death.

Thank God for Lisa. She gives Ouma a tremendous amount of innocent, unfettered joy.

This notebook doesn't much reflect the deep and mutual involvement between Lisa and myself. I watch her and play with her with endless fascination. The most important single development of the past few weeks is her discovery of the power of language — that words can conjure up what has been, and anticipate what will be. 'Stories' are now part of the daily routine — they deal with what has happened or is going to happen according to the routine of our days, and are peopled with familiar objects and activities — horsey, froggie, kitty, motorcar, daddy driving the motorcar. There is as yet no fantasy or make-believe. She listens attentively and gets very excited when the story reaches the climax.

I stepped out of doors for a few moments last night enjoying the warm aftermath of one of P.E.'s blue and beautiful days, and as I stood there on the pavement a little man, pipe in mouth, walked past then turned back and stared. 'It can't be,' he said. I didn't recognise him. 'Aren't you Athol Fugard?' 'Yes,' 'And me — don't you recognise me?' Seeing the puzzlement in my eyes, he tucked an imaginary fiddle under his chin and swept his bow down in a few bars of silent music. 'Of course,' I lied. 'You played the violin with Daddy.' It was so easy — his face lit up — I've seen this happen so often. 'That's right . . .' And then followed the usual few moments of memories and a little talk about the present — being old, work wasn't found so easily these days. He gave the impression of something that had 'shrunk' — not through age, just shrunk like a cheap garment dipped in hot water.

What I remember very clearly, and growing in beauty every time I think of it, is the silent music, the violin that wasn't there, those few chords from 'Ramona' or 'Harbour Lights' and, somewhere in the night my father, white-haired, at the piano. Their band was called 'The Melodians'.

Not a day passes now without me reading in the paper, almost as a commonplace, of some fresh outbreak of violence, another outrage to justice and decency. I turn with fear from the thought of the final reckoning. We will have to pay and with lives and hope and dignity for all of these that we destroyed. Lisa is the hold-fast for all my anger, and bitterness, and sometimes even despair. They have now finally succeeded in making a foul, corrupt, diseased world for her to grow up in. All that stands between her and taint is Sheila and myself. I do not imagine it will be easy.

May
Last night during a walk around the block, while Sheila was prepar-

ing supper, Lisa saw the moon for the first time. It was a beautiful, mild evening, the sky luminous as it can only be in these parts. On a corner Lisa stopped, and very excitedly pointed up at a rising half-moon.

Working hard — five to six hours a day, day after day. Getting impatient now. The end is in sight. Moments of confidence in the play.

Reading John Donne — beautiful. Sincerity, discipline, at times harsh, even brutal — all that is opposed to the morass of sentiment. Excellent instruction.

How much can a man love? Is he built big enough for all the loving his life is capable of? How destructive? How creative?

I now seldom see my hand holding the pen, or the pen crawling crab-wise across the paper. This is a sign of something — something good. In the same vein, I look less in mirrors these days and the part of my anatomy I know best now is my legs and feet — I often look down at them.

Last night we took P.D. to dinner at the local Chinese restaurant. For some reason the talk never came to real life.

Two points : What would one do in the event of a call to arms to all white men in this country to protect wives, families and homes because the Africans had risen in united and bloody revolt. P.D. said without hesitation that he would join the other whites, take a gun and shoot . . . I said I hoped I would not. This led to us discussing the purpose, if any, of making a stand like this — of saying No — because it will result in all likelihood in your being dragged out and shot by the whites as a 'kafferboetie' traitor. I said that even if this happened, and my life, and possibly that of wife and child, ended there — could one then say that the stand, the episode, had been 'futile'? What do we really know about the continuity of an action — how it proliferates and affects others long after the doing? Is it conceivable that a man could do *anything* that will not affect others? Is there any such thing as a really personal and private action? Even if one were the last human being alive on the face of the earth, and one did something, threw one's whole life into an act or gesture — suicide for example — could one with all certainty say that it would end there — that the gesture would be snuffed out like a candle in the dark?

I am not sure. I am very inclined not to believe it.

I must think about this continuity of action.

Two visitors in the past week and both resulted in a mood of guilty awareness of how selfishly I live with my 'simple' pleasures — how cut off I am from the physical realities of South Africa.

The first visitor was Norman Ntshinga, husband of Mabel Magada, a blues singer. His was the old, old request. Would I do a play for them? I say 'request', actually it is hunger. A desperate hunger for meaningful activity — to do something that would make the hell of their daily existence meaningful. He is coming again with a few friends and we will try to start a local branch of Union Artists.[5] The point about Norman's visit is that when he sat opposite me, I realised I was making contact with South Africa for the first time since my return from London. I found his presence 'strange' — his well-known 'blackness' strange — it was like meeting a well-loved and hated friend after a long separation. The truth of course is that I stepped out of the plane and into this room.

The other visitor was Eric Atwell. Among a lot of things he told me about the welfare organisation in Grahamstown devoted to poor relief among non-whites in the district. Unable to cope with all the demands from hungry or starving families, the organisation has laid down a minimum earning of threepence a day, above which no family will be helped.

Both Norman with his presence, and Eric in what he said, made me feel bitterly guilty. Not even the new play escaped the taint of self-indulgence.

Shell collecting at Cape Reciefe the other day. I knew what to expect because on the drive there I followed on the tail of a convoy of army lorries carrying Active Citizens' Force trainees and their guns to the nearby rifle range. The silence of the beach was persistently broken by the innocuous sound — and therefore so much more terrible — of rifles and automatic guns being fired on the range. Everything conspired to make the afternoon ominous. The sun went behind cloud, a cold wind came off the sea, the tide rushed in with savage fury. And all the time — pop-pop pop-pop pop-pop. I remembered those little toyguns we had as children, which fired corks.

Involved and finally futile argument with Sheila, provoked by my reading Kazantzakis' novel, *Christ Recrucified,* which she, as a Catholic, admired. I find it intolerable — sell-out Christianity. In it a wise and holy man starts off a parable to prove God's greatness, 'Once there was a village lost in the desert and all its inhabitants were blind . . .'

To me it is damningly revealing that a parable which is going to

81

state the God-Man relationship should have to afflict man with blindness and then still lose him in the desert.

I don't know if there is or isn't a god. What I do know is that the question is the most idle and meaningless I could ever find. 'This earth remains my first and last love' — Camus.

I keep remembering from time to time, and still see occasionally, in the street, one remarkable face from my youth. It is that of a man who for as long as I can remember could be seen at night, standing motionless against the wall on the corner of Jetty and Main Streets. The face is remarkable — large, unsmiling eyes, heavy lids, harsh sceptical mouth, long face. I must have seen it a hundred times — but I have no recollection of any expression other than this one of morbid withdrawal.

The last time I saw him was about 11 a.m. at the entrance to the public library; he had taken to standing there these days. I watched him for a few minutes. He stood absolutely motionless — staring at nothing, his face now bloated, his eyes glazed; shabbily dressed. Next to him was a young coloured man — neat, lithe — watching the white man beside him with amused contempt. Then my man said something to the coloured but without looking at him. The coloured smiled — openly showing his contempt — the white man lurched away down the street. He was dead drunk.

I remember my father. Dad had the same way of telling people, almost strangers, the next move in their enormously trivial game of life — and then doing it. 'I'm going home.' 'Make it an early night.'

Yes, that must surely be what fascinated me about this man — his similarity to my father. I can remember my father standing propped up against a Main Street wall with equal clarity.

And when I think of the places where this man could live, I get excited. The Valley for example. He is a P.E. story — and I must write it.

Johnnie — Dad. Jetty Street — the war years — Johnnie was nineteen years old. Pimped for his sister. Now she is married. Johnnie LeGransie.

June
So, *Johannesburg* again and another play under my arm. Vaguely ill-at-ease — discontented. The prospects ahead do not excite me as they would have in the past. Something is finally coming to maturity in me.

I look at the landscape out of the window and realise that South

Africa's tragedy is the small, meagre portions of love in the hearts of the men who walk this beautiful land.

I fully expect a rather bewildered public reaction to this play if and when it reaches the stage. Bewildered because it might seem to be about nothing – and I know everyone is waiting for more controversy. I couldn't care less – the play concerns people and, most important of all, 'the noise of living'. The noise we must make, as Milly puts it, 'to let them know we are here.'

Sunday and my fourth day up here. I again find it depressing, lonely, bitter. Specially Dorkay House – purposeless drift and waste of talent and aspirations.

And now in addition the air is thick with talk of leaving. For so many, life seems no longer possible here in S.A. Even those who have not yet had banning orders issued against them or been put under house arrest, cannot see themselves continuing. And these, in nine out of ten cases, are people who want to see justice done and believe in human dignity. So S.A. gets poorer and poorer.

It was put to me that I too should think of leaving. 'Second Algeria', 'what about your family when the bullets start to fly' etc. All of this is enormously depressing. How could I? South Africa is starving to death from a lack of love. This country is in the grip of its worst drought – and that drought is in the human heart. We all live here loving and hating. To leave means that the hating would win – and South Africa needs to be loved now, when it is at its ugliest, more than at any other time. By staying I might be able to do this.

I cannot say this way, my way, is right for others. It *is* mine. It is one of the final meanings in my life.

But it is bitter and desperate. I have my back to the wall.

I think I can find a good cast for my play up here – the problem is a venue. I don't want any segregation in the audience and this of course makes it virtually impossible to get a good theatre.

I have sufficient distance now to believe quietly, and unshakably in *People Are Living There*. It is very real and meaningful despite Ian Bernhardt's stupid remark: 'It is a good play but I don't know why *you* wrote it.'

But I also realise I am very tired and I want to be back in P.E. writing again. I want less and less to be involved with people. Possibly 'tired' is the wrong word. Life is getting simpler and the furious noise and activity of the past is now no longer possible. I miss Sheila and Lisa.

I have been giving serious thought up here to how much longer I can expect to earn a living from writing plays and working in theatre. Circumstances are becoming very hard. If I can do this new play things will be all right for another year. We've never lived with an horizon more distant than that. But after that? If this country hasn't started changing for the better, it will certainly be a lot worse.

On the train back to P.E. 11 a.m. Just left Cradock. Outside the aloes are in bloom, thousands of them. The Karroo is looking beautiful — as beautiful as I have ever seen it. The personal circumstances of this journey back home give me a direct and immediate sympathy with this land.

Going to the toilet a minute ago, the train was passing a cluster of non-white houses when I looked out of the window. A little African child — three to four years old — dressed in rags, her legs bent horribly by rickets, rushed excitedly down a little path to the passing train.

I want to cry and vomit at the same time.

Everything has conspired to make this trip so much more definite, deeper, provocative and at times warmer an experience than the journey up.

My company in the compartment: Mr Els ('Elsie') — an enormously fat, red-faced, walrus-moustached man working on the mines, and Nieuwhuizen — a 'loodgieter' of the S.A.R. returning home after a job in the Transvaal; almost my build but tougher, more muscle, hands scarred and calloused by his work and fifteen years older. I am sure his women always thought N. good-looking. Elsie was about fifty.

I don't think I will ever forget the extended conversation the three of us had in that compartment, watching South Africa slip past the window. All that is good and bad — and worse than bad, rotten and wrong — with the white man in S.A. — his generosity and incredible meanness of spirit, his shrinking heart, his wonderful and simple humour — all of it, as never before in one incident of my life, in our second-class compartment broke loose from our hearts.

Elsie: The depression years. When they hit the country he was a young boy — around fifteen years old — and was forced out of his home to take a job with the S.A.R. laying sleepers on the line to Graaff-Reinet. Lived on the side of the line in a tent — cooking for himself. Back-breaking work. Total physical exhaustion at night.

Bean soup and how it makes him 'poep'. Now takes a glass of Andrews Liver Salts immediately after a plate of bean soup to minimise the effect. 'Anders, ou broer, dan poep ek so dat ek van myself

84

af wil weghardloop.'[6] Farting a family trait. When his father looked to the left and right in the street, he knew a fart was coming. Once old Elsie sneaked out one while reading the paper with his son playing on the floor beside him. When the child heard it, he jumped up and shouted, 'Sabre Jet!'

Nieuwhuizen: starting with the fivepence farthing an hour he got as an apprentice — he knew off by heart and without any hesitation every increment in his earnings since the days of his apprenticeship. Summed up the past twenty-five years of his life as follows: fivepence farthing — sevenpence ha'penny — one and sixpence — one and nine — two and fourpence three farthings, etc.

Enlisted during the war. Served up north and in Italy.

Had a lot to say about Klipplaat, that tough, dusty hot-as-hell railway junction here in the Eastern Cape. 'Put a roof over it and a redlight outside and you got a hoerhouse.' 'As die man uit die voordeur wil stap werktoe — dan kruip die buurman by die agter deur in om die ou vrou te "slaan". Selfs die jong dogters, man — sestien-jaar oud — hulle hoer dat dit bars.'

Elsie: 'Hulle is ook maar mens.'[7]

Standard greeting at Klipplaat: 'How's your wife and my children?'

Nieuwhuizen knew a lot about and had a lot of respect for 'rooikombers kaffers . . . Ordentlike kaffers. Daar in die Transkei as jy op die sypaadjie loop dan stap hy in die straat, uit jou pad uit, lig sy hoed en sê: Môre Baas.'[8]

As for the educated ones: send them to Oxford and Cambridge but when they come back they'll wrap themselves up in a blanket and sit. They'll never change.

There was no escaping these crudities and blindnesses. Even when the subject was not kaffers. We found ourselves at one stage discussing court cases — and one in particular: a young mother in South-West Africa who had killed her one-year-old baby; she was found guilty and sentenced to six years imprisonment with hard labour. Nieuwhuizen: 'I would have given her six inches not six years.'

Nieuwenhuizen was also driven mad with anger at the thought of politically conscious Africans. He had two working with him in P.E. and one of them fell into the category 'A.N.C.' 'Hy sê altyd "Afrika!" God! Een dag raak ek die hel in. Hy sê weer "Afrika!" Ek gryp 'n hand vol sand.[9] "Do you want Afrika? Here it is. Here take it. Here's a piece of Afrika."'

Both of them recounted in great detail incidents involving the 'moering' of a 'kaffer'.

Conversations pungent with the smell of S.A. — dusty veld, rain on parched earth, sweat, flowers and 'Alwyn heuning'. 'Not 'n fok.'[10]

Elsie: 'Die mens is darem slim om die bergies so te poephol'[11] — said as we came out of a tunnel.

I got the feeling that Elsie was 'on the run' from his home and wife. From what he said it would seem that this had happened fairly often, specially during the good years when the mines paid by the hour. With £50, that he'd held back from his wife, in his pocket, he would take the train somewhere, book in at a hotel and have a week-long binge — 'Daar's 'n hoer in elke dorp.'[12]

One long, lazy hour talking about cats — simply, naively.

An earlier note in this notebook: 'Are you all I get to love?' I suddenly had this question in my mind when I wrote it down — unrelated to anything particular. It came back to me in the compartment watching Elsie and Nieuwhuizen. 'Are you all I get to love? You are mine. I will never possess anything as surely as I possess you. You make me poor and you make me rich; happy and sad; bitter and sweet. Are you all I get to love?' Morrie could have said it to Zachariah. Milly to Shorty and Don.

So that was my return to P.E. The nebulous, drifting ten days in Johannesburg erased from my mind by the violent, beautiful reality of these two men. The tasteless hamburger replaced by rusks and coffee which is my real diet. The simplicity I found so suddenly after London increases with every day — growing deeper and deeper into my life. I have been waiting for this for a long time. I need the peace and solitude I find here in P.E. for it to take deep and firm root in my life.

Port Elizabeth

Today is Tuesday. On Sunday afternoon — a lovely day — Sheila, Lisa and I went to Settlers' Park. Made our way to a bench on the side of one of the little koppies and sat there in the sun. Lots of coloured children had come into the park from South End — and kept passing us in little groups. We must have been there an hour when suddenly at least a hundred of these kids came running and screaming past — they were being chased out of the park by a park policeman in uniform and carrying a stick. There was an edge of ugly violence to the moment. The biggest children were shouting high-spiritedly, knowing they wouldn't be caught. But some of the smaller ones were genuinely terrified, and screaming and sobbing with fear. A few were so small that they couldn't run at all and were being dragged along roughly by elder, terrified sisters.

The idea I noted down earlier of the P.E. derelict 'Johnnie', stays with me. Last night I suddenly thought of a story about him, using all three 'persons' — first, second and third — in the telling of it. Not a confusion of identities, but a counterpoint: I — You — He.

Two ideas moving quietly and surely in my mind. The first dates back to London 1960, when my eye caught a newspaper story by Stirling Moss about his winning the Mille Miglia race. Two men — Moss and Jenkins, his navigator. I intend working this up into a TV play. The man who did *The Blood Knot* might be interested. This idea has been with me so long, is so definite in outline that I shan't go into it in this notebook.[13]

The second idea is of course Johnnie, and this still needs extensive exploration. I want Johnnie to be a P.E. story.

They are racking their brains in Johannesburg to find me a Milly for the new play.[14] I remain very detached. Those ten days up there have left me more than indifferent to the prospect of working there. The past five days down here, living quietly, new ideas stirring, add to my reluctance to return. If they said everything was ready I would of course go up and do the play. We need the money.

I see and feel Johnnie in terms of Jetty Street, the Valley, South End and his tireless vigil in the Union Castle corner at night, and beside Queen Victoria's statue outside the library during the day. Not to forget of course that that is where the bus-drivers gather with their tin boxes of tickets and timesheets. In Johnnie's heyday the 'Pop Bio Café' was still in existence — the grey flickering screen, sweet smell of a green cold-drink, the waitresses.

I will need to do something to earn money if they cannot find me a Milly. By the end of next week we should know what the shape of the immediate future is.

Last night read Gogol's *Diary of a Madman* — his 'laughter through tears' is of course very close to what I am attempting. Could it be said of me — as is said of Gogol in the introduction — that ridicule and laughter is a type of revenge on Life?

At the end of the evening we listened to Mahler's Fourth Symphony. One of those rare moments when from the very first note I was in tune with the work. The 'whole' had a ravishing order, symmetry and beauty that I perceived instantly. Sheila and I discussed how great music, like great writing, shares in a feeling of inevitability.

Each moment, logical and sure, leads with certainty to the end. In the presence of a truly great artist there is only one way through the experience — his way.

Incredible conversation in the café yesterday afternoon between Manie Swart and Mom — the subject: Radio quiz shows and the 'presents' given away to the winners. Manie particularly loquacious about the 'mystery tune' — 'I tell you, you must always go look around 1800, around there you know. The olden times. Look, like last week, it was the "Watermelon Fiesta" — that's an old one.' Mom: 'You know, Manie, if only Daddy had gone in for these things, there would have been a steady flow of presents. I always said to him, "Daddy, you *must* write away, man." Like the mystery tunes. He was always spotting them. And his wide knowledge about things — always reading — there was nothing he couldn't talk about. His common knowledge was very wide. He had encyclopedes.'

Last year Glenda won a pop-up toaster on 'pick-a-box'.

July
A letter from Leon[15] yesterday which makes it seem unlikely that any of my work will see the light of production in the near future. He wrote that it seemed virtually impossible to find a Milly for the new play. Sheila was much more bitter than me. But both of us asked the same question over and over again — what must one do to be given a reasonable chance in this country?

Despite these setbacks, or rather *because of them,* I find myself thinking and feeling positively. I am still young enough to take all this. *The Blood Knot* was written in the face of nothing. It is a congenial environment for my writing.

Sheila asked me last night: 'Why do you write plays? I mean, do you prefer to write plays, rather than novels or poetry?'

A question with a bewildering number of meanings and answers.

Looking back it is easy to find the accidents that seem to have led me to playwriting, rather than prose or poetry. And yet the conviction and assurance with which I turn to this medium time and time again, the freedom with which I think and feel in it, makes me want to believe that there is more to it than accident. After all, each literary medium can do something the others can't, and what plays *can* do I no doubt want to do. Though of course this could be an acquired ability.

Possibly the whole issue is as circular as any consideration of cause and effect. Which came first — the hen or the egg?

Nevertheless there is a present reality, regardless of its origin, and I feel I can say something about what 'is', even if I can't say how it came about.

In the theatre of course my fascination lies with the 'living moment' — the actual, the real, the immediate, there before our eyes, even if it shares in the transient fate of all living moments. I suppose the theatre uses more of the actual substance of life than any other art. What comes anywhere near theatre in this respect except possibly the painter using old bus tickets, or the sculptor using junk iron and driftwood? The theatre uses flesh and blood, sweat, the human voice, real pain, real time.

Which brings me to another fact about playwriting. As strongly, if not stronger, than the audience awareness of the actors and the living moment, there is the actor's awareness *within* that moment. Let me put it this way: there are two perspectives — from without, that of the audience; from within, that of the actor. This of course applies to music as well.

On the surface — plays, less so with music — exist, or rather are justified, by that first perspective — the audience. It it's not to amuse them, it's to enlighten them, or instruct, or to increase their awareness. One day someone must point out that as great a reality — in fact a *full half* of the *whole reality* — is that of the actor. It requires both. What happens to the audience is matched, is equalled, by what happens to the actor. These strange beings — men and women — are as deeply affected as those watching.

My wholeness as a playwright is that I contain within myself both experiences — I watch and am watched — I examine the experience and I experience. The motion of a pendulum — or if that is too balanced and sane a movement — let me speak rather of agitation between two poles of awareness.

To the circus yesterday. Lisa had a great time. Loved the animals, watched all the acts and was frightened of the clowns. Every time the latter appeared she came to my lap — said the funny man was going to bite her — and either tried desperately to sleep or wanted to go to the car.

I found the circus an unexpected help in my work on the Mille Miglia TV play. It came with the trapeze artists — two men and a woman — strangely aloof, in fact aristocrats among the hurly-burly of the other performers. Like Basil and Stevie they played with danger — risked it all for a few moments. It was fascinating to watch them — and the subtle operation of their sense of superiority. Nothing desperate — as was the case with all the other performers — sweating and straining to get a laugh or a gasp from the audience. The trapeze artists knew they couldn't fail — the danger was real, the risk total. They had no need to fawn. Dignity intact — and if anything, larger than most men's share.

'We have a right to our shadows.' There is Defiance. Leaving the earth for the trapeze, they leave God. I must work this out for the play. Basil and Stevie also leave God.

'Can't we pray?'

Why can't they? Because that race is an act of Defiance. We will go to Death and play with him — and our skill, and cunning and cheating if need be, will save us. That and that alone will save us.

Last night an incident — almost an image — that said more about pain and terror and desperation than I have yet been able to.

We were in the room, reading, when a sudden uproar broke out in the street. This is such a South African sound. Why is it I never seem to have heard it anywhere else? Somebody screaming — oaths, abuse — and invariably somebody crying. We went outside. There was a woman — African — falling about the pavement, trying to get her hands on a man — non-white — who was walking away. A little girl, not more than six years, had thrown herself at the woman, trying with piteous desperation to stop her following the man and when the woman broke loose to stagger after him, the child went at her mother again, 'No Momma — Momma!' — a terrified appeal.

A few white people stood around and watched from the balconies of flats, at front doors. No one moved to help or find out what was wrong.

Eventually two African men and a women sauntered up to the child and her mother. I heard a deep voice, placating the drunk woman, 'Haikona, Sissy!' and then words I couldn't hear or wouldn't have understood even if I had. We went back indoors. Once or twice the woman's voice broke out again, the child sobbed, then silence.

That little girl! She stayed with me at night — and I remembered another child, her legs bent by rickets, who I saw momentarily on my last train trip. In the next room Mom suddenly sighed in her sleep — groaning away the unvaried residue of pain felt in her long life. I remember Dad whimpering with pain like a puppy.

Is there any human predicament greater, more urgent, more beautiful in its source of meaning, or terrifying in its source of pain — than that we are made of flesh and blood — that we break and bleed and always feel, feel. I say predicament — I should have said, reality — the final human reality.

'Dressed for death' we live our days.

Since finishing *People are Living There* I have been pottering around with ideas and making the usual number of false starts, particularly as regards a TV play. At first this was to have been my old idea of the Mille Miglia,[16] but it never came to life and is now abandoned. My next idea was a group of white hobos I saw one day in Johannesburg. At first I thought of a play covering one of their days from start to finish — yesterday I suddenly saw the play covering only the end of their day — in an empty, partly-demolished house. *The Occupation.* What is it really about? Walls, I suppose. Why we build them, imprison ourselves and live our lives away behind them, why we hate, need, even destroy them.

This idea — the hobos and the end of one of their days — is proving much more dynamic and generative than the other and might well end up as a complete and completed piece of work. Just finished reading Robbe-Grillet's scenario, *Last Year at Marienbad,* and this is also at work as a goad and stimulus to finish at least one thing for the screen medium.

These periods between the finish of one play and the real start of the next one — these false starts, playing around with and examining ideas — are finally very important in their quiet and unobtrusive way. What they amount to, I suppose, is the equivalent of the training sessions and exercises of an athlete — keeping him fit for the next effort.

Busy three weeks ahead. Crawling out of my shell temporarily to work with Pieter du Preez in getting a new drama group going. He has a play of his own he wishes to do and has asked me to do something to go with it. I have decided to adapt Machiavelli's *La Mandragola* to a New Brighton situation — using of course an African cast. It adapts remarkably easily and if I can work out a suitably quick and light style for the staging it should be hilarious.

First rehearsal last night with the New Brighton group. We have decided to call ourselves Serpent Players. (Rhodes University, which had taken over the old museum and snake pit as part of their P.E. campus, offered us our pick for a place to perform — intrigued by the abandoned snake pit, with the audience looking down into the space, we have chosen that. Hence our name.)

91

The group — a clerk, two teachers, a bus driver and the women domestic servants or doing cleaning jobs. Most encouraging start. Potentially there are three or four talents up to Johannesburg standard. Enthusiasm incredible — their excitement almost that of a child given the toy of its dreams. They have transmitted this to me and I look forward with pleasure to the three weeks ahead. I am very glad I committed myself. It is a positive act — creating hope and meaning — it cannot but make life richer and more significant for me. It balances some of the selfishness with which I live.

I shall stage *Mandragola* very strictly in the Commedia dell'Arte style — bare stage, a few props but lots and lots of fun.

In the middle of our reading the Special Branch burst in. Five of them, with I believe a squad car of uniformed police parked outside the university. The cast and I took it easily. SB took all our names and addresses — read the play, went through the papers I had — but it would be unfair to say they behaved offensively. Du Plooy — head of the local SB — spent some time chatting to me about the London production of *Blood Knot,* wanting to know how it had been received, what the audiences were like, etc.

Still, I did remember later that he could have taken me away and locked me up for 90 days without any trouble.

What is Beauty? The result of love. The ugliness of the unloved thing.

Busy period — mornings spent writing TV play and afternoons preparing for the rehearsals of the two plays at the university while in the evenings from 5 to 9 we rehearse. The cast of local white amateurs for Pieter's play depressingly unimaginative. The New Brighton people are infinitely more exciting and stimulating. I always leave a rehearsal with them glad that I took it on.

August

The year turns on its side. Winter — the worst of it — is behind us. Nights of intense, dewy silence — like waking up suddenly in the dark, eyes wide open, aware of presence and being, but all the time lying quite still. The air, especially early in the morning, is drenched with that mist of smells and moisture that surrounds all new life — a haze, nothing is finally real yet, all is promise and dreams.

For some time now a strange and disturbing beggar has been coming to the door and also, quite often, always at sunrise, accosting me in Bird Street. Looks like an Indian though it could be that only one parent was one. Black hair, black eyes, dark skin. Heavy expressionless features — but this is inaccurate — there is a permanent wild, demented quality to the eyes. They never express any emotions like hope, gratitude, disappointment or fear. When he comes up to beg and you either give or don't give, nothing happens; he takes the sixpence or walks away empty-handed without a flicker of emotion.

I am sure he is mentally retarded.

Physically he is inert. Round-shouldered. No neck, his head rests on his chest.

How stupid I am in relationships like this! Making a point one day of saying aggressively, 'No, I've got nothing!' — the next time, making Sheila find any left-over food we have in the kitchen and giving it to him, I blunder and fumble and confuse the issue. Surely it is so simple! Surely, looking straight into that man's eyes, there is a truth as simple as 'I have' or 'I don't have' — an act as simple as giving? There can be no question — I fear him. I hide behind false charity (particularly when Sheila is handy to do the giving) or aggressive refusal. I have never stood simply before him, being myself, and listened quietly to his words. My personality makes such a noise in my ears and blindness in my eyes.

I am thinking of this man today because walking home from the cinema last night, we passed him being marched off by a policeman. A beautiful night — moon and dew, intense silence — and then the two of them. The policeman with his stupid mask of authority, hardness, determination — and shuffling beside him, the Indian — wild-eyed, dumb, disturbingly inarticulate and, most frightening of all, accepting. Going obediently because of the uniform and the hard white face beside him. I just *know* that his arrest is a mystery to him. Yet he accepted it. (Age — 20 to 30.)

Nights of such stillness that the noise of trains shunting down at the station and harbour reaches the room with remarkable detail.

Unseasonably, unpleasantly warm today. In the street this morning it is dry and feverish — sudden gusts of delirious hot wind. When Sheila opens the back door the wind moves through the house — as provoking to stillness and silent observation as the agitation of a stranger.

Reading Genet's *The Screens*. Am acutely conscious of the presence of a mind that has truly freed itself and can explore the furthermost limits of human experience. I look back on my small and bitterly-won achievement in this direction.

The New Brighton play has been a success beyond my wildest hopes.

93

I never for a moment thought we would enchant our audience and critics as much as we have. Laugh, laugh, and at everything, from the grotesque absurdities down to subtleties in the play which we ourselves had never seen. Acting — excellent. I could not have got better — or possibly even as good — in Johannesburg. It has been a pleasure working with them. And my God, do they work on that stage! I must certainly work with them again.

But possibly the most rewarding aspect of the venture has been the success of my production and my deliberate attempt to reproduce the style — lightness, elegance, tempo — of the period piece. A completely bare stage except for one black applebox, and then the actors — on and off, running about, etc. in a series of short, pithy scenes. For the first time I feel I really sense the potential in truly improvised theatre.

The applause at the end of each performance leaves absolutely no doubt as to the warmth and gratitude of the audience.

I've always said to others: Life? It's there to be taken. Put out your hands. Now I appreciate consciously what was sensed intuitively when I said those words.

Malraux — 'Man, the only animal that has learnt, and so badly, that he must die.' An even simpler statement which I prefer: . . . the only animal that knows he must die.

Resumed reading Camus's *Carnets*. I would be happy to spend the next ten years deepening my understanding and appreciation of this man — and rereading and again rereading everything he has written. Camus sounds out and charts the very oceans of experience, feeling and thought, on which I find myself sailing at this moment. His importance to me is monumental. Reading Camus is like finding, and for the first time, a man speaking my own language.

This quotation from his notebooks: 'The misery and greatness of this world: it offers no truths, only objects for love.'

'Absurdity is King, but love frees us from it.'

Camus, Malraux, Sartre — to be read again and again.

Lisa is now, slowly, mastering her first 'time' concepts. Tomorrow, this afternoon. Talking to Sheila about it I said that although it was a big step forward and another adjustment to the world in which we, the adults, lived, I was nevertheless very conscious of something lost — a pristine unclouded awareness of the present, the continuous living moment. Then I realised that for Lisa 'tomorrow' and 'this after-

94

noon' were the first steps towards the lesson which Malraux says, 'Man alone of all animals has learnt . . . that he must die'. Time and death: tomorrow and yesterday. Lisa is parting company, at two years old, with the innocent, animal spirits of this world.

Positive start with the second draft of *The Occupation.* The images I see, the idea as a whole, excite me. And no aversion to this medium − the screen − now that I am working for it. Whether I have any real ability or not is of course another matter. The medium is in no sense novel − I feel the experience gained in the small lifetime wasted away watching bad films.

Reading Robert Lowell's poetry.

The lavish, wild, tragic and naive beauty of the human heart and mind. Last night's fare: a chapter on Ukiyo-e prints; a few chapters on marine biology and, to end with, Mahler's Fourth Symphony while I sipped lemon tea.

Little candles held up in enormous and dark rooms − madmen muttering and singing in the corners. I was deeply moved by the richness, the beauty, the pathos of the human adventure. Those solitary courtesans in kimonos, the primeval mystery of the single-celled protozoa, Mahler singing! The candle burns brighter because the night is dark. Would the making of meaning be so moving without the eternal threat of chaos and nothingness?

Made the mistake of trying to tell Pieter about my TV play − *The Occupation;* a mistake because there is no question of being able to 'tell' it to someone. I must guard against this and make silence an inflexible rule when working on an idea. Talk *always* dissipates.

A long walk in the veld with him; strange landscape − cold, white setting sun behind windswept banks of clouds; the veld green, grass leaning to a long, clean, fresh wind. I said to Pieter: 'If Pasternak described this moment I would say, Yes. That is Russia. It is so foreign.' A moment that made me think of Barend[17] and his bed. Man must build a wall against a wind like that. It could wipe him away to nothing. Also thought of the false peace and resignation that they say floods over men in the arctic wastes, making them sit down in the snow and die. I could have sat down there in the veld and looked at the bending grasses and let time pass, and pass and pass . . .

A desolation − that could erase the memory of warmth and dreaming. As potent and ravaging as ecstasy itself.

The bluegums outside Pieter's house: whipped savagely by the wind and roaring back — not pain, but anger and rebellion or the threat of rebellion. And how empty a threat!

Why does the wind desolate me more than anything else in nature? Not even deserts — or night itself — render all action so futile or so effectively topple all achievement.

My note yesterday about man and his achievement — the candle in a dark room. Let me add, my pride to be one with author of the textbook and the artist of the Japanese prints and Mahler in his music. Proud not because we've won — how can we ever? Isn't losing inevitable? — but because of his lonely heroism, his courage. We haven't won; maybe we'll never win but nothing in life has fought as man has fought oblivion and nothingness.

Pride and Love — made all the more precious and painful because 'Absurdity *is* King ... Everything that exalts life adds also to its absurdity.' — also Camus.

Moments such as yesterday evening also have in them a keen awareness of the lurking futility of it all. I am drawing closer to a real understanding of what Camus means in the word — Absurd.

Ultimately — Pessimism. But heroic. Heroic Pessimism. 'Courage in the face of it all' — Milly in *People are Living There:* 'Surrender? Never!'

Have decided if all goes well to do *Woyzeck* next with the New Brighton group. My problem will be the name part — the rest of the characters and production style I feel very strongly. Meeting with the group last night, our immediate problems are to find rehearsal space and a backer for the play.

How different these men, and the local mood, are from Johannesburg. There I spent half of my time dreaming and bitching, with the Rehearsal Room group. Here we act. Also, these men are so much more responsible. I can see now how the patronage and 'help' of well-meaning whites has sapped away the initiative in Dorkay House.

In two weeks *The Occupation* will be finished — then I will prowl again in search of a new beginning.

September
Relationship between Mom, Sheila, Lisa and self in this flat. The flat is of course Mom's but Sheila and I have in a sense 'taken over'. Chaos of the evening meal — everyone shouting, crowded around the too-small table. The worst is yet to come. Next week Aunt Ann and

her third husband — Hendrik — move in with us for a week. Sheila in particular is squirming at the prospect. Those two old bodies — urinating, farting, expectorating — separated from us by the partioning between our and Ouma's room. Mom is giving them her room — she is moving in with Lisa.

Even without them life in this flat has always been marked by a fight for privacy — a feeling that it is too small for the four of us. Sheila avoids going into the kitchen when Ouma is there, specially at night because then the clothes-horse is also there.

An idea for a play: Hendrik, pompous, self-opinionated, prejudiced. Anna, big-bellied from all her operations — the two of them, sitting side by side.

Yes, the crux of the physical aversion in this flat is our use of buckets and chamber. The lavatory is outside. At night each room has its chamber — Ouma a bucket — anyone using one can be heard in all the other rooms.

Last night I found myself lying awake in the dark, tensed, desperate, listening to Mom wheezing and coughing in her room — her asthma has been very bad lately. I suddenly realised that this was exactly how I had reacted to my father in the months before he went to hospital. What does it mean? What does this say about me?

Never such a radiance, such a passionate orgy of freedom as Lisa when she finds herself on the beach. Space and the sea: the one inviting, the other provoking. She smiles and laughs and runs as at no other time in her short life. It could be the sun jumping beside me on two little legs. I watch her and the sea — her antique game with the waves, teasing, daring the broad tongue of foam and wetness as it comes hissing up the sand.

Nothing in her provokes so strong a feeling of responsibility as this happiness of hers. If I could choose, I could not help her more than by protecting and encouraging that excitement. Is there anything as innocent? I think of Camus's words: 'No life is wasted or meaningless that is lived in the sun.' Lisa on the beach has made me understand what he really meant.

Truth — an experience outside time — so that when it comes it flashes back, like lightning, through all that preceded it. Found in the deathbed it goes back to the moment of birth.

Esslin on the absurdities — Beckett, Ionesco: the old suspense — what is going to happen *next*. The new — what *is* happening.

97

The suddenness with which we find ourselves loving something. In a sense the sea broke into my life as suddenly as that. Now it is the wind — the long, clean, effacing winds which blow here in P.E. And a wind at night when everyone is sleeping — shaking the trees in the street. Or the moving beauty of wind in a curtain as a symbol of life — or rather, a statement of life.

Finished *The Occupation.* My final feeling is a good one. Over the past week I must have reread the script about six times — and every time there came a moment of complete fascination with the four men and their situation — the empty house. The one unevenness in the script is my usual realisation — it is very accurate and detailed at moments, sketched in in others and, in one or two places, it's hack writing. I find myself increasingly inclined to describe as 'provisional' and 'rough' any script which has not stood the test of production and been altered accordingly. Of course, I do not concede any alteration or tampering with the central image — once that happens you have a new play.

Last night before sleep, found myself thinking about Johnnie — the local street-corner derelict. I remembered my thought about a sister and suddenly I saw, and very clearly, the germinal situation of a play. Thinking about it this morning I am again excited.

Johnnie living with his father in a two-roomed shack in Valley Road. The father is blind and a cripple — victim of a road-blasting accident (SA Railways). Johnnie looks after him — feeding, washing, dressing, carrying. They exist on the old man's pension — old-age or disability. Johnnie does nothing else. His 'private life' consists of standing on one of the main street corners and watching. Drunk or sober — that is all he does.

One night — after a ten to fifteen year absence — his sister arrives unexpectedly at the run-down little house. All that she has in the world is in an old battered suitcase. Her purpose is revealed: she believes the old man was paid 'hundreds of pounds' by the SAR — 'compensation' for his accident. It is under his bed. (Before all this comes out she questions Johnnie about the old man and particularly his obsessive refusal to let anyone near his bed — she remembers this from the time before she left home. In other words, she has been thinking, brooding for years.) She wants the money — wants to steal it and eventually is prepared to kill the old man to get it.

Neither of these things happens. She leaves Johnnie and the old man together.

First problem: do we see the old man? Or only Johnnie and his sister?

Even if not see, his 'presence' must be felt — a hate, bigotry, resentment, meanness — as twisted and blind as the physical reality.

The sister, a common prostitute. Even before leaving for Joburg she had men — sailors (war years?) whom Johnnie, then a young boy, brought home from Jetty Street. These men were her reason for leaving — the father found out. Her past fifteen years in Joburg — an experience that has taken her to the limits of physical violence and crudity.

'I'm not a woman any more. What's a woman? Not me. They fuck me — but I'm not a woman.' All that is left for her is the 'happiness' in the box under her father's bed. She has a 'plan' for her share of the money. One of her schemes to get at the money is simply for her and Johnnie to leave the old man and let him starve to death — Johnnie is frightened (?) of her suggestion of physical violence.

Johnnie bogged down in his lethargy — cannot find the 'reason' to steal the money. She tries to rouse him: 'You want something. You must want something. A motorbike! What about a motorbike!'

What defeats her? Johnnie's lethargy?

Johnnie does not recognise his sister when she walks in with her old suitcase. She has to tell him: 'I'm . . .'

The sister — all hope (blind) and meaning in 'the box under Daddy's bed' — an obsession that allows of neither right nor wrong; yes or no. She must get it. This is what life has come down to. Apart from that there are only memories — and most of them provoke her to anger, hate or disgust. One other reality — her bruises, her physical self.

Johnnie's outings — a bottle of beer and a packet of lemon creams to the beach.

Johnnie — the old man, his cries, his pain, is a drug which keeps Johnnie numb. Johnnie has lived, grown up, with the old man crying in the other room.

The main headlines in today's paper: the shooting of Denis Brutus. [18] Both Sheila and I deeply shocked. The last we read of him was that he was in Swaziland. Apparently he slipped into Portuguese East Africa — was caught in Lourenço Marques and handed over to the South African authorites. In Johannesburg he made a last desperate attempt to escape and was shot — in the stomach. Hospital reports his condition is 'satisfactory'.

Two details in the newspaper report. He was carried by the man

99

who shot him. The shooting took place in Main Street, Johannesburg, outside the grey monumental Anglo-American building.

Suddenly I see and feel — acutely — the frailty of the man — the enormous horror of that lead smashing into his stomach. I wonder at the expression on his face. Did he laugh, swear or cry when they carried him?

A walk this evening just after sunset, to the Eldorado Hall in South End for another meeting with the New Brighton group.

The streets in the fading light, the wind and a tumultuous, feverish sky — particularly in South End where the poverty added an ambience — a human ambience — to everything. To one side of the bridge over the Baakens River two women sat, faces lost in the growing darkness and scarves, beside boxes of fruit. One could see the moment had come to pack up and go home. Why were they still there? Waiting for a man who would carry the unsold fruit home? Or, like everything else, simply sitting out that moment of peace . . . fatigue . . . yet another day . . . yet again . . . 'Ah dear! Some moments in life can be quiet and empty of everything except being — being here now . . . yesterday . . . I'll be here tomorrow.'

The water in the river is black.

In another corner of the bridge a bus conductor — one hand holding his timesheet and tin box of tickets — had a woman pressed up against the wall. Between them at that moment, holding their two bodies together was one thing above all others: he was a man, she was a woman. So obvious — but in the way a child writes its first word — enormous and naive. I can remember nothing of their faces except that in a different light I would have thought them crude. At that moment their very crudities were archetypal — her red lips and mocking smile; his eyes, his body.

And so on moment after moment until I reached the hall and began work.

All is hunger — hunger and wanting — mind, belly and loins — and then still more, so much more! The secret, unnameable wanting and desiring — of organs and parts no anatomy has named or reckoned with. That is why slums' backstreets are so disturbingly human — the hunger is of the crudest, and concentrated — so we smell it. The smell of man — of Life — hunger!

And now, at the end of today, the wind is blowing — judgment with compassion. All is ultimately nothing but Man, the sharp sides, the shapes of your achievement, whet me to a keen pity!

The wind as the great dispersal agent — scattering. Yes! This

100

thought touches the melancholy evoked in me by the sound and feel of wind. Nothing stays — nothing sinks. We float and are scattered. There are no anchors.

As a change from the sea I went bird-watching yesterday in Settlers' Park. Splendid time. Burchell's Coucal, and a colony of weaver birds. Watched one of the latter weaving his nest.

Returned home through the valley — setting for what could be my next play : semi-detached houses and the Hindu temple.

This is to be a period of rest and living — the next few weeks. I have *Woyzech* to direct and the Valley play to think about.

In this morning's paper a story of a woman celebrating her 100th birthday. No husband, children or living relatives. Her hobby: to stay alive longer. In her garage is a 1939 model motorcar which she stopped driving five years ago at the age of 95. However she still keeps it licensed and insured. 'It keeps me in touch with the Municipality.'

I feel almost certain that the next thing I write will be the play about Johnnie (Boetie) and Hester Smit. A number of disturbing ideas about their Valley Road semi-detached house have formed during the past few days. Ideally I would like to think about and plan from now until the end of the year, and then start working in the New Year.

How many themes does a writer really have? This play — the idea — is in one sense a fusion of elements in *The Blood Knot* and *People are Living There*. If I can realise it I imagine it will be closer to the former — tense and tight. One of my*problems in fact is whether to have only two characters — brother and sister — or whether the father should also be seen. I have my first and last moments very clearly — and a dynamic appreciation of the characters of Johnnie and Hester.

Ideally I would like to plot it with as many twists and turns, as many surprises and 'moments' as I had in *The Blood Knot*. But I must be very careful. There are already dangerous parallels in the relationship — brother and sister, and their physical situation. Another point of similarity: *B.K.* was serious with moments of comedy. *People* was comic with moments of seriousness. The new play should be the former.

Yesterday for one hour — from about eleven to twelve — a sudden and tremendous advance in my thinking about the new play. A sequence of about five ideas and images but the result is that suddenly

101

I 'see' the play — form and content. I am almost certain that again there will be only two characters: Hester and Boetie Smit. At a superficial level this thought nags a little — but when I forget comparisons and concern myself only with the reality of this brother and sister, it becomes pointless to consider 'adding' another 'character'. In Hester and Johnnie I find a *complete* expression of this complex of thoughts and feelings — another character would be redundant and uneconomical. I just don't need him or her. The father might eventually make one or two appearances but these are so unimportant to the whole that I will accept without any qualms whatever circumstances demand.

Two Acts: the First — Hester's arrival; her reason for returning; the first suitcase. INTERVAL. The second — suitcase after suitcase, box after box; their contents spilling out onto the floor — growing chaos as Hester finds her past, her promise, her life, and finally sees clearly their ruin — the present. And leaves.

Set: table and two chairs. An emotional continuity in that room and between the scenes. In fact, they aren't scenes but moments. The only *time* direction must be the insistent, repetitive: later . . . later . . .

Just when I think I am almost ready to write the new play, I read my first Proust (*Swann's Way*) and realise how far I have yet to go in understanding the implications of Hester 'finding her own self' in the suitcases and boxes from her father's room. Provoked by this realisation, particularly by incident of the piece of madeleine soaked in tea which ends the 'overture' of Swann's Way.

Sartre: Anguish = the fear of not making the time and place of the 'appointment with self'. I realise that the popular image of Beckett's characters is hindering our appreciation of other aspects of Beckett's writing — his existentialism. Vladimir and Estragon are Man in a state of Anguish, and Godot — their concern with the 'right place' and the 'right time' — is Man desperately trying to meet that appointment with Self.

These thoughts came at a most opportune moment and must undoubtedly add dimensions to Hester and Boetie.

October
A disturbing moment last night. I woke and for a long time did not know where I was. I am not even sure that I knew who I was. What does the 'me' — that I refer and relate everything to during my waking conscious hours — what does this 'me' really consist of? Memory? Our lives, our special and utterly unique 'selves', just a memory in action?

102

So Edward Albee provides us with our first banning in theatre. Last night's performance in Johannesburg of *Who's Afraid of Virginia Woolf?* was stopped by the Minister of Education. Matter referred to Censorship Board who now take the final decision.

Mom picked up the news on the radio last night. I remember feeling hopeless and depressed about the future when she told us.

I say to myself: Death is loss. To die means to lose everything, to cease to be. After death there is Nothing. And my mind says it understands this. But do I? I think that living, all we ever know of Death and its meaning is the smallest and most insignificant part of the whole — like a whispered conversation heard through a wall, of which only one or two words reach us clearly so that ultimately all we can do is guess at the meaning of the whole.

Death is the final experience of losing — but one we have been rehearsing for all our lives. And what is more, it seems to me that the rehearsals are worse than the performance itself. For having lost in life — possibly something loved as much as life itself — we have to go on living. I don't think there is anything after death — the pain of that loss cannot be felt. But of course being so well rehearsed we can anticipate.

Man — an actor blind to applause, the acclaim or booing and slating of his final performance.

It seems that this anticipation just referred to means that whoever does so anticipate, lives with his 'death' like the hard stone in the centre of a fruit. The indigestible core at the centre of life's sweetness. And who knows — possibly the analogy can be taken all the way — and Death is the real reason for the sweetness, the sun-ripened flesh — a man's Death is his real 'seed' — the germinative thing in his 'life'.

A man well-rehearsed for dying.

Paraphrasing Malraux — Man alone of all animals has put this thought of death, this anticipation, at the centre of his being.

What a story it would be if simply told: the gradual knowledge of Death in the human consciousness. This story most probably already exists in the history of our Gods.

Disturbed and restless. Inwardly agitated with my growing feeling for Hester and Johnnie.

Lurking in the background these past weeks, waiting for its chance in unguarded moments, a mood of uncertainty, doubt, a sense of failure.

103

In all honesty I think there is only one explanation — money. Our savings are down to a couple of hundred pounds. Except for a few vague possibilities the immediate future doesn't hold out much reason for hope.

Child-parent relationship = avarice. We talk glibly of the 'parent trying to live the child's life' — but doesn't this really only point to an earlier cannibalism? The child having swallowed up the parents' life?

I do not know of a single relationship in my life in which I wasn't eating or being eaten.

All of this because of the night when Lisa woke screaming in the middle of the night. I said to Sheila: 'A worm in my days. This is my life. Today was a day of my life, and she has . . .'

And it is true. Lisa comes at my life hungrily — a blind ravenous hunger to eat into and possess my life. I have to defend myself. If I don't and she does eat me up then I will be in her bowels, parasitic upon her, for as long as she lives.

Camus's 'no life lived in the sun can be a failure' — I understand this now, having discovered the sun and the sea, and the long hot hours on the beach. Simply to go there involves me turning my back, literally and figuratively, on this room and table, this world where the words 'success' and 'failure' have meaning. Down there on the white sands, with the long wind blowing and the taste of the sea in my mouth, they are empty sounds. A fine contempt is forged in the sun, tempered in the sea.

December
Woyzeck is over. Good reviews but none of the performances was more than 50% of my ideal. Production and staging good. But the acting failed completely to catch the subtleties, the light and shade in Marie and Woyzeck. Although for the group this production was a step forward after the Machiavelli, the final result wasn't anywhere near as satisfying. A long way to go.

South End: roughly a triangle defined by South Union Street at the bottom and then Valley Road and Walmer Road on the sides. Little semi-detached houses, some derelict some newly-painted; young girls leaning on stoeps chewing bubble-gum; fishermen; dogs; babies — seemingly neglected, crying in doorways; poky, untidy little Indian shops; fish and chips; a paw-paw tree leaning out of a backyard into the yellow light around where we ate curry and rice last night; the harbour down below at one end; a full moon in the sky; a warm breathless night. A place where men live — in fact vivid with the stains of birth and death, hoping and just waiting — yet open to the world; full of the moon and the sound and smell of the sea, the feel of the rain just falling. The haunting beauty of the pinched, deprived face caught in a moment of repose.

The little coloured girls wear boys' socks rolled neatly up their legs.

One evening I watched a man carrying his furniture from a room on one side of the street to a room on the other.

This must be the world those strange itinerant characters buying 'empty-bottle' in the respectable suburbs come from.

The sea — swimming and sun — as never before. It is more than just 'getting away' from my work. Conscious that an 'indifference', a 'silence' is being forged — learning to live without hope. Simply to Live — the invitation and the ideal. Courage and lucidity — and no 'appeal'. The only certainty is flesh — what it feels and wants.

Tremendous urge to kill now that I go into the sea with a harpoon.

And Mom, it seems at times, dying next-door like Dad. The same pattern: Lying awake and listening. We mentioned him last night — in between gasping for air, her asthma, she said: 'Yes. He had pain. Thank God I've got no pain.' It struck me as a monstrous absurdity — that pain could still matter when you were fighting for your life as she is.

'I'm dying without pain. That's something.'

Reading Camus's *Sisyphus* — tremendous!

Lying on the floor in the café was a Christmas tree. It seemed pointless and I felt ashamed, more so when I thought of how I was going to dress it up late that night so as to provide Lisa with a little novelty that wouldn't last an hour. I picked it up and carried it to the car — but as I stepped outside into the night a remarkable thing happened. A slight wind was blowing and as it swept into and through the tree, the little pine sighed and I was holding a forest in my hand.

Finished *Sisyphus*. Impossible to describe the excitement, the total sympathy that exists for me with Camus's thinking. In the harsh but lucid world of his writing I seem to have found, for the first time, my true climate.

Thinking continuously about the Valley play — Hester and Boetie

Smit. Difficulty in the mechanics of the climax — when Hester 'loses hope' and 'learns she must die'. Dissatisfied and suspicious of what I feel is a 'stock' pattern, a 'formula' which I seem to have used in all my plays so far, i.e. *growing desperation* leading to *emotional crisis* leading to the *leap*.

Thinking about it for a minute I realise I am wrong to see this as a formula, common to all my other plays. *The Blood Knot* doesn't have it. Far from 'leaping', Morrie and Zack wake up to find themselves heavy, hopeless, almost prostrate on the earth. I think my trouble is simply that whereas consciously I think of one thing — unconsciously I write another.

Yes. That is it. What I am searching for in the new play is the moment when Hester 'wakes up' and finds herself prostrate on the earth. Three experiences: loss of hope; knowledge of death; the only certainty = the flesh.

What is more obvious than that I should be drawn, be overwhelmed by Camus. Morrie and Zack at the end of *The Blood Knot* are men who are going to try to live without hope, without appeal. If there is anything on that stage before the curtain drops it is lucid knowledge, consciousness. In effect, Morrie says: 'Now we know.'

Reading Sartre's *Nausea* — one of the characters telling the story of how she was taken into a bedroom to see her dead father 'for the last time.' For the Last Time ... When I read those words I went cold with horror — realising acutely for one instant the finality to death, the Loss ... of everything. It seemed impossible that there would come that moment, when others must take their last look at me ... I who live so much in other people's eyes. Or rather ... I am always looking at myself, and I too must one day see myself for the last time. Yes, that is it.

Mom went into hospital this morning under circumstances which provide an uneasy parallel to those of my father. The past 24 hours have been sheer hell. Nothing to record but the stupidity and horror of her struggle for breath and life and the even greater stupidity of my helplessness. To stand by with empty hands, a foggy mind and sleepy eyes while her asthma and desperation reduce her to terror and trembling until she feels the darkness closing in on her — this experience, four or five times over, has left me drained of every normal response. My life must assimilate this experience, I know, but it's like trying to swallow a mouthful of nails.

106

Christmas morning — Lisa bewildered and confused by her new toys, all of which are a great success, particularly the tricycle. Otherwise, nothing. The celebration of that birth 2000 years ago is totally without meaning to me.

On Monday a day on the Tzitzikama coast, Klaasies River — staggeringly beautiful with the Indian Ocean rolling in over the horizon to thunder onto a wild rocky coastline. Went into a couple of Strandloper[19] caves, now occupied by bats, birds and occasional wild animals. The caves provoked depression. I couldn't romanticise them — they stank of darkness and fear. They were too perilous — the human hold on those damp walls too frightened and insecure. I must be more precise — not the mortality of those lives but the lack of consciousness. Revolt (meaning) can only come with consciousness. I am sure I would have felt differently if there had been paintings on the wall — because in that I would have seen consciousness.

Without that consciousness even the sunlight and sea become as black as the night that stuffed the inside of the caves.

Consciousness — the sun in man's life — our only light.

Without consciousness we become victims instead of actors — even if it is still only a question of acting victims. And in this make-believe of our lives the audience is self.

Days passing without difficulty — swimming, hunting. I have never lived so lightly and happily. But at the same time I am ready and receptive — waiting for the impulse that will lead me back to work. Still thinking — sometimes just 'seeing' — Hester and Boetie Smit in the Valley.

The story of Dimetos in Camus's *Carnets:* falling in love with a beautiful but dead young woman washed up by the sea, and having to watch the decay and corruption of what he loves. Camus: 'This is the symbol of a condition we must try to define.'

When I first read his note on Dimetos I was excited and immediately thought of it as the germinal idea of a play. Yesterday I re-remembered it.

Dimetos goes mad watching the decay of her body.

Spring tides tomorrow. Still waiting for the 'big kill' in the sea. My best so far has been a 20-inch barbel. Delicious eating Sheila agreed, but for her every mouthful was haunted by the hideous face of the fish, with its four pairs of feelers. Mom also ate a portion, but vomit-

107

ed it all up when I told her the fish didn't have scales and looked vaguely like a snake.

The wind on my body when I lie on the sand after a dive — the feel and sound of the day passing, time passing, sun moving, earth turning, my life living and also passing — soft ineffable melancholy that carries me numbed through all this sad passing. But at moments it stops, just briefly, but long enough for the heat to nail and hold that one living instant, my body on the earth. It is a moment of shock — mind and body burning; then the wind starts again and the sand of my life runs out, runs out.

Time to talk about the Kill — that electric, orgiastic moment when the harpoon shoots out of my hand and runs through a shining, sea-clean fish. This morning it was fair-sized, fat harders which we will eat for supper tonight. All attempts to think and write about it, here at this desk, are uncertain, as if the essential experience, that part of me which hunts in the water, eludes memory. But it seems, as I remember here and now, that my whole being shrinks to an intense focus when the chance comes — and that after taking this chance — shooting and spearing — there is yet another experience, occasionally the certainty that the fish is mine. There have been kills without any of this excitement, and afterwards a flat stale feeling as if luck or circumstances had given me the fish; at these times I did not draw the last vital impulse of that silver body along my harpoon, something else had killed it. The other, rarer experience is that absolute certainty that I killed it, that it was my moment. I shot my big barbel under those conditions.

This killing, the keen excitement I get out of it, does not worry me. I have, again, a vague memory of it when I sit here and consciously think, and I have a few phrases which lift me over the hurdles, e.g. It's more honest. I prefer to do my own killing. The ease with which I elude all difficulty makes me think seriously about my idea of a memory, a level of being which eludes memory.

The end of the year. Nothing could mean less to me. I have felt acutely and with nostalgia, melancholy, or anticipation as the occasion demanded, the passing and coming of the past four seasons. But this moment, this artificial point (Auld Lang Syne with the O.K. Animated Choir; the tugs and cars blowing their hooters) leaves me stone cold sober. I will lie in bed tonight and, as I have done so many nights, watch the shadow of a tree on our stoep through our opened doors. The curtains will breathe gently, with a soft wind, and the

108

shadow itself will move, clotting into blackness on the cool stone or breaking apart into the agitated contours of leaves; and, as on so many nights now, I will fall asleep in the unimportant labyrinth of a dialogue that I follow through as if learnt by rote. First my mind consciously analyses the phenomenon of a shadow, the fall of light, etc., and assures me that a shadow is nothing. Then with my eyes, with all the sense of my living mortal body, I look at 'it' — 'it' — and savour the beauty of its being. Yet it is nothing. My mind has told me ... etc. And my wonder increases, encompassing now not only the beauty of the shadow but the duplicity, the paradox that runs so richly through all this life. And then sleep.

1964

January

Today is Friday. I think I will start work on the new play (Hester & Boetie) over this weekend. Am I ready for it? I don't know. To be honest there is a feeling of being unprepared. On the other hand, I am impatient to be working again.

At times it seems that all I can remember of the other plays I have written (remember of the actual 'writing' that is), is the feel of this pen in my hand and the waiting, intimidating blankness of the paper. Either my techniques are unconscious or I really do 'learn' nothing from play to play. My thinking is awkward, my 'solutions' crude; I could almost hear myself asking some other writer: How do you write a play? — with the emphasis on 'How' and not 'you'.

This time a strong — stronger than ever before — feeling of exploring my idea and situation with the actual writing. Like walking into a labyrinth. I know where I must come out — I need the luck of the Gods to find the right way.

Wrote Act 1 at the top of a blank sheet of paper yesterday morning and started writing. The night before, I had bad insomnia — during the two hours I tossed and turned in bed I thought out a few radical changes to the plot (the father dead and buried instead of alive and in the other room); also reduced all action to one night instead of two. Am working along these lines.

Horrible feeling that the whole thing might miscarry.

Diving opposite the country club on the Marine Drive yesterday afternoon. Splendid. Incredible number and variety of fish. Brought home a delicious supper of four grey mullet.

As expected, a miscarriage. Five pages which I reread and then tore up. Dull and prosaic — 'Knock on door. Johnnie leaves the table and opens the door. Woman (off) . . .' etc. Have always squirmed with uneasiness and frustration within the realistic convention. This time I must break free. My feeling for Hester and Boetie is untouched by this bad beginning.

Flowers, a noise in the night, night shadows on the cool stones of our stoep, the wind in the trees — all we can ever hope for, our 'most' is to wound eternity, to draw blood by making moments mortal.

The dream of new and strange beauties seems to disturb, to provoke me less with each day. My obsession — growing with every day — is with what I have — what 'could be' or is somewhere else, hardly crosses my mind. No yearning. In its place a profound and sweet melancholy for my here and now. The thought of ever travelling again is unpleasant.

Bird Street at nine o'clock this morning (Sunday). Walking home with a pint of milk; Lisa ahead on her tricycle; no-one else in sight and plentiful sunlight and air. Silence and calm — all of it broad — a generous measure of a good day on our earth, under our sky.

A fresh start on the play (planning on paper as with *B.K.* and *People*) is producing encouraging results. No doubts now about the first attempt: I was unprepared. Fortunately my idea has sufficient resilience and power to withstand this messing about.

Mom back from hospital — the fist of old age cramped tight onto her piece of life. Wheezing, coughing, retching, sneezing, she lies nextdoor in her room, thinking of nothing but herself and now, like my father in his last days, living for and on pills, tonics, capsules, Vicks Formula 44, Nerve pain specific, etc. etc.

Sheila said: 'Can't you tell her to turn on her wireless and listen to Springbok Radio or knit or read her School of Truth prayer books? Anything rather than lie there.'

I tried to suggest listening to the radio — the suggestion threw her into a panic of protest and refusal.

The fist of old age — one would break one's own fingers trying to open that hand and give more. It is impossible. All she will ever have or know of life is already hers, already held and held too long — squeezed dry. When do we harden our hold like that? The beginning of death — loss of possibility.

The new play: second start, about ten days ago, has been promising. Have thought and felt myself deeply into Johnnie & Hester. I believe I have really started this time and will finish. Title: *Hello and Goodbye*.

My father never 'made a noise' so we didn't really know he was there. Then at the end pain made him articulate. Something like shock finding him cluttering up our existence.

Mom — that is the difference. There is not the same angry resentment when I listen to her at night. I've always, in a sense, known she was there.

Milly was right: we need to make a noise.

Visit from one of Serpent Players — deceptive appearance of acceptance and resignation, then suddenly he revealed an enormous bitter resentment, anger, frustration that has several times brought him to the point of leaving. 'Anywhere in the world!' I'd never suspected it.

Talked about the nausea brought on by reading the newspapers — mornings when the headlines recording Verwoerd's latest move made him throw the paper away, too sick, too appalled by the hopelessness of the situation, to read further.

His experiences as a detainee during the Emergency (after Sharpeville) — interrogation by a senior police officer from Pretoria:

'Do you like the Government?'

'No.'

'Why?'

'Ag, man, hell — I could give you a thousand reasons.'

'Give me one.'

'One? Why am I here? I don't know why I'm here! You don't tell me. That's one.'

Govan Mbeki[1] organising the detainees in hunger strikes. They were in the same cell. Certain mornings Govan would say: 'We don't eat today. The plates are rusty.' They all obeyed.

The old dilemma — stay or go.

Something else that sickened him: old men labouring for five rand a week — utter hopelessness. They did not even know there was an alternative, another way of living.

February

Very rough outline of first half of *Hello and Goodbye* down on paper. Hester and Johnnie are as real, as complex as anything I've written. Seems as if *People are Living There* was really an exercise preparing me for this. Definitely a return, possibly a development of the *B.K.* style and technique which wasn't really present in *People*.

Overwhelmed by my first real reading of the Greeks: Euripedes' *Women of Troy* and *The Bacchae*.

Meeting with the local group — Serpent Players — again. Have decided to attempt 'pure' Commedia dell'Arte. So far so good. In three meetings we have hammered out a good, funny and intricate plot. Now we start improving and building the scenes. I am relying on three factors to provide the fluency, tempo and excitement necessary: Complete understanding of character and its possibilities. An equal understanding of plot and requirements of each scene. Co-operation or, better still, 'ensemble' playing.

Moods and moments of such beauty here in this ugly little city that I find myself inarticulate in face of their subtlety, their movingly human nature and stature. And mortal! These are the ingredients: flesh and blood, sea, wind and sky; dirty little streets; faces under street-lamps late at night; never rich and most times poor, poor enough for too much hope . . . all that makes this earth my here and now and gives it its little meaning.

One day it was the faces of women — young and old housewives and office workers — trudging up Russel Road after a long hot day. How can I convey the richness and complexity of that moment? A woman knocking and the door opening to let her in . . . The startling reality of curtains hanging in a window . . .

Another day it was a little girl, very neat — and how much was said in that neatness! How much defiance and courage in the home she was going to as she crossed the pool of light under a lamp.

Tonight it was a cat, crouched, tense with cunning and excitement, watching something in a gutter — and a beggar digging out and eating discarded grape berries from a pile of rubbish outside a fruitshop.

It is my understanding, my total knowledge of the shape, sizes and feel of these moments that makes P.E. what it is in my life: necessary. It is like a love — needed and necessary. And Hester and Johnnie are an expression of it.

The snake incident at Malay Pool. A group of coloureds, Sheila, Lisa and myself watching — standing in a circle in the sun — the death agonies of a puffadder they had found in the lavatory. Body undamaged and beautiful, but the head smashed to pulp — writhing, twisting itself into knots and all the time, all of us watching. Laconic comment: 'Pofadder.' 'Ja.' 'Gevaarlik.' 'Sê nou net iemand het op hom getrap!'[2]

So much of South Africa in that moment — the watcher and the watched. The snake beautiful and dangerous, deadly; our senseless killing of it, our moral complacency in watching; the sea, sun and sky as indifferent to us as we to the snake. The truth is we have not made

113

a good job of sharing this earth. Is there anything alive that can compare with Man in deadliness?

Too much hope at the moment: the premiere of *Blood Knot* in America,[3] and the invitation to Northern Rhodesia. I almost wish this period was more barren. It's hard, of course, but once you've stomached hopelessness, Life really begins.

March

Tomorrow *The Blood Knot* opens in New York. I have forced myself to expect the worst. Tynan's legacy[4] is a certain fatalism and growing indifference. The critical asp has had its bite and I've bred antibodies.

June

Between last entry and this: Northern Rhodesia and three weeks in New York. Both experiences are too detailed for me even to attempt recording them in retrospect. Both so special I cannot see myself forgetting any part of them.

So today life starts again and this time it's The Haven at Schoenmakerskop.[5] A view of the sea and the silence and privacy I've wanted so long. I feel ready for work.

Looking out of the window a moment ago I saw afresh the moving, restless nature of the sea and the solid — am almost tempted to say 'stolid' by contrast — weight of the earth. It is cold today, a keen edge to the wind after days of mild warmth. Overcast sky; rain squalls passing far out at sea; the sea itself flecked with white and running with the wind.

Major revision of *People* in terms of form. Beginning to appreciate the lesson John Berry taught me through his cutting of *The Blood Knot* production in New York.

Yesterday for the first time observed the habit which gives the Butcher Bird (Fiscal Shrike) its name. One of them had impaled on a thorntree just outside my window, a small fieldmouse which it had just caught. Spent the morning feeding off it. A few minutes of tearing off and eating pieces of the body and then a half-hour or so at the top of a telephone pole or Agave spike, obviously digesting this, then back to the 'kill'.

When I went for a walk at sunset about half the carcass remained. This morning that was also gone. Some other predator must have found it during the night.

And so the score is one dead and two full bellies, in the middle of this harsh winter.

These first two weeks here at Schoenmakerskop make me doubt whether I would ever accept living in a city again.

July

My fourth dive yesterday — still without harpoon — but for the first time since my return something of the old exhilaration: a fluency in the water that kept me in, prowling around for at least half an hour. Cold water. A small feeling of desolation always just before and as I go into the water and leave behind the accustomed firmness of land. Then the excitement and fascination of that alien world in which I am an intruder, grips me: sense of liberation, of living — until I feel the cold — on a higher, more intense physical level. An ascetic purity in the experience — the very opposite of sensualism even though it is apprehended with all of me that must die.

For the first time in what must surely be ten years, I put something into the earth yesterday — four of ten poinsettias for the back fence.

For all the obviousness of the remark — it sounds the worst type of cliché — living here does take us back to nature. The elements just don't have the same consequence in the city. Going to bed last night I noticed with keen hope that the wind had dropped — and sure enough, here it is today: sunshine, clear skies and a calm sea. Our west wind brings rain. You can smell it in the air, usually about noon. The sea confirms it — wisps of spray lifted off the waves and carried falling along their length. This is what 'nature' means in a situation like this. There are no more 'answers' here than anywhere else, but what happens does so in a pattern that you can define and fit into. I think back to Bird Street where the 'weather' was a 'bad day' or a 'good day' in the street outside my window, where the wind when it blew was a nameless agitation in my clothes and in the trees, where rain was wet and fell from skies and made rooms dark.

Farm Funeral: Dr Meiring's wife, Billy.

We arrived at Kirkwood to be told that they wanted me to be one of the pallbearers. But did I have a 'dark suit'? Of course not. I was wearing a sportscoat and grey trousers — my best, in fact. I'd even put on a white shirt and tie. But it was not a 'dark suit' and so that was the end of that. Instead I took Lisa into the orchards where she played for about two hours, leaving Sheila free to do her best and her duty.

115

The faces of the women — fat women with small ungenerous eyes behind spectacles — congealed with ... what? Not grief. Self-indulgent sentimentality; kissing each other with wet eyes and broken voices. And black ... so black it became at times the substance of that moment with the sun shining and the sky blue and the orchards green. The last 'look' — '... do you want to see Billy for the last time?' — the cracked face of a man after that 'last look'. Most terrible of all, the thing in the coffin. Bitter half-mooned mouth, loveless stuff that had been flesh, stark resentment. Total stupidity of it all. I was shocked. Never reckoned with 'it' being 'dead'. Completely eluded my imagination ... I mean the fact that she is *dead*. Not just asleep, with eyes closed, unmoving ... but dead, 'no more'.

During our two hours in the orchard while the service was in progress, found a dried piece of thornbush — the thorns bleached white — which I brought home with me, it is so beautiful. Looking at it — the incredible purity of line, the stillness and beauty of its death — thinking of Billy in the coffin, I could only ask: why don't we die like wood? What do I mean? Something to do with survival after the event — yes, this is it — survival of the substance.

A long dusty drive from the farm to the cemetery. There, on the other side of the road and about a hundred yards into the veld, was a laager of abandoned rusted shells of motorcars. Two donkey-carts and several coloured women with great loads of firewood on their heads, passed quietly and leisurely down the road during the service. A donkey brayed raucously twice.

Winter with us again today. Rain squalls sweeping along the coast in a wild cold wind. The sea shrunk to a few yards of boiling white water beyond the rocks — the rest hidden in a grey void of wind and rain.

Weather that runs with the wind, constantly changing : one moment a splash of weak sunlight — ten seconds later, grey again and rain; needle-sharp, slanted, hurrying rain. No respite.

Lisa, now five, and Paul du Preez, the same age but much bigger. Normally she is on the receiving end in a bullying, aggressive relationship — but not always. One afternoon he arrived here with his mother after a long sleep and, as is usually the case with a child, was disorientated and vague. Lisa, on the other hand, was wide awake. They played in the garden, she jumping around, spinning out a web of fantasy so fast and ceaselessly that, although his natural inclinations were to refuse to play, she caught him as surely as a spider catches a fly, dragging him through game after game much against his will. It is an apt image — she is ceaselessly on the move, mind as well as body, the thread of make-believe (Shall we be three monkeys?) seemingly endless.

August
The wind has dropped. Moonlight and the pure shimmering white of the water where the waves are breaking. A solitary bird crying at the water's edge. The promise of a perfect tomorrow in the dewy sky.

The thunder of the surf is a faint sound here in the room where I sit thinking about tomorrow's work on *People*. I imagine I can feel the echoing vibrations of each wave as it falls in the floor under my feet. While the high piping call of the bird pulses out again, an ascending scale and then dying away on the top note. The useless, absurd splendour of this moment. That sea is the silence into which we cry and laugh.

Disturbed of late to realise how much of the 'here and now' I lose or waste, pledging it for some hazy, ill-defined promise in the future. Admittedly there is less of this than before, but still enough to frighten me into wondering how much of my life I really live. To live as if this were my last day. I know when I achieve this by the moving and beautiful melancholy with which the moment is suddenly invested.

After the long sweat of reshaping and rewriting, now entered a phase in my work on the third act of *People* which I can almost say I 'enjoy'. My line is sketched out roughly on paper so there is no longer any of the tension involved in moving from moment to moment, and of finding those moments. But it is a rough line. Now I refine — going over it again and again, fixing, clarifying and elaborating. Somewhere else in the notebooks I have spoken about this — likened it to a passage of time taken out of time, a mechanism which once evolved can be wound up again and again and allowed to run down. I watch the antics of my little toy: to begin with the thing squirms and wriggles around almost blindly when I put it down. But I know the shape of the movement I want. I tighten here, lengthen there, loosen here ... at the end I wind it up and put it down again, the wheels turn and it moves as I had intended. Does anyone want to buy it?

Yesterday found washed up on the beach a dog-fish egg-case, intact and with a live embryo inside. Now in a bucket of sea water here in the study the squirming little embryo with the shape of the adult

117

fish already discernible, linked by an umbilical chord to the yolk sac. Something mysterious and disturbing in this dumb, deaf blind blob of life struggling, wriggling on to maturity while it lay there on the beach, and again now, the same small pulse of life in a white plastic bucket ... Remembering the beached dead adults I've sometimes found on my walks — five feet long and 30 lbs in weight. The embryo must be about half an inch long.

Hester gives me a chance for the ruthless honesty I admired in Faulkner's *Wild Palms* — statement of Camus's 'courageous pessimism'. No other character of mine is as close to the 'bone'. Even in Milly there is too much 'meat', something soft that must rot away before the harsh white truth is exposed. I can achieve this with Hester. Also the verbal density, 'weight' of the *B.K.'s* texture.

It is Hester and Johnnie I am thinking, brooding about today with the seemingly endless wind buffeting the birds on the fence outside my window, tearing them off the crust of bread I spike on one of the poles every morning. Beyond them, the sea — heavy, lurching, spilling over itself in a sort of bestial truculence, whipped eastwards by the light-footed, impatient wind.

The major question — why and what does Hester find in the boxes when searching for her father's 'compensation'? When I know the answer, I have got my play.

September

Today's paper: one of the 90-day detainees[6] committed suicide by jumping to his death from the seventh storey of the Special Branch headquarters in Johannesburg. Happened during interrogation.

Sartre's *Men Without Shadows* — the suicide at the end.

Also: 'Fascism is not distinguished by the number of its victims, but the manner in which it kills them.'

Hester — moral anarchy. The world she lives in.

'I have seen ... so why shouldn't I ...'

'God, volk and trek' — rejected. It's a lie — the images, idols of decency, cleanliness, godliness.

'*They* pretend and they don't see they keep alive the lie that God's in heaven and on our side.'

Two days ago a long letter from Irving Schneider, the American producer who is interested in *People*.[7]

He was appalled at the changes I had made and urged me to get back closer to the original. My first reaction was extreme confusion. I was so convinced that what I had done was right and a major improvement. As usual I wanted to abandon the work and go on to something else. Forced myself however to examine carefully all of what he has written and now must admit that he is right.

I cannot seriously consider abandoning the play. Like Schneider I am glued to it — more so with every thought I give it. At times Milly's predicament — those five hours in that Braamfontein kitchen — has a tremendous and moving relevance to all I think, feel and do. She deserves her chance.

Struggling with apathy and confusion in the group to get *The Caucasian Chalk Circle* understood and started. By and large they are as bourgeois in aspirations and morality as most white people in this country. Masters and their slaves. The fight is for a slice of the same cake. No-one wants to bake a different one. This is the hardest — showing that the *Chalk Circle* is a different recipe.

And for myself again the suspicions and doubts about my work that contact with Brecht always provokes. Above all else I am overwhelmed at this moment by the 'usefulness' of the *Chalk Circle* — so much a tool, the edge honed to a bright decisiveness by this great dramatist. A man wants to dig a vegetable garden — I talk to him about the nourishment and health to be had from vegetables; Brecht gives him a spade and seeds.

Self-indulgence.

I have it now — my pessimism! Brecht has optimism. All is not said in that of course — there remains anti-individualism as opposed to my inability to see man — a man — as the sum total of his social relations; but pessimism and optimism define modes of thinking about man before we have even reached diagnosis and prognosis.

Disturbing to realise how much a product I am of Western morality — and what could possibly be a better school in that morality than the back-streets of Port Elizabeth, and how different had my milieu not been so anarchic but productive of a social conscience.

Milly — jungle morality — threatened and threatening. Or — even better — Hester.

'Concerning Poor B.B.' — Brecht's poem about himself. That withering cynicism and self-contempt, strikes a responsive chord. 'Here you have a man on whom you can't depend.'

November

Bought the Schoenmakerskop house.

119

Lyndon Johnson President of the U.S.A.
Chalk Circle alternately promising and depressing.
Schneider and I still arguing about Milly.
And Wind Wind Wind.

December
Preparing for township performance of *The Caucasian Chalk Circle*
when my Azdak was taken in for ninety days. What the papers don't
report is that this warm and wonderful man — a school-teacher — was
savagely assaulted by the police in his home (1 a.m.) in front of his
family, then dragged away to jail crying for mercy. I felt suicidal. If I
hadn't had to go on as Azdak, I don't know what I'd have done.

1965

January

Hello and Goodbye — a dedication: 'To my father, who lived and died in the next room.'

Resumed work on the play just after New Year. 1st Act in rough draft. 2nd Act in outline and a mass of notes. Returned to the play with a strong sense of Hester's moral anarchy. Have abandoned my idea of Hester forgetting about the money while she searches through the boxes for a bonnet (or some other specific thing) which she had as a girl and which, when found, triggers off a cathartic reliving of a moment in her girlhood. Instead, she still forgets the 'compensation' from time to time in searching for something she *doesn't* know, *can't* identify — a meaning to her life? Something that will give point and purpose to the welter of second-hand rubbish she is floundering in?

What does Hester want? To begin with: the compensation. *To begin with,* because she walks into that room unconscious of her life; 'in it' as she says at the end. But one level of experience to the boxes and all that comes out, is a growing objectivity, a removal from that intense 'being myself'. At this level she ends up wanting (searching for) something that will remove the absurdity that spills out of the boxes.

Then: what does Hester 'see' and 'feel' as the boxes vomit out their contents onto the floor? Easy words come to mind — 'meaninglessness', 'waste', 'poverty' etc. — but they aren't accurate. Theoretically (philosophically) sound, but nothing else. I need the 'feel' of Hester. And now a new one — 'hopelessness'. That provokes! Image — the woman, holding her baby on the pavement outside the Braes o' Berea flat, New Year's day a few years ago.

Important step forward yesterday — plotted the sequence that takes the play through to the last box and Hester's climax discovery that the next room is empty, her father dead. What follows after this moment has not been a problem at this level (sequence of incident and emotion). Two major gains in the line I have drawn roughly on paper: firstly and specifically — I see the way to a full, complete expression of the absurdity that overwhelms Hester ('There is no

God!'). Secondly, and more generally, I see a pattern, not just a plot; a chance to weave together all that Johnnie and Hester mean — the 'simultaneous' moment with all its complexity in design and depth that I achieved so unconsciously in *Blood Knot,* and couldn't repeat in *People.* The unpolished images — Johnnie's recounting his father's dreams, Hester berserk in the welter of rubbish from the boxes — suggest that same ultimate residue of obscurity, that membrane of mystery, that surrounds Morrie and Zach.

February

A question I can't fully answer (yet? ever?): what is it that draws Johnnie to the crutches? Any number of little answers. Am tantalised by the thought that there is one final answer that as yet eludes my thinking — because I *feel* the absolute reality of that fascination and see him, without any shadow of doubt or theatricality drawing closer and closer to the moment when he goes onto them permanently.

To master the idiom — thought and speech — of a character. The problem is not 'what' does Hester or Johnnie think, but 'how' do they think it.

March

Piet and his wife. Their house in Algoa Park. Piet — simple, naive; the 'heaviness' of the Afrikaner, mentally and physically; fluent English but with a strong Afrikaans accent (his love of poetry — quoting endlessly); for a number of years a Bus Inspector, now trying to sell insurance but unsuccessfully; he is looking for another job; very active politically (Congress of Democrats[1]) — his views strongly left.

His wife, Gladys — English; well-educated by comparison with his J.C. certificate (or Standard 6?[2]). Writes poetry — nothing published. When their house was searched recently by the Special Branch, they found her poems (love?) and read them all — traumatic effect on her (rape?), leading to nervous breakdown. Mentally disturbed for a number of years — several visits to Fort England mental home in Grahamstown; the last time she had to be taken forcibly after Piet's cajoling, pleading and threats had failed to get her voluntarily into the ambulance.

Contrast: Piet's sober sanity — the feeling he gives that he is indestructible, that you'd have to kill him, that you could never drive him mad. And herself — highly-strung, neurotic at her best, really unbuttoned at the worst — the refinements in sensibilities that go with this instability. She is a qualified shorthand-typist but has seldom kept a job for longer than a month because of the recurrent delusion that any new appointment in the office where she is working is a S.B. spy placed to keep an eye on her and Piet.

Piet — the story about his friendship with the African boy in his youth on the Alexandria farm where he grew up. The African returned as a man, many years later and was in the last stages of T.B. Piet was then a man, running the farm. Severe drought at the time when the friend died. Piet had to pull down the roof of a dairy he was building, to provide wood for a coffin. At the graveside: 'Here lies a man.' Then into the veld by himself to weep.

The ornamental pond he has laid out in the small garden at Algoa Park — stocked with little plastic fish, rubber crabs, pretty stones and two rubber ducks floating in the water. 'When I left the farm I took a vow — never again a living thing. Pets are a problem.'

No children.

Piet is widely suspected here in P.E. of being a police informer.

April

The happiness machines (The Second-Hand Happiness Machines): I don't know when we were ever new, or if we'll ever be . . .' 'We were made for Happiness — look at us! Think of what a man really is, what he's made of, what makes him move, think, dream, love or hate . . . he's meant to be happy, isn't he?'

August

The old woman on the road from Cradock where Barney Simon, May and I had gone for the first day of Norman's trial.[3] We picked her up about ten miles outside the town — she was carrying all her worldly possessions in a bundle on her head and an old shopping-bag. About fifty years old. Cleft palate. A very hot day.

Her story was that she had been chased off a farm after her husband's death about three days previously. She was walking to another farm where she had a friend. Later on she told us that she had nine children but didn't know where they were. She thought a few of them were in P.E.

I told her to tell me when to stop. When she'd got into the car she had said she was going very far. After driving about fifteen miles it became obvious that she would never have reached her destination on foot that day. We asked her about this and she said she knew it and would have slept in one of the stormwater drains.

She cried frequently. The first time was when I took the bundle

123

(it was very heavy) off her head and put it in the boot and she realised she was going to get a lift. She told May she couldn't believe it.
'It was like a dream.' Then in the car, telling her story, she cried
again, May comforted her. Finally, when we reached the gate where
she wanted to get off and I gave her two of the three shillings left
in my pocket, she cried again. I put the bundle on her head; May carried the shopping-bag down an embankment to the gate and set her
on her way. My last image of her is the thin, scrawny ankles between
her old shoes and the edge of her old skirt, trudging away into the
bush.

I suppose she stopped to cry a little and then went on, cried
again later and went on, went on and on.

Barney — about her bundle: 'She still has a use for the things in
her life.' And just her life; still using it — feeding it, sleeping it,
washing it.

The bundle consisted of one of those heavy three-legged iron pots,
a blanket and an old zinc bath full of other odds and ends — all this
tied together with a dirty piece of flaxen twine. In the old shopping-
bag I spotted a bottle of tomato sauce and Barney spotted a packet
of OMO.

Finally only this to say: that in that cruel walk under the blazing
sun, walking from all of her life that she didn't have on her head, facing the prospect of a bitter Karroo night in a drain-pipe, in this walk
there was no defeat — there was pain, and great suffering, but no defeat.

How many put all of their life that they haven't got in their hearts,
onto their heads and make that walk?

Hester does in her fashion, and Milly rolls up her decorations. Hester and her suitcase is another person making that walk.

THE WALK.

Where to begin?

Norman found guilty and sentenced to five years.

Back to Cradock yesterday with May. He called me as a witness in
mitigation.

So what is left?

A coat goes back to New Brighton.

In a stranger's shopping-bag.

The two men who preceded Norman. 'Number One accused' —
aged fifty-eight with a wife and ten children. 'Number Two accused'
— forty-three with wife and children. Both found guilty — similar
charges to Norman. The old man grabbed May when she was talking

to Norman afterwards in the cells — took off his old coat (it would be taken from him now that he was a prisoner) and gave it to May, asking her to go to his family and tell them what had happened and give them the coat to 'use'. So May carried it back to New Brighton in her shopping-bag.

To Sheila: 'The continuum of first-degree experience. What can I say, or write about today that could have even a hundredth part of the consequence of that coat going back. Even the greatest art communicates only second-degree experience.That coat is first-degree, it is life itself. That man's family will take it back, smell him again, remember him again, it will be worn by a son or, tonight, will keep one of the small children warm in her blanket on the floor — move into her dreams, put her father back into her life. That coat withers me and my words.'

The message he gave May for his family: 'Wait for me. I'll be back.'

I'd forgotten there was an anaesthetic — the Law itself and its formulas. When I walked into the courtroom and saw the two men in the dock and realised that I would have to sit through their judgement and sentence (the lawyer had told me their case was hopeless) before Norman's case, I prepared myself for great pain. Then the Magistrate appeared, and in his soft, almost gentle voice (which threatened to make the ordeal even more terrible), he started to speak. I looked at the ceiling, I looked at my feet; I couldn't look at the accused or the Magistrate. But I was also listening: '. . . there is a precedent in the case of Rex versus Nkona . . . Law Reports page 356 . . . in terms of Act 26 of 1941 as amended . . . it was ruled that if there is corroboration . . . judgment handed down in the Grahamstown Supreme Court . . .' on and on and on — until I was looking at the Magistrate with his over-shaved blue face and then, finally, at the two men; watching them with little more than a memory of my pain when the fatal words fell softly on the air: 'Guilty. On Count One I sentence you to two years . . . Count Two . . .' etc. etc. etc.

Yes, the drug. On the first visit to Cradock, Barney had been shocked by the levity, the joking, the tea-drinking — all of this in court with Norman present — of the court officials. How could they? Norman was there — waiting, watching!

It was the same yesterday. Those two men were sitting in statuesque dumb misery in the dock, and the Prosecutor was giving a demonstration of the 'conductor' who had led the singsongs at the rugby matches during his days at Stellenbosch University.

We were all drugged.

His words, his voice, as soft as smoke. Three years of my life are turning to ash.

In each case, just before passing sentence, the Magistrate gave a little speech (using the identical words) that left me stunned by its blindness and ignorance. Looking at the accused — who are in that court only because they are black; their wives and children rendered destitute by their arrest — looking at these men, he then gave his little speech which included phrases like, 'Murder! You deliberately joined an organisation that had as its aim the murder of a section of the community ... just because their skin is of a different colour ... innocent victims ... wives and children.'

Is this then all there is to it? Blindness? Men who have not looked into their own souls?

The most subtle frame-up of all — that the accused were forced to commit the crime *after* they had been found guilty of it. The Magistrate found them guilty of the *desire,* the intention, to murder. I don't believe this was ever there. Certainly not in Norman. But I would not be surprised if, having heard that incredible final speech, he did not go back to the cells with murder in his heart.

Norman's lawyer said the Magistrate was in tears when he went to say goodbye to him in his room — after the case. He said to the lawyer: 'There are things you have just got to do.'

September

Sequel to the last visit to Cradock: the S.B. arranged for May to visit Norman when he was brought here as a prisoner. He tells her this story —

After sentence he was taken back to the cells. A few hours passed, then the door was opened and the Prosecutor came in. He was on the point of returning to Johannesburg and wanted to say goodbye to Norman. Then a short conversation along these lines: Norman must not think he (the Prosecutor) wanted it this way (five years). He was only doing his duty. He *had* to. He hadn't brought the case against Norman. It was the Special Branch ... etc., etc., all the obvious phrases that might offer an escape from his very obvious sense of guilt. When he got up to leave he asked Norman if they could shake hands. They did.

I remember too how, after my address to the court in mitigation of sentence, he turned down the opportunity to cross-examine me — he hesitated for a moment after the Magistrate's question: 'Any questions?' — stole a quick look at me, then half-stood and said: 'No questions.'

If there was evil and wrong in that courtroom, where was it? The

126

hearts of a few men — Magistrate, Prosecutor, Special Branch? Or in the Law? If it was the latter, what morality, what moral dimension was there to those who execute it? The real stink of that courtroom — the surrender of conscience?

South Africa.

For a Christian there is no morality left — hence no salvation, neither heaven nor hell — when the 'simple act' between two men — be it giving or taking, loving or killing — is delegated. Something else — a form of Non-being = depravity.

The organisational victim.

Spiritual depravity — something that is neither good nor evil.

In a sense then, the 'doing to' Norman that day in Cradock, was a castrated act and blighted of all consequence. It was the 'doing to' *themselves* that will have a history of cause and effect.

In organisations men no longer 'do' to others, they 'do' to themselves. And even this is so much like masturbation — what can it lead to? The way into my life is through the 'other man'. And to reach the 'other man' we need the simple act, we need responsibility.   *

Johannesburg: Hello and Goodbye
Third day of rehearsals (four weeks). So far just straight readings. Barney[4] spoke of Johnnie as 'mad'. I jotted down these notes: numb — drugged (not complete — there can, and does come a moment of response). For example in the opening monologue, what must I communicate? A horror — not an intensely-felt pain. Johnnie = a dead frog's leg twitching when touched by electrodes. Fear of 'feeling', of Life — *as himself* (inadequacy). Hence resurrection = 'different me'.

In one sense then Johnnie's line is his progression to a moment of conscious pain = the assault and subsequent speech.

The ideal Hester is carnal, flesh that has said fuck-you to the spirit.

The danger is hysteria — a thin and screaming instead of thick, bruised anger.

Hester knocks on a door and gets no reply; opens it and walks, hesitantly, nervously, holding her big suitcase, into the kitchen-cum-lounge of 57A Valley Road . . . the first clause.

Two hours later she opens that same door and walks out . . . last clause and full stop.

Johnnie's madness — a better word, 'dwaal' (numbed). Lost as in the scene where he tests Hester's belief in the father's presence ('Smart little Errol Flynn moustache') — and the truth consists of him telling a lie.

127

Hester rushing into the father's room at the end of the play — what would have happened had he been there? Hester would have collapsed on her knees and begged his forgiveness. 'Vergewe my, pappie!'[5]

Her assaults on Johnnie — an index of her hunger for love. 'You can't hate anything more than you can love it.'

Love and hate in the play. Barney: 'An eternal triangle — Hester, Johnnie, Father.' Something I had never seen before is the strong impulse in Johnnie to make Hester jealous of his relationship with the father.

Ambivalence in Hester's return: why does she come back?

Have now sketched out movement and business of first act. The nucleus around which my Johnnie is growing in rehearsals is the fantasy of the father in the next room — starting with the moment when Hester, right at the beginning, slips into the belief that 'He is lying there with only one leg left . . .' etc., then to the first timid lie from Johnnie, 'He's sleeping' — all the way through from there, with moments like the cocksure 'play' of the moustache and 'he's getting fat . . . plump' and the staggering achievement of sucking Hester ever deeper into the fantasy by making her panic and help him mix the medicines at the point when he pretends the father has awoken and is groaning: 'If there's a stroke we know who's to blame!'

Morrie and Zach: Hester and Johnnie — a fundamental difference. Johnnie never awakens to the reality of Hester's existence. She at least does have a moment of tender awareness at the beginning and then again at the end. Morrie and Zach never escape each other.

November
Train to Cape Town after five weeks in Johannesburg and Pretoria. Final verdict — a success.

December
Back in Port Elizabeth after final performances in Cape Town. Dennis Brutus and my decision to play before segregated audiences.[6] When I left P.E. several months ago — still undecided on this issue — he seemed to reveal a tolerance in terms of the dilemma and a preparedness to accept the decision to play before segregated audiences even though he felt it was wrong. Then in Johannesburg — after a week of non-segregated performances in a private venue — I took the plunge and went into the Library Theatre with *Hello*. I explained my attitude in an interview in the *Rand Daily Mail*, which was quoted in

P.E.'s *Evening Post.*

A letter in the *Post* (nom-de-plume 'Cicero' and obviously Dennis) attacks my decision to play before all-white audiences. Refers to me as having become an 'ally of apartheid' and having contributed to the 'erosion of human decency' in South Africa.

My only answer — if there is any — lies with Johnnie and Hester.

Finally I suppose I talk to white South Africa not because they can possibly profit from hearing from me but because I *must* talk. What is my life without the reality of a 'here and now' in which I belong: how can I cut myself off from it?

Not even a question of efficacy but the meaning and content of my life. 'I am . . .' Choosing to be *me,* I can't escape talking to South Africa — even under the compromising conditions of segregated performances.

What am I trying to say? That a man can't ever escape the need to talk to his brother? (Himself?) And this involves love — not politics, or morals, or slogans. Love . . . Hate.

What next? *The Coat?* I feel I should write something about New Brighton, about Black South Africa. Or, the woman on the Cradock Road! I'll never escape her. The old woman — the load on her head. Talking: two voices — distinct and clear as she walks — her own, cleft-palate. When she puts down the load to rest. *Sisyphus* — Camus.

Exceptionally high Spring tides today after two days of a fresh South-Wester pushing in the seas. Waves were breaking over bush at the bottom of the headland. But most exciting of all, a seal on the rocks just below me. The animal was struggling badly in the chaos of waves and rocks — I thought it just about finished, but then it managed to find a firm footing on a large rock a few yards out. Here it gained a measure of safety even though waves broke over it from time to time. This was at about four o'clock. My last image of it was at sunset (around seven), when it stirred after being prostrate for about two hours. No blood or sign of any other visible damage.

A magnificent animal. Primordial beauty of this strangely-fashioned, ungainly creature when seen against the background of the violent open sea.

Hard to believe that the seal is not dying. Still there tonight. I went quite close — all it managed to do was lift its head and snarl. Before I had taken three steps away its eyes were closing with what seemed an ineffable desire to sleep and then it slumped down on the rock again. Someone had placed two fish near it on the rock, but these were untouched.

And behind it all the time, restless, destructive, vital — a violent sea. That vigil in the rocks is now into its fourth high tide.

Disturbing contrast between the black, unmoving rock, the flicker of life in the big animal, and behind them, around them, over them, *the sea.*

The seal appears to be recovering. Neighbours saw him sporting in one of the gulleys today.

1966

January

Four or five dives in water of moderate clarity. I seem to be growing out of my obsession with the harpoon in my hand, the possibility of a Big Kill. My dives were all 'prowls' — looking for a ray, a big cod, etc. But lately I've found time to just poke among the rocks and look at things. Dived down to a deep ledge where I had seen a fish — forgot all about it in my surprise and wonder at an exceptionally large white anemone under the ledge.

These past few weeks the sun and sea bleaching my life to a sensual innocence. Man does have a capacity for regeneration. The inevitable squalor that goes with a production — *Hello and Goodbye* — has been washed away. Again I am aware of how much of my life is in *my* hands. So much of my 'all' is already here. I must learn to know and use it.

Milly: 'I want more.' Hester: 'I'm used to it now. It's strange, you know. I can see myself . . .'

I could never have written Hester — her acceptance — without first having made the impossible demand through Milly.

Nothing, ever, in my life seems to stem from my asking a question and needing an answer. My consciousness of self and the world around me is, most times, the best times — like now — as smooth and solid as the sea tonight — hardly able to push up a wave after two days of easterly winds.

I don't think I live negatively — the impulse to write is a vigorous, affirmative one, but it never has its origin in the need for answers. Terrible things like bigotry and prejudice — I never (consciously) seem to get past the fact that they 'are' — the reality is sufficient.

I do ask questions of course, but always in the context of a Hester or a Morrie — *their* reality. Never in my own life. And if that reality — no matter how superficially limited it may seem (Hester and the compensation) — is seen with enough Truth, all the other questions will be there.

When it comes to writing I have always had a total indifference (contempt) for my own life and its issues. An element of subterfuge of course — because I find them again in Morrie or Hester, in Zach or Johnnie. So it's turned full circle. I *do* write about myself but never

131

what is uniquely 'self' — a self that has something in common with at least one other human being. If it concerns *him* or *me,* the chances are that it concerns *you* as well.

I'm unable to ask the 'abstracted' question. Must be rooted in a life, a here and now, and relate to the apparently trivial content of that life. Why does it always work? — given the basic conditions of Truth, Compassion, Love, etc. That a man — anywhere — concerned with the petty issues of his life, can end up talking to all of us about our unique selves.

Man is *one* experience, one pattern. There are others, of course, but *we* have one, and all creative activity is an endless, inexhaustible exploration of it.

Faulkner: *The Sound and the Fury* — All we are left with finally is the possibility of a dignity and the price of that is the Truth.

Veeplaats, a coloured area, is now being encroached on by New Brighton and Kwazakele townships. A wasteland of stunted thorn-bushes and litter. Corrugated iron. Donkeys, pigs, goats, little children walking home from the Chinaman's shop with a bottle of paraffin or a loaf of bread, the earth tramped hard and bare by generations of poor men going to and coming from work, children playing in the dust, women bent over washtubs — all of this in that wasteland — prickly pears and every thorn with its scrap of paper. At the bottom of every fence paper is banked up, flattened against the wire by the wind.

While white surburbia consists of men in cages, in these locations I find no anonymity unless it is that which makes all faces harden, and human, when turned into the winds of adversity. In the most ramshackle of these homes, more so possibly than in the others, I find a definition of the human condition — a symbol of our lives, our clumsy hands, and few but final needs.

Newspaper — bread, fish and chips — empty cigarette packets, brown paper-bags. Why this species of rubbish more than the others — bottles, tins etc? More obvious? Most paper bleaches white from exposure to rain, wind and sun.

Hester and Johnnie, Morrie and Zach — exposed. All of their lives involved in the trivia which with us adds up to boredom.

Poverty = the violence of immediacy.

Immediate (dictionary) = (of person or thing in its relation to another) not separated by any intervening medium; (of action) direct.

Immorality Act case at De Aar. Coloured Anglican missionary and a

132

forty-year-old white woman, a librarian. The police caught them in bed, pulled back the sheets and took photographs.

Darkness. Suddenly a blinding flash of light like a photographer's flash; a split second later a woman screams. Then stage lights up to reveal an office desk, chair and — to one side — a filing cabinet. Standing at the desk, examining a police file, Sergeant . . . He takes out a set of photographs — 'They'll get four months' suspended.'

De Aar. Heat. Dust.

'Three statements after an arrest under the Immorality Act' — Woman Man Sergeant.

July

London — Hampstead season almost over.[1] An incredible disconcerting success. Full houses the past week; reviews unanimously good, many of them raves. I know that our work is 'African' in its most meaningful sense and is therefore unique, but is it that good? William Gaskill (Royal Court theatre), after seeing our production of *Brother Jero* by Soyinka, talked very excitedly about its impact, humour, vitality, etc.

The success of this 'cosmopolitan' African company (Ghana, Nigeria, Sierra Leone, Uganda, S.A. African and Coloured)[2] raises with fresh controversy the establishment of an African group in London. Wole Soyinka doubts whether such a group could lead to anything and have an identity. He refers to the idea as a 'theatre of the dispossessed'. I am probably in agreement with him but one cannot deny that this motley collection of individuals has become a group as far as the Hampstead season is concerned.

Unlike the critics and our audiences I am nagged by the lack of polish and discipline in our work. At least three of my productions in South Africa — *Godot, Chalk Circle, Mandragola* — were much better, both as productions and in the unity of style of the cast.

Zakes — a splendid achievement, deservedly applauded as Jero and Zachariah. Impressive development as man and actor.

Femi Euba — most exciting potential. And Jumoke Edabayo.

During the crises of these weeks I turned to the books of marine biology I've bought here, a reminder that there is more to living than writing and directing plays. The result: an intensive course I might never have stuck out under normal conditions — I am splendidly equipped for my return to S'kop and the sea.

At least one performance of *Blood Knot* at Hampstead that I would like to remember. Any number involved a marvellous response from

133

the audience — but this one was special for the quality of our work on the stage. An overwhelming sense of rhythm, of pattern, of the shape of the 'whole'. Voice, body, every gesture moving almost without effort from one moment to the next. Thinking back to my own performances — completely relaxed and in control; a harmony between self and part — both factors present, consciously so, yet an equation that resolves. Once I realised what was happening, I knew I *couldn't* go wrong. Zakes and I looked at each other with amazement in the dressing-room.

Echoes of it in the two final performances that followed.

So many now say of this *BK* that it is the best ever — the same people having reserved their judgment when we opened in Brighton. A subtle yet important change between our performance there and in Hampstead that I am not at all conscious of — Sheila speaks of a ratty, vicious Morrie at Brighton while Mary, lamenting the change from the South African original Morrie, ascribed it to the fact that 'things' have changed and that, at Hampstead, there was 'a return to innocence'.

August

Back at S'kop after three weeks in Crete. A return to silence against a background of the sea, wind and birdsong in the beautiful early morning.

Wrote to Mary: 'As for being back, what can I say? The obvious: that once I realised I was back, once I was living here again the months away in London and Greece seemed fat and flaccid by comparison. I am tense here, my mind is taut. Lowell exactly captures the feel of it in his lines — "My heart grows tense/as though a harpoon were sparring for the Kill" — it's so obvious isn't it — I mean the fact that being here makes me want to write.'

Last night in the silences in our talking, the sea was a metaphor of the 'trouble' that hovers behind the blandest moment here in S.A. — and which was suddenly with me again when we arrived in Johannesburg. After the placid months overseas, stewardess in the airways bus: 'Hy't 'n kaffer doodgery.'[3] — and suddenly it was all back.

So much of my happiness at being back again relates to the privileges which go with being white. If I had returned to New Brighton . . .?

September

Verwoerd dead — an act as lunatic as everything associated with that name. Newspapers and radios sickening in their god-inflicting all-for-

134

getting praise of the dead man.

The violence he did to thousands has been paid back in small measure.

I can find no sympathy — hardly even for his family.

Olive-green house-snake in the compost-heap which I killed, not knowing it was harmless.

Besieged in the house by September weather — wind and rain. In a week's time the Spring Equinox.

I want to write but I am helpless until the right image surfaces. Reading through one of my notebooks has added to my frustration — there is so much! What it did also do though was sharpen my perception of this world (P.E.) — its textures. Slowly rediscovering the smell and feel of it.

Also my desire, with the country in its present state, to commit myself more deeply.

Themes: Norman and Cradock. The old woman. Piet (informer). Bodies Beautiful. New Brighton. The Coat.

Spent yesterday hiking up a valley, just outside Patensie. Unspoiled indigenous bush — massive yellow-woods and Cape fig tree growing beside the little river, Camdeboo stinkwoods, wild gardenias. Incredibly rich bird life. At least five loeries and, at one turning in the valley, a troop of baboons barked down defiantly at us from the opposite rock face. Cycads in two places.

Provoked by my notes on the old coat Mabel brought back from Cradock.

Actress (Mabel): I went to Cradock today for the end of my husband's trial. He was sentenced to five years. Before his case, two other men . . .

The Coat: Images — prickly-pear sellers at Smelly Creek.
New Brighton — stones in the roads. The wife and mother is folding the coat — behind her the actors sit and watch her —

Actor:	It will get older.
Wife:	Yes.
Actress:	It will get mouldy.
Wife:	Yes.
Actor:	And crumble.

135

Wife:	Yes, yes, yes, yes: To all your questions, yes; to all my feelings and fears, yes; to God, yes. To you, my husband, yes. To my children, yes.
Also:	The informer.
Actress:	(handing over the coat to the Wife) He said you must use it.
Actor:	Something hard and real to hold.
Wife:	I've still got the coat.

What is the coat? = our time; our poverty; our uselessness; our need; our shape.

Actress:	I went up with Njikelana. We left when it was over. The van with prisoners passed us near Cookhouse, going very fast. A man was looking out of the window. It might have been him.
Wife:	Tell me about the road.
Actor:	The child is sick. (etc.)
Wife:	Then I must sell it.

Why did he send it? What is the coat? What does it mean?

There are no victories. Memories fade, the heart forgets, whatever happens the man himself will one day die. We are here a short time; and at the end of that short time one of the few things we can have is the dignity that comes from courage and truth.

Wife:	I am not here forever.
Actor:	Then your children . . .
Wife:	They are not here forever . . .
Actor:	What are you trying to tell us?
Wife:	A man wore this coat.

The Coat: three temptations — a child is cold; a child is sick; hunger.
'Give it to the child!'
'No.'
'But he said use it didn't he?'

'I am an actor. I live in New Brighton. Today, a worn old coat came back to the township in a stranger's shopping-bag. We want to tell you about it, there are certain facts. There are also questions. For

136

some of these we have guessed at the answers. For others we have no answers.'

An actor called Mulligan . . . John . . . Humphrey. An actress called Mabel . . . Nomhle. (Five chairs on an empty stage. The actors enter and sit. Mulligan comes forward and speaks to the audience.)

The Coat: moving on to foolscap paper. Notes becoming extensive — possible form also emerging. Not yet clear in my own mind as to what I am after. Encumbered by what I would *like* to believe, i.e. the woman *not* selling the coat. Maybe she does. Either is possible of course — the point is Truth and honesty in dealing with either alternative.

The point *not:* to sell or not to sell, yes or no. But *yes and no,* conflict, irresolution and finally just a posture = I am flesh and blood, bewildered, blind, desolate. I will cling stupidly to this one thing. Already a life is crystallising around it.

Last night May filled in a few details about the coat. She said it was quite a good one, worth possibly two Rand. The wife was about sixty. In front of May she went through the pockets — all she found was a little twist of brown paper containing some powder. This turned out to be medicine bought from a witch-doctor to reduce the court sentence. The old woman said it had worked. She'd heard stories about men getting life sentences and had expected the same for her husband. Instead of which he only got three years. She asked about her husband, said she would wait.

Brecht's *Messingkauf Dialogues* provoking my thinking about the coat.

First change is a shift away from the cold statement I had been working out, i.e. five actors telling an audience, etc. Better: does she sell the coat? Let's find out. (It will certainly create more of Brecht's 'ease' and a chance to talk and think about it. The audience will participate.)

October
The extermination of the Jews in Nazi Germany and the Slave Trade in Africa. Comparison. Atrocities, and in numbers, in the latter equals that of the former. Slave dhows from Dar es Salaam to Zanzibar = the cattle trucks to the concentration camps. Long marches of slave caravans from interior to coast = forced marches. With the Jews, however, it was the persecution *of* a foreign minority

137

whereas in Africa it was by and large persecution *by* a foreign minority.

Reading Fanon's *The Wretched of the Earth*.

The most moral of all conscious acts: Rebellion. 'I (we) have had enough! ' An awareness (discovery) of self and circumstances.

African Nationalism: Frantz Fanon.

Some progress with *The Coat*.

I should do the same — 'an actors' exercise' — with the old woman we gave a lift to on our first trip to Cradock.

October

During a game in the garden yesterday our neighbour's small daughter pretended she was a white housewife and her brother that he was an African garden-boy. His role consisted of being incredibly stupid — pulling up the wrong plants, not knowing what a weed was, getting drunk, neglecting his wife and children, and so on. Her role was to abuse him, insult him, rant and rave about his stupidity. He had several names: Phillip (who is a real person and has often worked in our gardens), Shorty, John and November. They found the game very funny and laughed loudly with every twist in the plot — for example when he collapsed drunk in his 'madam's' lounge.

Piet — his sleeves rolled up, short trousers, shoes and socks, a pair of pruning shears in his hand. His garden — statuettes of animals. He is quoting Dylan Thomas, musing aloud, talking to the trees and birds. It is a fine spring day. Gladys appears with a canvas garden chair — she is going to sunbathe,

Gladys — Natal English.

Steve — a coloured teacher, banned.

Piet's English-speaking friend: E.

Special Branch policeman.

Piet's friendship with E. strained by latter having heard and suspecting that P is an informer. Comes to a head when they have it out — E. confronting him with the rumours: Are you or aren't you?

'I loved animals for a long time. They were among the first things I learnt to love. I can remember a little goat — given to me by our neighbour — I carried him home in my shirt.' (Then: Gladys, the drought, his African friend and —) 'Living things! No man. No more pets.'

Act ending: Piet carrying away a screaming Gladys to the waiting ambulance.

Piet: the house has just been bought. He is building up the garden. When the friend comes he brings a few cuttings and plants from his own garden.

The animal statuettes are established in the opening scene with Gladys. He has bought a new one. 'I've put the frog under the gardenia.'

Drought forced the young Piet to abandon the farm and find work in P.E.

Gladys uses his full first name. Peter.

Act ending: the SB have come, searched Piet's house and taken away Gladys's poetry. She is speaking — a taut hysterical note increasing — 'They will take them and read them. Those filthy swine will read them.' (rape — outrage)

Isolation — Piet through suspicion. Gladys through madness.

Piet is a member of a committee (legal defence of political accused).

He asks Steve when the next meeting is to take place. Steve is evasive. Then Piet finds out that a meeting was held without him. Police raids.

The raid: Piet and Gladys in their pyjamas.

Sequence: Piet asks Steve about the next meeting. Steve evasive. The meeting is held. The raids. Steve and others convinced in their suspicions that Piet is an informer.

Or else: Piet already withdrawn from politics — with the exception of his friendship with the coloured school-teacher — and isolated by the suspicion that he is an informer. Gladys: 'Why doesn't Lionel come any more?' Piet: 'They think I'm a police informer.'

Gladys: 'Sometimes I think you like it.' (Isolation.)

The school-teacher, Steve, comes to supper and in the course of it they are raided.

November

For about four weeks now I've been working steadily on 'the informer' (Piet). Four hard, frustrating, often doubt-ridden weeks. So many times the idea of Piet suddenly presents itself as two-dimensional and superficial. I then fight my way through to a renewed appreciation of its potential depth — only to find I've lost it again. Most worrying of all is a lethargy and prosaicness in my thinking. I am skating on the surface, instead of sounding its depth. I need to break through into the freedom of space.

I think these problems and anxieties occurred in the initial stages

139

of all the plays I have written. An aggravating factor is the more blatant politics of this idea — and the bellyful of clichés about South Africa that I've got to vomit out of my system before I can start writing meaningfully. I need to locate Piet, Gladys and Steve in a world of real things, not ideas: Steve with a fishing rod in his hand and the memory of his mother digging for mudprawns; Piet holding his pruning shears and wondering what to do; Gladys with her pencil, trying to write a poem but feeling out their loneliness.

There has of course been progress. At this point I have a strong and fairly well-detailed story-line; the main points in the development of Piet, Gladys and Steve are felt and appreciated.

But now I must face myself. I must stop plodding. Let me develop some of Brecht's 'ease'.

I am also working on *The Coat* with the group. We have been asked to do something for a 'Theatre Appreciation Group' here in P.E. in four weeks' time, and we've decided to spring this on them. This is a tremendous opportunity.

At last. An image which defines a human predicament and Piet. Thinking back to the drought, he cries out, 'I am frightened of being useless!' The logos behind his humanity, his politics. He escaped the horror of his impatience on the parched, dying land, by a life of action among men. And then the second drought — and again alone — just himself, empty-handed, useless. Piet face to face with himself — the absurdity of himself, *alone.*

'A man's scenery is other men.'

Read *Hello and Goodbye* at Rhodes University, Grahamstown, last week. Made me realise how far I am still from a synthesis and unity of all the elements in Piet's story. And even greater deficiencies — above all else that focus and concentration of character in an incident or reality — Johnnie and the crutch, Hester and her mother's dress, both of them and the boxes. Embodiment of *all* levels of action in one reality.

Piet is still down the middle — doing one thing, and thinking another.

This is what I mean by carnality — the idea in, or as, flesh.

The image of uselessness (the drought) persists and is provocative.

A MAN'S SCENE
Make the stage a blank page on which to scribble and sketch a few images in public.

Tremendous urge to abandon the logic of chronological sequence ... but for what? What other logical ordering of 'things' is there? Again: not 'what is going to happen next', but 'what is happening'.

Here is the problem: the idea of Piet, what he is, his predicament, and failure — to communicate this not by 'on the basis of a pretence' but ...? I have got three dimensions and silence. When my actor moves from point A to point B I want my audience to see an actor cross the stage, and not try to bluff them that Piet has moved from the gardenia bush to the water tap.

The setting — an empty stage.

A relationship between audience and stage that starts off similar to that between reader and the blank page that preceded the poem; or, more accurately, *is* blank until the first line is read.

I open a book to a page . . .

I sit in the theatre, the house lights go out, the curtain rises, I see a stage . . .

The final image, the absurdity of a man alone. A man's scenery is other men.

'A man without scenery'.

To find for (in) Piet, Gladys and Steve the inner logic, dialectic that motivated Morrie, Zach, Johnnie and Hester — that *dialogue with self* that gives them their touch of madness, compulsion.

A last visit to Kirkwood to collect the car we have bought from the estate.

The garden neglected, dry, choked with weeds: the house empty, most of the furniture already carted away, except for a few pieces scattered about the bare, hollow rooms; strangers moving through there like vultures among the remains of somebody else's feast. Even the trees in orchards which come right up to the house, seemed to be sinking into a final fruitlessness. And silence — everywhere a final whispering silence. I thought back to the house's heyday — its well-stocked cupboards, the laden tables of its mealtimes, Sheila's father and his second wife in their chairs in the lounge as if there for all eternity.

On our way back we went to the graveyard. Here I was strongly moved by the beauty of its setting, its loneliness, the poverty of the graves — poor because of what they'd lost with death. Strangest of all, for me personally, a sense of loss. I know I was never loved by the Valley (which was after all the Meirings') — at the best only tolerated — but I loved it. I am sorry we are now severing all links with it through the sale of the farm.

141

Sheila though is glad.

My first drive to the Valley, alone, eleven years ago, to meet Dr Meiring. Sheila and I had met in Cape Town and I already knew I wanted to marry her.

The local Native Commissioner has given his permission for a play-reading by Serpent Players before the (white) Theatre Appreciation Group provided three conditions are observed:

1.   It must not be public — members only.

2.   Serpent Players may not use the toilets at the hall.

3.   They must leave immediately after the reading — no social gathering or discussion.

The group expect us to be reading a comedy by Soyinka. We have been working on *The Coat*. I am a little frightened — there could be repercussions. And if there are, what were my motives? — vanity, foolhardy recklessness plus a genuine desire to shatter white complacency and its conspiracy of silence.

Serpent Players tonight — what should have been our last rehearsal for tomorrow night's reading was instead a moving, absurd, sensible and idiotic discussion — given all the pros and cons — of whether, with the possibility of the Special Branch being in our audience, we should proceed with *The Coat* as a group venture or as a reading by myself alone.

Why lie about it or pretend it isn't there — an anarchistic, destructive core to my being. Tonight, for example, I made it easy for the cowards to be cowardly, I fostered the cowardly impulse behind a smokescreen of apparent honesty and 'facing the facts'. And the foolhardy are invited to impulsive action. Do I really need to destroy all around me? Create a desert so that my achievement is the better seen?

What happened is really too complex for a straight-forward account. Four of us — Mulligan, May, Humphrey and myself — were publicly pursuing a dialogue with self. And of the four, only Mulligan was decent in the sense that he affirmed, he had faith. He was the only one who did not at some point or other say: No, Athol, I cannot read. There are chances involved that I dare not take. He stood in the centre of the lounge, looking with withering disgust at all those who had just declined to take part, and shouted: 'Voetsek! Shit. Voetsek, man!'

The reading of *The Coat* a considerable success. Full cast was at the bus terminal at seven. I gave a few notes beforehand and the reading went off very well — my faith in the actors, in our subject, the shape and content of the audience's experience of us, completely justified.

Wrote to Mary about it and spoke of Serpent Players' moment of 'posthumous glory'. The extent to which fear shattered us at one moment means that we just aren't a 'group' with a solidarity and identity over and above that of us as a collection of individuals.

Or, I said to her, it was a resurrection. I told how in four weeks we had put together a script and our analysis by way of improvisation and discussion of the coat. With the actors using their own names. Mulligan started the ball rolling with a friendly chat to the audience (we had about 150) about the group, our approach and methods — and hence the coat. 'But just before we start let me answer any of you who might be asking, why the coat? Why not the man who wore the coat? Isn't a man a better subject for an actor's exercise? Yes, he would have been better, but, you see, it was the *coat* that came back. May brought back the coat.'

Mulligan sits down, May comes forward: 'I brought back the coat from Cradock — 160 miles away. I had gone up there for my husband's trial. The coat isn't his. It belongs to another man from New Brighton. There have been a lot of men from New Brighton in the Cradock cells. The charges are mostly the same: membership of a banned organisation; contributing to its funds: holding a meeting . . . distributing pamphlets . . . etc.'

You could have heard a pin drop. The audience's complacency shattered — they sat and watched us with the horror and fascination that freezes you a few feet away from a puff-adder.

The piece is pure Brecht. The *Messingkauf Dialogues* did it. Improvisation and discussion, improvisation and discussion — and behind an apparent easy carelessness, a logic, in our case centred on the question: 'Would she ever sell it?'

December

A man without Scenery ground to a halt for the third and, I think, final time. What happened? Cart before my horse — consciously evolved my 'idea' and then tried to embody it in a place, a time, a man. It is no good, I just don't work like that — that part of me that wrote *B.K.* and *Hello*. I returned from London determined to 'commit' myself more deeply in my writing and now I am sure it is this that has led to the present barren and frustrating impasse — a fine 'idea' with a strong message that I just can't breathe life into. With

Johnnie and Hester, Morrie and Zach, the act of writing was exploration — this time I tried to *make* it — tailoring — and I have failed. I must be careful here not to imagine a conflict between heart and mind — emotion and intelligence. It is not that. But the stage and writing for it only becomes compulsive when I approach it with images and not ideas. The image of Johnnie on the crutches; Hester with a suitcase, looking at the door she is about to open — these provoke any number of ideas — conversely any of the 'ideas' is only a fraction of the potential, only one side of a many-faceted reality.

It is so obvious now looking back over the past six weeks — the flat, stale taste of my hours at this table.[4]

Welcome, released about a week ago,[5] came out with the group last night for what was supposed to be a small Christmas reunion party. It proved impossible for any of us to get 'high' and gay — his stories about Robben Island, the thought of Sharkie, Norman and Simon still there and the new spate of trials — 77 now recharged and found guilty just as they were on the point of release — all of this kept us grimly sober despite the wine. And then also T. At the end of the evening this down-at-heel man suddenly produced an expensive camera and flash apparatus and wanted a picture of 'the group', all of whom scattered in panic — two through a window, one to the toilet — and the evening broke up on a sour note of suspicion and fear. I must admit the camera was very suspicious. He has never breathed a word about photography or an interest in it, in all the time he has been with us.

May and the trip to Robben Island. She goes down to see Norman once a year, and is allowed one visit of half-an-hour. The last time there were three other women — middle-aged and all from New Brighton — on the tug that takes visitors and provisions once a week from Cape Town to the Island. At the other end they were lined up and marched to the visiting cubicles. As they went in, the policeman called out, 'Ntshinga 18! Jolobe 4! . . .' etc. and so went into the appropriate cubicle. Sat down in a chair and faced a blank wall, in which was a small little window (about one foot square) and through this saw Norman's face. He was in a similar cubicle on the other side. Two policemen came in and stood behind each of them while the thirty minutes ticked away.

The tug back: they stood on deck and just as the tug started to move a policeman came up and warned them that they would get wet and should go below. May says they looked up but could not see a cloud in the sky and decided he was just playing the fool with them.

Once they cleared the harbour they realised what he meant — a wave broke on deck and they were drenched to the skin. Immediately all rushed to the gangway and they were drenched a second time. Down below, May got violently seasick.

Welcome described prisoners' transport to the Island. They travel down from P.E. to Cape Town in large vans. The prisoners are chained together in two's by their *outer* legs as they stand side-by-side — in other words they have almost got to skip when they want to move. Inside the truck there's a bucket for urinating and another of drinking-water. Two over-night stops in which they are locked in police cells at George and Swellendam. The chains are only taken off as they board the tug for the Island. In other words, when you want to urinate or shit during those three days, the other man goes with you.

The work teams on the Island: the Quarry Span — the biggest; hundreds of them in the rock quarries. The Vark Span — looking after the pigs. The Kalk Span — the 'big' boys: Mandela, Sisulu, Mbeki, etc., who are all kept rigidly isolated from the other prisoners. Sometimes a group of prisoners are halted and told to face the other way when they — Kalk Span — pass.

Weekend: Lunch at 11 a.m., supper at 2.30 p.m.

Welcome finds New Brighton 'fast' — too 'fast' after his years inside. No immediate plans except to enjoy his 'freedom'.

Last night Lisa's annual outing to Playland and Happy Valley.

The happiness machines: one of the children's rides was a swing of little aeroplanes and flying saucers; the attendant, as with all the rides, an African in faded blue overalls. His behaviour, manner, slightly odd — chewing a match nervously, muttering darkly to himself as he leant on the lever that had started and would stop the machine. His eyes — abstracted intensity. Before the ride started he seemed lost and uncertain as to whether he had taken all the tickets. One little boy leaned out of a flying saucer — 'Boy! Hey, Boy!' and gave him his ticket. During the ride the same child started monkeying around — standing up — the African stopped him with a sharp, savage whistle, fingers between his teeth.

After a few weeks at Humewood for the whites, Playland moves out to Korsten for the coloureds and Africans.

Characters for a play (a film?) — the African operators, the white man who owns the show, his wife, the young man who runs the gambling side-stalls. Incident: the African who doesn't stop his machine — lets it go and on and on — laughter turns to screams. The whites trapped in the Happiness Machine.

145

Empty stage — suddenly a coloured couple come running on, each carrying impoverished items of household possessions — an apple-box, mattress, pots — repeated several times until a little pile of junk has collected centre stage. 'Okay, baas!' Out of breath, they then stand and watch the demolition of their house off-stage. 'Bulldozer!'

The man doffs his hat. 'Give me a cigarette, my baas!' Exit — returning immediately with a butt.

The man and woman sitting among their possessions.

Woman: There's that one in the uniform coming again.

Man: (jumping up) We're on our way, Baas!

The man wants to abandon everything — a sense of liberation. The woman loads it all on her head and follows him.

Man, wife, a friend. The two men who collect 'empties' — 'The white man's drinking himself to death.'

The Happiness Machine: 'It's forever, my baasies and madams! (The screams start) It's forever. For ever.'

Foul weather within and without — east wind, a dirty sea, a confused mind — a barren time so it seems.

The coloured derelict and his wife: exposure of a life that has known innocence and the loss of innocence; been the victim of brutality and itself brutalised, hoped, despaired, laughed, loved ... Then the roof is torn down, the walls pushed in and it is naked, destitute itself.

After the demolition: 'Where we going?' The empties — a sack of broken bottles.'A whiteman slept with me. A good looking whiteman.' 'She's trying to make me jealous.' Where would they go? Bethelsdorp, Missionvale, Veeplaats, Kleinskool.

An old man — tuberculotic — holding a blanket, in the first mad scramble on to the stage — it was all he had in his nest. He is dying. He sits with his back to the shacks that are being demolished, coughing quietly. The others stand and watch the demolition.

Finally a place where they start to put together bits and pieces for another hovel. 'Nog 'n vrot ou huisie vir die vrot mens.'[6]

The old man following them: 'Voetsak Hond!' 'Maybe he's my father!' 'He was our neighbour.'

After the demolition: 'There goes the Kaffir! Where you going, blackie? Let's follow him. Maybe he knows a place!' (To the old man) 'Go with him, Outa. He knows a place!'

'You can't come with, Outa. We're going far. Go to hospital, man. (To his wife) Walk fast. Walk, man!'

146

They walk off — the old man bundles up his blanket or, dragging it, follows them.

Then the old man dies. The man and woman are frightened: they will be blamed for his death. After the fear — anger. They beat the body, then load up again and leave furtively.

1. Demolition and departure.
2. The new place and old man's death. 'They'll say you did it!'
3. Boesman and Lena.

Boesman, Lena and Outa. For about six months Boesman and Lena have been living on the resale of 'empties' which he collected in the white suburbs. A sackful smashed in the scramble out of the house. Lena, at times in her past, a domestic servant.

Guilt! 'You beat him. They'll see the marks. There's always marks on the body. When you beat me I go blue . . . Why do you beat my life. I'm a woman.' (A cry. Protest)

Re Outa: Lena, 'He wants us.' Boesman: 'Us? (pause) Why? What for? (pause) Don't talk rubbish.'

'Nog 'n vrot ou huisie vir die vrot mens!'

Vrot — rotten, bad, useless, falling apart. A piece of corrugated iron, a bit of sacking. Another rotten place for rotten people. Rubbish — 'nest of rubbish,' 'rubbish nest'. Rubbish — old sacks, rusty iron. Stink. 'Another rubbish nest. And us. Rubbish.'

Outa becomes 'Hond' (dog). 'Hey, Hond!'

After seven days of easterly winds, it changed today and came in evenly, gently from the west. Tonight the miracle — rain, softly on a chorus of frogs. It is in my hair and dripping onto this page after a walk with the dogs. Not mercy, nor compassion, just the goodness of (in) life itself. Good and bad — just so much of both. And a thought for Boesman — a rock-bottom sobriety:

Lena: He is dead.
Boesman: Ja. He's *just* dead.
Lena: I'm tired.
Boesman: Come.

1967

January

Finally, it comes down to the ultimate — a gesture of defiance in the face of nothing — and nothing will win. Time will efface us, our meaning, our value, our beauty. There are no victories. Outside our human environment is the world of stones.

Hopeless innocence. Innocent loss. Boesman and Lena. Yes.

Mulligan last night: the question he asks himself about our friendship 'Is it just sympathy for a black man or is it because I am Mulligan?'

March

Back in S'kop after five weeks in London for the BBC TV production of *Blood Knot*. Myself as Morrie, with Charles Hyatt as Zach. Robin Midgley directing.

Midgley reduced the play to 90 minutes. We rehearsed daily for three weeks and then had three days — long and arduous — in the studio recording. Five cameras. A wonderful set.

Midgley — unlike John Berry — never really talked about Morrie and Zach on any level other than that of race conflict. I was not unduly worried about that though because the other realities that I like to think are in the play, look after themselves if that at least is treated with honesty, i.e. the existential 'hell' of another existence. But operating on that level Midgley did manage to dig up things that had been missed in all the other productions. Most exciting was his treatment of the first letter-writing scene — 'Address her' — which he turned into an essay in illiteracy — two levels: Zach sweating as the words clot in his mouth, labouring to put three sounds together and make sense, terrified by paper and pencil, and then Morrie squirming with impatience and frustration, or radiant with pride when he gets down the 'introduction'. Both men damp with sweat and effort at the end, looking in amazement at the piece of paper and its childish scrawl.

Midgley was always asking of other Zachs (James Earl Jones, Zakes, etc.) 'Did you believe he couldn't write?'

Morrie underwent important changes in his hands. Less of a spider jumping around Zach and spinning a web of words, more silence and

148

strength. This was hard for me — I don't think I quite reached what he was after.

The sheer luxury of total professionalism — got everything we needed to do the job. But can't believe that TV has the potential of the stage — both for actor and audience — the reality of the living moment, the transience of its communication.

After four days of indecision decided tonight to turn down an offer from PACT[1] to stage *People Are Living There*. Offer was extremely generous — large advance royalty etc. At first I was quite confused — so many principles seemed involved, on both sides, for and against. Most important of all was my distaste at the thought of association with a Government-sponsored theatre, but if I said No, did this involve surrendering my right to talk here and now, even under segregated circumstances — a compromise I'd already accepted with *Hello*. Then tonight a sudden clarity. It comes down simply to decency and doing the job properly. I just couldn't work in that complacent, self-satisfied world. I couldn't make 'good' theatre under those conditions. No question of principles, but of taste. I'd rather work here, decently, with impoverished Serpent Players.[2]

One of the raw materials of good theatre is a 'moral' tone. I don't think PACT would have the sort I am used to working with. The debacle with our *Antigone*[3] was front-page news at the time in the *Rand Daily Mail*. Not one of those actors or managements protested. Five of our actors are in jail — I doubt whether those up north even know about it.

Also: my life needs an affirmation, not still more compromise. There is enough of that already. I am left tonight with something hard and real.

Yes, it is right and good.

Mulligan, in a letter to Norman on the Island, urging courage, said, 'Jump into your coffin and pull down the lid yourself.'

July[4]
Lisa, wishing she could see herself, holding a cupped hand in front of her face: 'If only I had two eyes here in my hand.' Lena, and the dog in the corner, watching her. 'Two eyes somewhere in a corner of my life.'

August
Winter walks. The exotic splendours of spring are two months away. These days a walk in the bush behind the house is a couple of bulbuls,

a robin and small moments with the small ones — neddickys, bar-throated warblers, prinias — and everywhere windy silences, the sun without strength, derelict cobwebs. And underfoot the gnarled, grey battered triumph of the stems of the scrub — buchu, blombos and many other anonymous little bushes. A good time — sobriety. 'This is all there really is to me.' It is enough. So the love-making starts.

But also surprises occasionally. This afternoon two new species — yellow canary and orange-breasted sunbird — both at work on a patch of heath in flower. Most splendid of all, an old favourite — giant kingfisher down on the rocks, exactly as it was when I first saw it three years ago. I hadn't seen it since. And arum lilies coming into bloom. Pindy, the dog, was in a mood of senile abandon on the sands beyond. Peace. The old happiness felt again. Here and now. Flesh, flowers, feathers and a tide far out.

Winter walks . . .

The Dickson family at Knysna — boycott by parents of the school where they'd enrolled their two children because the family was regarded as coloured, even though they could produce white identity cards. Mother had been educated at the same school.[5]

Afrikaans family fishing off the rocks at Sappershoek. Old man and woman, in their sixties, a young man in early twenties and a boy of about ten. The young man joined me on my rock and we talked for about an hour. Fishing-rod and tackle very primitive — his sinker was a smooth rock, size of a fist, from one of the gulleys. Addressed me as 'Uncle' — bummed some of my tobacco to roll a brown-paper 'zoll'. He was full of wild enthusiasm for the big fish that were about to come into the gulley which we were fishing and which we could catch (we didn't).

The small boy caught him a clinid in one of the pools, to use as bait. He was gutting it beside me. Suddenly, in an awed tone: 'My God, kom kyk! Die kleintjies. Liewe Here! Kyk net.'[6] The fish, a female, obviously on the point of giving birth, disgorged a few hund-red small jelly-like quite transparent except for black eye-spot, small fish from the gash he'd made in her belly. Half were still in little membraneous sacs, but the free ones jumped about on the rock. 'God! Is dit dan nie 'n sonde nie?' He meant it: 'Haven't I sinned?' We managed to scrape half of them into a little pool where they start-ed their long and precarious fight through to survival.

September
An evening with Norman, who was released ten days ago, after two

years in gaol — most of that time on Robben Island. He talked almost non-stop, acting out his hilarious-terrible stories about life on the Island.

In 'solitary' — 'Man, if a fly comes into your cell you nurse it, you look after it. When you wake up, you look for it. You get worried. Where is it? Where? You take a shirt or something and wave it around until you find it. Ah! There it is.' Similarly with ants — spent hours watching a line of them moving up and down his wall. They had left a faint track. Norman drew his finger across this, at right angles, and then watched their reaction. Those coming down, stopped — 'What's this now?' and then went left along the new path. Those going up likewise, only they went to the right. Norman collapsed with laughter. That was something to tell the boys when he got back to them.

Nomhle's brother, also on the Island, and his laziness: working in the 'Vark-Span' — studied the symptoms of T.B. and then put up such a good performance that he was admitted to hospital where he spent two weeks, during which he was X-rayed etc. ('That's the only place you see a bed.') Then one of the orderlies in his ward told him the X-rays had come back and his were negative; he was going to be sent back to work next day. He quickly had a little bottle of pig's blood smuggled to him. When the doctors came round in the morning to discharge him, he produced a blood-soaked handkerchief as evidence of his terrible coughing during the night. He stayed on.

A marked decline in prison brutality — manhandling by warders etc. — as a result of the Strachan exposures and subsequent case. (Confirmed by a number of other sources.)[7] One time his 'span' was being chased back to the cells by warders, being beaten badly as they ran; a number of them lost their shoes in their frantic hurry to get back to the safety of their cells. Once inside — collapsed on the floors, out of breath, bleeding — they looked around and saw each other's cuts and bruises. As Norman then tells it, a man, oblivious to his own injuries, would put his hands tenderly on those of his neighbours, wiping away the blood, trying to clean the wounds, but in turn another man would see to *his*, and yet another to *that* man's. Chain of sympathy. Always some men present who tried to raise their spirits. In this case a man stood up and, wiping away his blood, snot and tears, gave the 'weather forecast and news bulletin': 'It will be warm from Mngandi Street to Walmer Kwazakele will be cold...'

'Bulletin! Black Domination was chased by White Domination, and beaten. Black Domination lost their shoes and will go barefoot to the quarries tomorrow.'

151

Norman says that in the end their laughter had them helplessly rolling round on the floor and hurt them more than the beating they'd received.

The man, 'T.V.' who would put his mug to his ear at night and have a conversation with someone in the outside world: 'Yes. Yes. (pause) I see. But can't you ... Oh. All right ...' etc. He used these conversations to criticise the behaviour of the other men in the cells — their cowardice, subservience and fear of the warders as he saw it. He was a difficult man and frequently threatened defiant action that would land the whole cell in trouble. The others were always pleading with him to keep his mouth shut.

Usually the last sound in the cell at night was the clatter of the mug as it rolled out of his hand when he fell asleep.

Absurd tasks when they ran short of work on the Island. A prisoner given a bucket and told to empty the sea. Five men told to uproot a tree bare-handed.

The long hours in the cells at night and over weekends were passed with stories in the form of 'improvised bioscope'.[8] The man chosen to tell that night's 'story' would first work up interest by 'directing' the background music, all the inmates of the cell contributing to the sound. 'If you think it's a bit weak in the bass, you will fill in you see — da-da-dadada' etc. When this reached its climax the story-teller would then give the title and credits: 'Hairstyles by ... Camera supervisor ... featuring ... Directed by ...'

This done he then told the story of the movie as he could best remember it. The story-teller always had dead silence and the total attention of the other inmates. At the most, they would whisper among themselves, 'Is it interval yet?'

When your turn came to tell a story you had to; if not you were called a 'vampire'.

Norman developed a very close relationship with a young boy in the same cell. He was fifteen years old when he first arrived on the Island, seventeen when Norman left, and he faced another two years. His father was also there. The usual charge: membership of the banned A.N.C. From what Norman says it is obvious that the boy hero-worshipped Norman. When the time came for Norman's departure, the cell decided to give him a 'salad supper' as a farewell. Most of the men were at that point working in the vegetable gardens — each one was given instructions to steal something: a carrot, tomatoes, a few beans, cabbage leaves, etc. Over a week a little stock of vegetables was accumulated in the cell — Norman was not supposed to know about it, but it was obvious to him. Then on the night in question a grater was fashioned out of the lid of a small tin — holes were punched in it. The salad was made and served. When the time came for a speech the men backed out one by one, from embarrassment and pain. The boy appealed to each of them to say something. When they all refused, he stood up: 'All right, Boet Norman, I'll say it . . . It's been a long time, we have learnt to love you.' *And:* 'When you leave here you'll forget us. Yes, you will. The way the people you left behind in New Brighton have forgotten you, Boet Norman, you'll forget us. But don't worry, we'll never forget you.'

At this point he was in tears, breaking off to cry in a corner and then coming back furiously to say more, then breaking into tears again. 'No, let me say it. I'm not finished. I love you! You have taught me!'

They all cried.

The grape-eating orgy when a veld-fire broke out near the Island's vineyards and the prisoners were sent to fight it. The men ignored the fire and went into the vineyards — Norman: 'we were like baboons, man! It was fresh fruit!' He pulled off a bunch of grapes, took a bite and then threw it away . . . then another bunch, one bite and thrown away. Grape juice dripping from their mouths, onto their chests, arms, feet. When they saw the warders coming to round them up, the men began frantically stuffing grapes into pockets, shirts, trousers — anywhere they could squeeze in another bunch. Then on the walk back to the prison these bunches were pulled out — but almost with boredom because they were sated — one bite and the bunch was tossed away.

Next morning on their way to work they remembered the discarded bunches and were down on all fours looking for them. A second feast.

One of the 'stories' he remembers most clearly from the nights in the cell was 'The fastest gun alive'. The story-teller had a friend in the cell who had also seen the film, and together they acted out the more dramatic moments. Good man and bad man.

Serpent Players resurrected tonight. A meeting — about twelve present — Norman presiding — in the lounge of a little house in Korsten. Marvellous! Provocative discussion and disagreement, at the end of which we decided to mount a programme for the end of October. *The Coat?*

Norman: 'One day they'll say to me, you can't leave New Brighton . . . When that day comes we must see to it that there is an audience there, so that we can go on working.'

The ship carrying Steve away from South Africa on an exit permit, was out at sea when I walked the dogs at nine tonight. A day of bad weather — sudden squalls of wind and rain off the sea . . . the authentic S'kop spring — tolerable because of the promise that tomorrow will be good. Even so Lisa and I found a break in the weather for a marvellous walk on the rocks — just rocks, sea and a cold wind . . . and a doll with a dislodged left eye that I promised to mend when we got home. It proved beyond mending but we didn't do too badly removing it and replacing it with a ball of putty with a glass bead embedded in the middle.

And so, Steve. His last story — two days ago in Korsten — of an interview with the S.B. He is convinced they tried to drive him to suicide. After one spell of questioning which lasted an hour, they pushed him into a room and into a chair beside an open window — six storeys up. The policemen with him sat at least fifteen feet away, smiling. Every five minutes or so, the door opened and a captain just stood there, laughing mockingly and gloatingly at him. For Steve, a moment of total despair. This interview took place three weeks after the date on which he had first planned to leave. Pretoria had not yet granted him an exit permit.

My last meeting with him in his little house at Schauder Township. A number of elderly coloured women were there — family — making us coffee and digging up the plants from the garden. Steve: 'Where's that little guava tree?' Aunt Betty: 'No, he's out. Down at Johnny's place. I took it out this afternoon.'

The African, Lucas, who came round to say goodbye and offered a ten rand note: 'Buy fruit for the children. They say it's expensive in England.'

A two-year-old child has been lost in the bush at a picnic spot about five miles along the coast. Lisa heard me talking about it tonight to our neighbour. Later she asked me about it and I told her the story. At the end of it she asked: 'And if it was me? And I had died?' I replied with her own phrase (when discussing mine or Sheila's death) 'I'd cry my whole life.' She looked at me, smiled sadly and shook her head. 'You'd forget. You would have to forget.'

October
Boesman = self-hatred and shame — focused on Lena who is, after all, his life . . . tangible and immediate enough to be beaten, derided and,

worst of all, needed. His jealousy of and bewilderment at her relationship with Outa = her discovery of value, of herself as having value.
Boesman's loneliness at that moment.

Boesman and Lena facing each other across the scraps and rem-
nants of their life — 'I'll carry my share.' 'This is all we are, all
we've got.'

Love. Desertion.

Still the hardest for me to realise is that it is 'Here and now' — that,
in final honesty, the moment must be taken as it comes, for what it
is — that it can never be 'capital' in a later, impoverished time. An ultimate hurdle this — that when as tonight, I looked at a pattern in
the clouds, I must say 'now!' — and have it. So much, most? of my
'present' hangs, depends on a future when I will look back — and
appreciate. No!! *Now.* Try NOW, and then forget it, leave it, surrender it.

'Once, and never again ...' Rilke. To live out the conscious
moment for what it is — a candle in the dark ... with the winds
blowing. Forget that you saw last night's sun set, and will most
probably see tomorrow's rise.

Live prepared for death.

Boesman and Lena. 'Here!' 'Tonight, here ...'

'Here' — what better word to start a play with. (with which to
start a play)

'The fight back.' Where have I been?

A pond in the moonlight — a remarkable dulcet chorus of frogs. I
had rolled down the car window to hear a train approaching a level-
crossing.

My problem (predicament): an almost total loss of all sense of value
— my world shrunk, shrivelled to a pathetic core of 'self' and a blind
impulse to affirmation which, of all absurdities, has become catching
a big fish. My few friends and, worst of all Sheila and Lisa, 'things' of
convenience — I will apparently do anything, blunt my emotions, lie
to them and to myself, in order to make (keep) them convenient.
Suddenly — my life is without Love and Honesty. Is it any wonder
that Boesman and Lena remain frozen in a few trite phrases written
and rewritten a hundred times on my immaculate sheets of foolscap.
And drinking myself every evening into a wild, maudlin, emotional
stupor so as to fool myself that I still feel!

How do I get out of this hell. How do you say to your heart:
'Love!'

155

For example: have fooled myself successfully for two days now by saying that the play (Lena and Boesman) is bogged down because I do not yet have 'images', 'poetry' that provokes me. How can these ever precede 'love'?

My glorious 'carnality' is suddenly a desert, and in the middle of it — pathetic and stupid — myself trying to survive.

Lies.

The rubbish I talk! And then peeved because Sheila shows her impatience with the drivel I mouth! And what does it consist of . . . an attempt to hypnotise myself and my life into a fat complacency.

The coward who can't say 'No'. And never forget that that failure also eliminates the ultimate 'yes' in your life. To be frightened of using the one means foregoing the other.

An essay on the translation of poetry — the whole problem of the form and content of one language as opposed to another — prompted the thought that an important aspect of my writing is an element of 'translation' — the language spoken by Morrie and Zach, Hester and Johnnie and now, Boesman and Lena.

Who else? Bosman, Schreiner, Pauline Smith.

Particularly conscious of it this time with Boesman and Lena. To begin with phrases were all in Afrikaans — some are still, and still defy 'translation' e.g. 'nog 'n vrot huis vir die vrot mens'. Texture. Lowell's 'mutation'.

Drawing tremendous encouragement and strength at this moment — the most hellish and arid period I've ever experienced as a writer — from a book on Zen Buddhism. Trying to find my way back to a free flow of 'intuition'.

Lena . . . 'that' day . . . starting with their eviction in the morning, the beating from Boesman, the long walk, her exhaustion . . . every detail . . . and it's one day too many. The rebel (Camus); finally: No! Too much. So far and no further.

Boesman and Lena — Laughter! Brecht's 'ease'.

November

'Time'. So often just a word. But yesterday, sitting among the scrub and coarse grass with my glasses and the dogs, waiting for birds . . . a long empty wind off the sea . . . the shift and movement of everything as it passed . . . a small bird piping away somewhere . . . an intuitive feeling of what 'Time' really is . . . not even becoming — just being here and now. At the centre of it, of the illusion of passage or passing or succession ... the reality, a perfect stillness. Our terrible segmentation — days, hours, minutes, last year, next year, past and future — when all we really need is one word: present or, better still, a new word, or no word at all because the reality is all of it, past, present and future. Regret and nostalgia make the past, desire the future; the present? The limbo of becoming — the fulcrum between one mistake and another — the perpetual seesaw we think is living.

Instead, stillness and being what you are, here and now.

Quasimodo — 'Until one day ends forever.' And before it ends for ever, it lasts for ever.

The terrible world of opposites. Zen.

Mom doctoring Maria with Bob Martin's (dog's) conditioning pills for the pains in her legs. Uncle Manie heard about them in the Transvaal. Fished his little bottle out of a waistcoat pocket to show Mom, who now also takes them.

'They work! Maria could hardly walk. Now she runs.'

'But you must remember to order for the "medium" dog. You get them for small dogs, medium dogs, and big dogs — you know. Great Danes. Well, the medium dogs is the one for human beings.'

Maria: an old African woman, sixtyish, who has been working for my mother for more than ten years.

After a badly dislocated four weeks Serpent Players have found a church hall in Korsten which we can have at one rand a rehearsal. Our next production is to be *Brother Jero,* and I estimate about six weeks rehearsal. Have sent an SOS to ask Mary if she (via a rich friend) could help us find £25: R30 for the hall and R20 for production budget.

1968

March

Writing a play — a long voyage. At this stage not yet started but some inkling of what might lie ahead suggested by the equipment coming aboard. The ship herself looks seaworthy enough to survive — why then the raft they are lashing to the deck, the strange and primitive equipment of survival being stowed away?

April

Long chat last night with Mulligan, Zack, John Kani and Winston Ntshona, who recently joined Serpent Players. Intended continuing our readings of Genet's *Death Watch* which we hope to adapt and make our next production; but found ourselves talking so well and easily that we were loath to stop. Started off in the car coming here to S'kop with the Olympics situation — South Africa being given the push (having only just been re-admitted) because of the threatened boycott of the games in Mexico City if S.A. did take part. From this to the predicament we face and the basis for action — love of B or hatred of A (B's opposite)? A total appreciation on their part of how crucial the choice is: of how differently a man will act, think and feel, depending on what he chooses, even though the two alternatives might seem to lead to the same thing.

And also, to what extent as survivors, or men concerned with survival (ours and others), do we impede the very historical process and changes that we so fervently hope will take place? Our lack of ruthlessness — inability to sacrifice ourselves and others.

With the exception of Mulligan, they are young men (John and Winston matriculated a couple of years ago). Incredibly 'whole' and 'decent' — not yet deformed by bitterness and hatred.

Barney, Ian[1] and I plan to do *People are Living There* in Johannesburg next January. Am going to try to finish the new play and, if it is any good, do it instead. Yvonne Bryceland as Lena — an exciting and provocative prospect. Thinking of Y. as Lena helps me in a small quiet way[2]. She would have been a very good Hester.

158

May

My work of the past ten days disturbed by a sudden resurgence of the playwrights' boycott issue. Sparked off by an interview Laurens van der Post gave on his arrival back in London in which he quoted me (correctly) as saying that I thought it was time to lift the ban.

Firstly two incredibly agitated and irritable letters from Mary. Was v.d. Post right? Surely not! Timing of statement appalling – death of Martin Luther King, Olympic Games, racial trouble in Britain etc. etc. Would I please write straight away to *The Times*, giving a full statement.

Spent the whole weekend trying to examine my conscience and feelings for a reply (personal) to Mary when the papers were on the phone for a statement. I gave the following:

'When I first advocated the boycott by overseas playwrights five years ago, my decision to do so related directly to the circumstances then prevailing in South Africa. I felt the gesture might provoke some reaction among the theatrical managements in this country who had accepted the principle of segregated audiences long before they were in fact forced to do so by law.

'Now the laws are on the statute books and the timid and indifferent among us have a perfect excuse.

'But the five years that have passed have seen far profounder changes in our society than the loss of just this one opportunity. Virtually all significant opposition has been silenced – either in our jails or by being despatched into exile, by banning orders or just blatant intimidation. (Also censorship.)

'The ultimate irony is that the same period has seen the emergence of the myth of an "outward-going" South Africa; of a policy (apartheid) that given a fair chance would show itself to be ultimately decent.

'One of the consequences of this is a complacency among the majority of whites in this country that is as dangerous to our stability as any threat of invasion from abroad. It is frightening to see to what extent people are accommodating the appalling consequences of the policies of this Government. We are witness to a wholesale sclerosis of the emotions and sensibilities that is not the least of the terrible things happening to us today.

'My point is obvious. Anything that will get people to think and feel for themselves, that will stop them delegating these functions to the politicians, is important to our survival. Theatre can help do this. There is nothing John Balthazar Vorster and his Cabinet would like more than to keep us isolated from the ideas and values which are

159

current in the free Western world. These ideas and values find an expression in the plays of contemporary writers. I would like South Africa to see these plays.'

Meanwhile, I was receiving copies of letters written by playwrights to *The Times*. Fifteen playwrights, including Harold Pinter, John Osborne, Doris Lessing, Edna O'Brien and David Mercer, strongly supported the continuation of the boycott — they asked: '. . . does anyone believe the S.A. Government would permit the performance of any play which seriously challenged its vicious mythology of human relationships, or its bigoted and inhuman conception of a "just" society?' The radicalising role of drama, they believed to be negligible. 'Change comes through human action informed by political awareness and exacerbated by intolerable humiliation, suppression and deprivation.' (They had said that since the Government maintained the subjection of black South Africans by force, their ultimate victory would most likely come through armed rebellion.) Their conclusion was that if there is a moral obligation on playwrights, 'it is to refuse complicity with the sophistries of vested interests in the S.A. theatre, and to expose the self-delusion of those who pretend that the performance of their plays to segregated audiences is some kind of tangible contribution to the cause of African freedom.'

Frank Marcus wrote that their letter did not shake his belief that a cultural boycott of S.A. was of no practical value:

'I have lived under a Fascist regime. Hope can be kindled by indirect means; communication with the outside world can give encouragement. The plays written by the signatories . . . contain ideas, and ideas can be infectious. Is exile really preferable to resistance?' And Lord Beaumont wrote that 'The history of almost any totalitarian regime shows instances of "liberal" plays, books, etc. which have helped to keep hope alive among those struggling to maintain their standards and beliefs.'

Among those supporters of the boycott who nevertheless had films running in South Africa were John Osborne and Robert Bolt, and Osborne wrote to explain that the economics of film-making prevented writers and actors from having any control over their distribution, while Bolt pointed out that 'very brave South Africans, black and white, who are actively resisting their own Government do favour the action of artists and athletes who refused to take part in segregated events.' A point affirmed by John Mortimer as chairman of the League of Dramatists, who said he preferred to be guided by those engaged in the struggle — as for the suggestion that royalties from plays performed out here could be used to support black theatre in the townships, the African National Congress had made it clear that they would rather have the protest than the money.

A 'white South African visitor' who was quoted by the *Times Literary Supplement,* suggested that the only effective boycotts would be those which 'interfered with the pleasures of the average middle-class whites' — South African cinemas are packed, he pointed out, while Sammy Davis and Ella Fitzgerald can be heard on the state propaganda radio — 'the real victims of the playwrights' protest would be a handful of white and black intellectuals.'

My reply to Mary was on a very private and personal level — an attempt to explain to her (as much for myself) my 'philosophy' of survival. In the course of the letter I said:

'. . . for me it is not as simple as having "views" on one of the tactics of a campaign. The whole question of the boycott . . . relates with terrible and agonising immediacy to the problem of survival here — my own in the first selfish instance, but then others as well; of what "good" there is left in this society . . . [which is] fighting hard to survive the death-wish both within and without.

'I can now not function on any principle other than that of survival — the withdrawal of my passport and my decision to stay on here regardless leads inevitably to this. This is the basis on which I now live as a man and function as a writer. But could it be otherwise? My decision to throw in my lot "here and now", to *witness* — what? — if not those people, ideas, values, which left me — the man that I am — with no alternative but to align myself with them. What brand of spiritual deceit would it be to bear witness to the extinction, or at the least, mutilation of something I value, having contributed to that diabolical process?

'There is a profound dilemma here for me. To what extent in this alignment do I stand as an obstacle to the changes which I know will take place sooner or later? Could it be sooner if I chose to sacrifice? Maybe. But I can't. I'm back to where I started. I always knew the act of loving was a tightrope. Now I also realise it doesn't end. If you don't choose to jump off it, it goes on forever.'

I said I hoped this didn't sound vain — no-one could have as precarious a balance up there as myself. The horror of what this government and its policies have done to people and the account for which it must one day answer in terms of suffering, of destroyed and wasted lives, has built up such an abyss of hatred that at times, I told her, I'd been quite prepared to take the jump and 'destroy' — but, so far, 'by some miracle, the company of executioners remains loathesome.'

161

When it came to the specifics of how effective the boycott would be in provoking change, I said I do not know the answer. As a gesture of solidarity with the victims of apartheid — to give them courage — I have very profound doubts. But my contacts are limited.

The issue is people — as I wrote to her: 'it's the fact that men can be good, that the good must be sustained and that it's almost impossible to imagine a situation on this earth where it is harder to survive with any decency than here and now in South Africa. I can't think of any moral dilemma more crucifying than this one — to destroy the evil at the cost of what little good there is, or to seemingly accommodate the evil by sustaining the good. *I am not sure. I do not know.* I don't think I ever will. But to sit in moral paralysis while the days of my one life — my one chance to discover the brotherhood of other men — pass, is obviously so futile and pointless it is not worth talking about. So without the support of reason, or a clear conviction as to the consequences — relying only on an instinct (blind as it is) at the core of my life, I choose and act . . .'

(On May 5 the London *Sunday Times* reported that 'After weeks of furious discussion British playwrights have closed ranks to support a continuation of the cultural boycott.' David Mercer was quoted as saying 'There is a moral obligation' for this 'unambiguous rejection of the present regime in South Africa.')

I wonder whether Wilfrid Owen's poem is relevant? 'None will break ranks though nations trek from progress.' Or — the dead 'enemy' speaking —

> For by my glee might many men have laughed,
> And of my weeping something had been left
> Which must die now . . .
> Now men will go content with what we spoiled,
> Or, discontent, boil bloody and be spilled.

Nadine, Alan, etc. have all reconfirmed their faith in the boycott. The past ten days have been sobering. And provocative. I've been forced to examine my function and validity as a writer in a way that I've never done before. I think I know now what is involved.

Serpent Players last night — we are meeting here at S'kop for the moment. Reading and discussing Genet's *Death Watch* which we intend to do next. The problem of a second half for the evening came up and the group suggested that we try and do something like *The Coat*. I agreed to have a try, inwardly anticipating that we'd flounder around for at least a couple of weeks before we found our idea. I couldn't have been more wrong. In reply to my, 'Any ideas?' Zack told us the following (he'd obviously been thinking about it for quite a long time):

At the bus-stop in Cadles where he gets off to go to work, he passes every morning (early) a large number of young children running very urgently down the street. One morning he stopped one of them and asked where they were going. It turned out that they had come on foot from New Brighton and were going to Brito's Bakery to buy at a much reduced price a loaf of stale bread — usually two days old.

Zack looked at us with a little embarrassment: 'I thought that might be an idea. A loaf of stale bread.'

Pressed further for a situation, he suggested the following: 'A municipal labourer (R7.50 a week — a wife and children) — in other words, below the breadline. On Thursday night there is no food in the house. He sacrifices the few cents he'd put aside to buy himself something to eat at work next day. It barely produces enough to stop the children crying from hunger. There is still the problem of Friday — morning and afternoon — what will the family eat until he comes home in the evening with his pay? He does the last thing possible — sacrifices his busfare so that they can buy two loaves of stale bread. He will walk to work.'

Yes, yes! we said. That's it. But now what? We need a question that will give our improvisation 'form'. We found it immediately. Boy asked: 'Is he angry?'

We had it. A man, in the circumstances given above, and the question. Is he angry?

To begin with, one of two obvious answers: Yes, or No. Rebellion or resignation.

Two improvisations:

Resignation: the lunchbreak at work ... the men sitting round eating and drinking ... and then one of them notices that our man has got nothing. They share with him, talk, and he tells his story; questions are asked.

Rebellion: The same man, waiting at the bus-stop, early morning — a cold morning. Buses pass but don't stop because they are full. The men talk. Then they see our man coming. But he doesn't get into the queue with them — he walks past. They call to him. He stops ... etc. etc.

I wanted a third possibility. I knew there was one. We found that immediately. 'Yes! But ...' One actor alone, talking to the audience. Is he angry? 'Yes! But ...'

163

One of the most exciting evenings I've ever had with the group. After waiting so long the ideas are beginning to come from them — are 'growing', taking root.

We've decided now to meet twice a week — one evening the Genet, the second 'Friday's Bread on Monday'.

I can't begin to tell. Simply because I don't know how — in talk, in conversation. The tree tonight with the frogs croaking in the tangle of weeds around the base — the furred massive presence of the thing, the knowledge of roots, the droughts, seasons of rain, seasons when the rain failed . . . and after all this finally, alive!

The boycotting of trees.

It must be hell to leave a house with a real tree growing in the garden.

Session with Mulligan and Winston. Was to have been a reading of our Genet but only the two of them turned up at the bus terminal in town. After waiting half an hour for the others, Mulligan suggested, weakly, that we call it a night. I should go back to S'kop, they to New Brighton. I would have been spared the trouble of bringing them back at ten, and then the long drive home again. I almost said yes. Instead we drove back here for an hour or two of talking and drinking.

Our subject — emerging in the chat in the car as we drove here — honesty, with self, with the world we live in; 'being oneself' as fully and uncompromisingly as we are capable of; disgust with the double game — talking with 'A' about 'B' and a few hours after, with 'B' about 'A'.

And then this question — a black man in S.A., how far can he, short of suicide, really afford to be honest with the world in which he lives? The vulgarities (swartgat, bloubek etc.), to stop each time and say 'No!'?? What price survival? One's soul?

Survival can involve betrayal of everything — beliefs, values, ideals, — except Life itself.

Fanon on this subject. The schizoid condition of an oppressed people. The cure? Obviously nothing short of a revolution in the social order can give a man in that condition a chance of hoping (striving) with some possibility of realisation, that he can achieve this integration (balance) of self with the world in which he lives.

Really felt the loss of my passport for the first time these past two weeks. Re-examining and reworking *Mille Miglia* for Robin Midgley in London. The BBC have invited me to London for the filming. His first reading in ten days' time.

June
Have put aside Danie, Lena and Steve (Fairview — A man without scenery)[3] for the moment to take up Boesman and Lena. Why? Just by accident, paging back through this notebook, the entries in October 1967. Plus a sudden realisation of how lacking I am in tolerance towards Sheila. These made me see Boesman and Lena as being the story of Sheila and myself — knowing it, the situation, without any desperate dependence on myth-making or imagination, a reality of my life as if Morrie and Zach were myself and Royal: Johnnie and his father, myself and mine.

Surprised to find how fully realised the Boesman and Lena story is. Why had I shelved it? And the images! Boesman shouldering all they have, then Lena taking her share, joining him, etc.

We'll see what happens.

Zen and the art of angling. Every cast is a cast into your own soul, your own potential. Also: Indifference.

Interview with two Special Branch policemen on the rocks yesterday afternoon. They found me down there after being told at the house that I had gone fishing. Someone had phoned them with information about the Black Sash organisation and said he was Athol Fugard. Who was playing games? And with whom?

The art of angling ... the anatomy and moods of 'self' ... Rivers (Bitou and Bushmans) the turbulence of gulleys and surf.

Never strike without conviction.

The parallel with judo — defeating something with its own strength.

The cast.

July
Just over a month now with Boesman and Lena. First act out in rough draft, skeleton for the second. Characters and lines of development well established, but more difficulty than I expected in finding the substance to this relationship — a struggle for objectivity and distance. For example: Boesman's hatred and abuse of Lena ... easy enough to formulate, but a struggle to reveal it, in depth, in incident and dialogue for what it is.

165

Unrelieved squalor and poverty of their situation demands that I write this one more 'beautifully' than ever before. 'Flowers on the rubbish heap.'

Realised that the genesis of this play lies possibly in an image from over ten years ago ... a coloured man and woman, burdened with their possessions, whom I passed somewhere on the road near Laingsberg. It was sunset, and they were miles from the nearest town. Then of course, also the old woman near Cradock on the drive back from Norman's trial.

Again: Brecht's 'ease' *(Messingkauf Dialogues)* — lightness and laughter.

Fishing on the banks of the Swartkops River: saw her as we were leaving our spot on the canal wall. Lena. Either drunk or a hangover from the previous night's drinking. (A number of bait diggers, coloured fishermen, had spent the night there. It was bitterly cold. Bottles of cheap wine to help them live through it.) Doek on her head, faded maroon blouse and an old blue skirt. Barefoot. She stood to one side and let us go first over the little bridge which crosses the canal. Unseeing eyes, focused, if anything, on the ground just ahead. We were merely 'white men' — nothing could have been more remote from her life. Walked like a somnambulist. A face shrivelled and distorted by dissipation, resentment, regrets. Bloated stomach.

The texture of that place — the mudflats — and its possibilities, exactly as imagined. Specially Outa. Back with the play today after a few days' break with a conviction and certainty that I don't think I've had before.

Strangely, no surprise at seeing Lena. Just a sense of the possibility of sacrilege, of the demand that the truth be told, that I must not bear false witness.

Another coloured woman who might have been Lena. Lived somewhere in the bush along the Glendore Road. Worked for us for a short period about two years ago. Sense of appalling physical and spiritual destitution, of servility. Did the housework without a word or sound, without the slightest flicker of her 'self'. For some reason left us after about two months. Then some time later came back to see if we had any work. A stiflingly hot day ... Berg wind blowing. In the course of the few words I had with her she seemed to be in an even more desperate condition than when we had last seen her — not so much physically, though that was still there, but poverty is poverty and at its worst there are no grades — it was a sense of her disorientation, almost derangement, of only a fraction of herself committed to and involved in the world around her. The Rest? Where? (The vacancy of the Swartkops Lena when she reached the bridge, realised we were coming and stood aside to let us go first. 'Things' in her world.) After telling the woman we had no work, she left us to try a few other houses. An hour or so later, the heat even more fierce by then, I left the house with snorkel and mask to do some skin-diving in the gulleys. I would not have moved out into that sun if it hadn't been for the prospect of the wet cool sea. I looked back at one point, just before going over the edge of the headland and down to the rocks, and saw the woman, empty-handed and obviously unsuccessful in her search for work, starting up the hill on her way back to Glendore.

That hill, the sun, the long walk. Possibly even a walk that Lena has not yet made . . . but will one day in the time that still lies ahead of her when she walks away with Boesman at the end of the play; a walk beyond the moment of rebellion — that possibility past, even forgotten — a walk beyond all the battles, the refusals, even tears. Surrender: Defeat. A walk into the ignominy of silence, the world's silence and blindness, burdened now as never before by Lena's unanswerable little words: Why? How? Who?

'Can't I stop now. Just lie down and die?'

The young Boesman and Lena who passed in front of the car one night when I was waiting at a traffic light. A shared life in the beginning — at the end each other's jailer.

Boesman's self-hatred — his own failures.

After a good start, just over a month ago, have been floundering in the first act of Boesman and Lena this past week — specifically her first long soliloquy when she tries to unravel and order her memories of the past, tries to work out how she got to where she is. I have such a clear image of the function and 'feel' of this moment, yet so far it has eluded me. The same really is true of the whole first 'movement' of the play — from their arrival to the appearance of Outa — all of which appears to be tantalizingly on the brink of realisation, but which so far I've not been able to push over the edge. I'm sure I experienced the same problem with *Hello* — made a note about skating on the hard surface reality and waiting for the ice to break and being forced to survive in depth.

My first movement — Boesman and Lena, their relationship and predicament (her sense of one day too many, Boesman's self-hatred focused and working out on her) — the dynamic element coming

167

from her disorientation (How did I get here?) then the soliloquy where she thinks she discovers or remembers a short sequence of their whens and wheres . . . temporary elation until Boesman, viciously, destroys it, pointing out her mistakes but not giving her the truth . . . leading to her awareness of the hell of it all (it must be witnessed) and the moment when she calls Outa to their fire.

I'm sure the Zen precept is right — the harder you 'try' the more it will elude you. (Beating a drum while hunting the fugitive.) Spontaneity: I must rediscover this in my writing — I don't doubt that without it there can be no marvellous accidents. Will leave the first act for the moment and sketch, wherever I feel I want to, in the second act. Must free myself of 'labour' and use more 'delight'.

So often the paradox in writing: discover your beginning when you reach the end.

Boesman and Lena — their predicament, at the level at which it fascinates me, neither political nor social but metaphysical . . . a metaphor of the human condition which revolution or legislation cannot substantially change.

Also — the problem of identity. What am I? Coloureds and Africans; Morrie and Zach. Possibly one of the reasons why I have not used an African character and township setting in any of my last three plays is that I think and feel about it in too shallowly 'political' terms.

To be careful that I do not pitch Boesman at a level of monotonous hatred and abuse. Not just the technical problem of variety of tone and tempo — the more basic issue is that it is not as simple as Lena being the victim and Boesman the oppressor . . . both are ultimately victims of a common predicament — and of each other.

So, for Boesman, as total a statement as for Lena. What is mutilated, and why? The key I am sure is to reveal and dramatise his 'self-hatred focused on Lena.' What he really hates is himself. Why?

Title?

Lena: a sense of injustice implying therefore a value of self.

Boesman: no value.

Something dangerous, lurking and suppressed, deepdown in Boesman. If it comes out . . .? Then like Lena a sense of injustice, the hell of unanswerable questions. What is it?

The price of his apparent acceptance = the denial of value. His fear and loneliness when Lena chooses the old man at the end of Act I.

Boesman's fear — discovering his own value.

168

Coega to Veeplaas	— the first walk. One night in an empty shed at the brickfields. At Veeplaas Boesman got a job at the Zwartkops Salt Works. To begin with rented a small pondok — later built one of their own. Lena's baby born — six months later dead. First miscarriage. *Three to five years.*
Redhouse	— working for Baas Bobbie — farmer. *One year.*
Kleinskool	— Job with Vermaak the butcher. Labourer for building contractor. *One year.*
Bethelsdorp	— Farm labourer. Brickfields. *Two years.*
Missionvale	— Salt works. Aloes. Lena's second miscarriage. *One year.*
Kleinskool	— Odd jobs. Theft — six months in jail. Lena did housework for Vermaak. *Two years.*
Veeplaas	— Odd jobs. Saltpan. Chinaman. Prickly pears. *Two years.*
Redhouse	— Farm labourer. *Six months.*
Swartkops	— Building labourer. Odd jobs. Bait. *Two years.*
Korsten	— Odd jobs. Empties. Lena's third miscarriage. Boesman in jail again — knife fight. *One to two years.*
Veeplaas & Redhouse	— Prickly pears. *Six months.*
Swartkops	— Bait — odd jobs. *Six months.*
Korsten	— Empties. *One year.*

... or something like that. As Lena finally says, talking from the inside of the experience, it explains nothing. I, though, have reached a point where I need to know — if this is to be another palimpsest with the past blurred behind the present, and in turn blurring it. Exactly as there is a shallow and pointless reduction of Boesman to the oppressor, so also there could be a shallow reduction of their relationship as a whole to violent, bitter discord. They did laugh, they did love and share ... it is because of this, what they have in common and has bound their lives together, that they are each other's fate.

As much Hate (real) as there was Love.

Patience needed. Two good signs: the idea, the complex of central images, survive the frequent assaults of my doubts about validity, significance, etc. Not only this, but the idea and images have become increasingly obsessional ... the time I want to spend thinking and working has spilled into the afternoon (when I normally never work). I find I don't even have time for the new Serpent Players project — we are still meeting twice a week but my contribution consists of what I find during the rehearsal — they are doing *all* the homework, and very effectively.

But any number of blanks remain to be filled. Lena and the Old Man: I do not yet have my image of her 'choice'. Why and how does she choose to sit out there in the cold with him? Any number of 'Ideas' as answers — I'm waiting for the image. I had that problem with Johnnie in *Hello*. 'Why does he go onto the crutches?' And Hester: 'What does she find in the boxes? What is that one important thing?' Finally: Nothing.

Drank coffee outside tonight. Our third day of easterly wind. When it came in on Sunday it was cold and uncomfortable . . . tonight (it will obviously change before long and come in hard from the South-West) it was like velvet; a warm languid agitation among leaves and in our hair. The sea muffled and muted. Still moving when I walked the dog about half an hour ago though now with a touch of the frenzy that precedes the change to the westerly and the harsh, withering assault from the sea.

The St. Francis lighthouse very clear. And spring is still months away.

Still Lena and the Old Man. Why does she call him in? Does she?

Daan — the African who occasionally works in the garden; lives in Walmer Location; wife dead, two daughters of sixteen and thirteen. Going through a very hard time at the moment; obviously hungry, clothes in rags. At the most, two or three gardening jobs a week. Some weeks none.

Their life in that room in the Walmer location (his two children are with him and 'loop skool'). 'Die lewe is swaar né, Daan!' 'Here, Baas . . . elke dag is dit iets anders. Elke dag iets anders.'[4]

He came originally from the Alexandria district. I doubt whether he is legally in P.E. He'll be caught sooner or later no doubt and then endorsed out, back to Alexandria.

J.,on a visit from England (originally from Johannesburg), told how she had given a lift to a coloured man and tried to use it as a chance to talk frankly to a 'non-white' about his life. Frustrating experience. He evaded her questions. She asked how I would have tried to get him to speak. I couldn't quite formulate my answer but, later, thinking about Daan, realised what it was. It's the whole business of my having chosen to live and write here, where haphazardly and mostly by accident I have mastered the 'code' of this place and time.

How can the full reality of a life here and now be stated? 'Are you happy?' 'Do you hate the white man?' 'Do you think things will change?' etc. Journalism! And if replies were possible they'd be journalism. Daan isn't a journalist — he's a man living out with desperate earnestness, his life; and the richness of this in tears, sweat, frustration and courage is to be read in the torn and filthy jacket he was wearing yesterday, the image of his long walk from the location to S'kop, the hands that come out for the R1.50, the look back at the car after I dropped him near the location . . . and then, with all this noted and deciphered, the totally expressive, 'Elke dag iets anders.'

One of the reasons, I suppose, why I write for the stage — beyond, or before, all the spoken words there is the possibility of this code — the Carnal Reality of the actor in space and time. Only a fraction of my truth is in the words.[5]

Lena: as simple as this possibly. Loneliness drives her to call in the other man. A loneliness made all the worse by Boesman's withdrawal. As the action proceeds so does her demand — finally conscious — that her life be witnessed. Development as she talks to him, as he sees — of her awareness — finally obsessive — of the old man as a witness.

John Kani's stories about working at the Ford Motor factory:
1. Old Terblanche: 'Luister vir my nou, seuntjie. (The Afrikaner 'boy' relationship.) Die Goewerment gaan 'n end sit aan daai ding.'[6]
2. The visit of Henry Ford Junior.
3. Translating for the foreman, 'Mr Baas Bradley'.[7]

August
I have said often enough — in company, in interviews — that to leave South Africa (one-way exit permit) was an intolerable thought . . . I've known it was so, but until this afternoon never felt out exactly what would be involved. Didn't need to, I suppose, because it is the truth, that to leave this country is unimaginable. Anyway — a walk with Azdak in the bush this afternoon ended up on a high sandy ridge — almost a dune — where the harsh grey scrub was cropped close to the earth because of exposure to the South-Westers. One was blowing, long, clean and cool; in the distance the sea, brilliantly blue and settling down after three days of rough weather. But it was that

171

scrub underfoot . . . the nameless deformed little grey bushes, half their roots exposed by the shifting sand . . . the thought that I might possibly one day never again walk over them in that silence and innocence . . . a keen pain, intolerable sense of loss.

Then tonight, talking to Sheila — telling her that the idea had come to me yesterday at this table, that my life's work was possibly just to witness as truthfully as I could, the nameless and destitute (desperate) of this one little corner of the world. This is what could be lost . . . those little grey bushes in the shifting sands of the dune.

And so Olson:

> I have no longer any excuse
> for envy. My life
>
> has been given its orders: the seasons
> seize
>
> the soul and the body, and make mock
> of any dispersed effort. The hour of death
>
> is the only trespass.[8]

No longer any excuse for envy. My life has been given its order: Love the little grey bushes.

These thoughts about my development since *Nongogo*: not 'what is going to happen next?' but 'what is happening?' Revelation from the first line. A pattern of images rather than the logic of a story.

And time — the density of the palimpsest (past, present and future) rather than the false chronology of calendars and clocks.

In working on Lena and Boesman these past few days, a sense of the 'word' again, of playing with it on paper and in the accidents of the game making discoveries. More than anything else I suppose this reveals the extent to which I try to function at the poetic level (the Image) — surrendering to the authority of colourless, black ink (Pasternak). Right because it's unreal. Also since *Nongogo* — greater honesty about, and use of the unreality of the stage.

And efficiency — to use *every* moment, line, pause, gesture, to reveal.

Days on end when I sit at the table, not thinking about Boesman and Lena, but staying/remaining with the presence of these two. That and no more, but allowing the sense of them to grow.

172

A few more days of good work on Boesman and Lena. Suddenly a strong and clear sense of the 'dynamic' to the 1st Act . . . Lena's involvement with the Old Man, the effect of this on Boesman and his relationship with her. Again, this did not come as an 'idea' — I've had that almost from the moment I started writing — but as a discovery as I wrote my way deeper into the situation.

Most important consequence is that Lena now has a 'drive', is moving and not just sitting there in the mud floundering in her predicament. Next problem is to carry this over interval and into the 2nd Act.

Reading Laing's *The Politics of Experience* and *Bird of Paradise* has added a lot to the depth of my feeling and image of Boesman and Lena.

Lena, ontological insecurity? Maybe, in her demand that her life be witnessed. Not just a sense of its injustice.

A growing sense also of the pattern of the experience, of being able to find the right (and only) moment for images, actions.

A few more days and I will have, for the first time, a properly worked-out rough draft of the 1st Act.

The accident in writing: A powerful example when sorting out my ideas and images for the ending of Act I — Lena at the fire with Outa, sharing her mug of tea and piece of bread — kept hearing her say, 'This Mug . . . This Bread . . . My life . . .' Suddenly, and almost irrelevantly, remembered Lisa the other day reading a little book on the Mass — and there it was = Lena's Mass . . . the moment and its ingredients (the fire, the mug of tea, the bread) because sacramental — the whole a celebration of Lena's life.

And, with that, the first, rough draft of Act One.

September[9]

Bombarded with cables from New York where production of *People are Living There* is being set up, and as a result running round in circles trying to get passport, or permission to travel, yet again. Helen Suzman has agreed to act on my behalf and has an interview with the minister next week. She doesn't hold out much hope, but is also not prepared to say my chances are hopeless. I think they are.

Two or three more days and I should have a skeleton outline for the second act of Boesman and Lena. Good development these last few days, to the dynamic and line in Lena's predicament. Two fulcrums (up and down): 1. Calling Outa into her life — the sense

of her life, her feeling for it, growing intensity of involvement, and
2. Outa's death — alienation. 'I'm alone.'

'So that is all. Hold on tight . . . and then let go.'

She lets go. But you can't be dead before you die. So . . . give me
mine.

Hester — any difference? Not really I suppose. And even if there
were, what they have in common is so much more important — the
return to what they are, for example.

One of the differences — of degree — Lena has less hope . . . not
that Hester has much, but she is comparatively young. Lena is at the
end. She takes back 'herself' for her *last* walk.

It has been asked of Hester: what is going to happen after she
leaves Johnnie? In the case of Lena, the answer is simple = nothing.

I can't say it all here — that's why it's a play. Boesman and Lena
have become . . . what? . . . a sea, and myself adrift on it . . . the
victim of dark and deep currents. The naiveté of these notes! . . . like
the maps of the world before they discovered the world was round.

What remains to be done . . . Boesman's poem of destruction;
Lena's poem about meeting herself, the memory of herself; Boesman's poem about . . . etc. Still to be written but at least I begin to
see the need and place for them . . . the cracks in the 'surface reality'
where I must fall in and drown.

Significantly, in my days at this table now, I don't look at the map
of P.E. on my wall any more, but at the blank foolscap paper on the
table. It seemed impossible to start with — the enigma and mystery
of that little stippled expanse beside the washed blue of the river
where Boesman and Lena spent the night . . . fruitless hours staring
at it. The truth lay in the still greater mystery (untold stories) of the
blank writing-paper.

Before even the magic of the word, the clotted choking reality of
blank paper. Every — but every — possibility. I must choose one.

The thought that *Boesman and Lena* is the third part of a trilogy that
if anything should be called *The Family*. The two generations —
parents and children, and thus:
1.   *Blood Knot* — (the children) brother and brother.
2.   *Hello and Goodbye* — child and parent. (Hester and Johnnie
     with the father — not with each other).
3.   *Boesman and Lena* — parent and parent.
In biographical terms — myself and Royal; myself and father (or
mother); myself and Sheila.

No reckoning with a 'stranger' — all knotted together by blood and habit. Fascinating, and depressing, to think that seven years of work has amounted to an exploration and statement of this one nexus in human relationships. Also the personal revelation involved.

What next?

This, in a letter from a friend in Johannesburg, urging me to leave South Africa: 'Well, I know how highly regarded you are overseas, but they are getting bored with this passport set-up, and don't forget when they can't get you because you won't move off your comfortable arse (play-acting Pasternak to your tribe of admirers) they are going to forget about you altogether. Anyway you are only mimicking an idea that had currency at the time ... I was also scared to go and also scared to jump out of the aeroplane with a flimsy parachute — but once I did I was free forever.'

As Sheila says, he accuses me of cowardice and of complacency.

The Group: performance at Livingstone Hospital[10] tomorrow night of Genet's *Death Watch*. By and large directed by Mulligan (who arrived in England yesterday where he will study). Two or three run-throughs in the garage this past week — I find myself very impressed. Their performances make more meaning of that cell and the relationships between the three men than any of my readings of the script have been able to. Possibly the most sustained, convincing and committed performances that Serpent Players have ever produced.

Have almost forced myself to this notebook tonight. I would so like to parallel the writing of one play with a diary of its ideas, problems and solutions, images, sudden development etc. Anyway I came back to this one after fourteen days of steady and good work, none of which is reflected in the last few pages here. Where am I in the play? The usual swing of the pendulum — sometimes Boesman and Lena seem as valid and real as anything I've ever done, sometimes just so much paper, defaced by my horribly selfconscious scrawl and its attendent mannerisms — a few words and then fullstops, commas, etc.

The thought that it is a 'third part' of something, stays with me.

The point at which this play touched my life already passed. No more than I look at the map any more do I think of its personal references. Boesman and Lena *are* ... themselves ... and the only discoveries I make now, can make, are found by venturing into the whiteness of blank paper.

175

Thank heaven for one thing — my 'taste' seems to be intact. Although at this point I am not concerning myself (too much) with detail, I find myself responding to and deleting over-statement — that one fatal word too much — my pen sometimes finding the line which, coupled with the actor's gesture, will say the 'whole' and not one jot more or, better still, the line which *needs* the actor's gesture to complete it. The secret of dialogue.

Seven years — six characters: Morrie, Zach, Hester, Johnnie, Boesman and Lena.

Boesman's *shame* — not an incident, a 'one day', but a pattern, his life ... possibly an image which sums it up, but not one that 'explains' it.

Visit from Norman — ostensibly to discuss a play he is trying to write but ending with another outpouring of his incredible stories about Robben Island.

'Satan' — the convict in charge of burning all the rubbish and old paper on the Island, standing beside his fire with a long pitchfork. An important man as he was the only source of the brown paper used for rolling zols. (Horseshoe or Springbok tobacco.) The brown paper was usually that in which the warder had got their meat — blood and fat-stained. It was strongly believed on the Island that the fat-stained paper made the finest zols. When Satan couldn't provide any paper you fell back on the brown-paper covers of your exercise-books.

Norman's description of trying to smoke secretly at night under your blanket (the zol too short to pass around). Somebody else crawling around on hands and knees, smelling the air like an animal, until he located the smoker. Cigarettes lit with a small piece of razorblade and a piece of matchbox 'strike'.

Smuggling in the 'greens' for Norman's farewell salad — one man producing tomatoes out of his trousers, cabbage leaves from his shirt, etc.

'Give us a brush.' During their 'shows', so as not to draw the attention of the warders, they rubbed their hands together instead of clapping.

Jake — unsung mime artist of Robben Island, a 'must' at every show: 'We want Jake!' One of his sketches: bus queue in Johannesburg — argument between two men, one of whom is trying to push in; then the old Zulu municipal policeman gets involved, the bus arrives and the conductor gets drawn in too. Finally a white inspector arrives on the scene and he also gets involved — Jake switching from one character to the other without a pause, changing body, voice and even language (Zulu, Xhosa, Afrikaans, English) so fast and effort-lessly that finally there were a dozen people on the stage.

Another of his sketches: a convict being dragged off to the cooler by white warder, protesting violently. Every few steps, 'Wait! Wait! Now why, man? Why are you doing this to me?' 'Kaffir, you're being taught a lesson.' And off they go struggling again.

At the 'authorised' shows he often caricatured one or other of the prison officers, and warders sitting in the front row — 'Old Porridge' for example, a much-hated officer who, baton under his arm, liked nothing better than to find a prisoner committing some minor breach of the rules in the long food queue, and then to take his plate away from him.

The news and weather forecast: 'Black domination was running, chased by white domination. Black domination got the shit beaten out of it. Black domination lost its shoes.'

October
The first swallow of spring dropped past my window this morning. The season is emphatically here now — flowers in the veld; the sun, given half a chance, already very warm; and our wonderful winds, long and clean, straight off the sea. In the garden everything is grow-ing. At the warm midday hour I delight in standing with the hose in my hand, pouring out gallons of water.

Two nights' fishing on the Kowie River at Port Alfred with Denis. Between us, ten grunter. Bitterly cold but a marvellous rediscovery of the African night — its vast silence, the intermittent noises (night calls, the night jar) that only emphasise the overall solemn silence. Our rods out . . . watching the tips . . . waiting for the first flicker that will indicate the fish are on their way up or down the river. When that happens, an hour of electric activity and then, nothing . . . so to sleep — the first night in a tent, the second in the car.

Boesman and Lena progressing. Seems certain that we must do it rather than *People* in February. What I have down on paper seems to fall so short of its potential, however I work steadily, and good, if small, things do happen every day. These past two weeks I've spent almost all my time, energy and consciousness on Boesman. It is now not *all* Lena. Boesman: There are secrets in my heart as well.

Thinking about them today I realise that whenever I do go back to them my task is to go beyond the mudflats as the context of their predicament and into their minds (their visions and lunacies); if they are not yet 'mad' enough, to make them so. Add a thousand years to their experience of life if necessary. The anatomy of their souls, their vision of life . . . not just a catalogue of their experiences.

December
Lena arrives at the mudflats tired — 'It felt old today.' Boesman is the hell-in — the failure to stay 'free'. He works out his self-hatred on her — driving her to a realisation of what her life, her predicament really is. She chooses Outa. She stumbles accidentally on his function as 'witness': 'Watch now, Outa.'

Talking to the Group last night about *Boesman and Lena* — my struggle to find a new form for the experience: John said, 'Boesman and Lena are the rejects of the white man's world.' (Boesman: 'We're rubbish. We've been thrown away.')

Yesterday another Boesman and Lena . . . around five o'clock they came down the hill, turned right at the bottom and went marching off towards the Reserve. Side-by-side. Most startling of all, Lena was leading a dog. Typical location mongrel. She had made a lead out of a length of flaxen twine. A doek on her head, the same doek, but the blazer had disappeared. In its place, an old jersey . . . only two buttons. The man had a large sack (provisions?) slung over his shoulder. Hatless — head shaven bald. (Jail?) They talked to each other as they walked along.

Another encounter with the local Boesman and Lena. Driving to a Christmas Eve dinner-party last night, we passed them on the road just outside S'kop. Both obviously very drunk. The woman had fallen and was rolling around on the ground at the side of the road. As we approached I thought he was trying to help her to her feet. Looking back in the rearview mirror though, when we'd passed, I saw him pick up a large stone and threaten to throw it at her.
    Half-an-hour later we sat down to a lavishly decorated and burdened table with French champagne to drink.

For some weeks now have been reading Ernst Fischer's *The Necessity of Art* — his Marxism and advocacy of social realism seems finally to be expressed in his description of an artist as being 'commissioned by his society'. My whole dilemma, specifically in *Boesman and Lena,* focused on this. Do I want a commission? Have I got one? Must I function without one? Is my context irremediably bourgeois? Can I

178

align myself with a future, a possibility, which I believe in (hope for) but of which I have no image? My failure of imagination?

More than ever before in my life a sense of how much the blindness, apathy, indifference of people holds us back, bogs us down in this morass of self-indulgence and limp, useless consciences. Our hell (history) is man-made, to that extent it can be unmade by men.

1969

March

Committed to an opening of *People* in Cape Town on June 14 (CAPAB); thereafter two performances of *B & L* at Rhodes University. Sudden and surprising charges in thinking about *B & L*. Thus: the local two I've seen here, from the shell-crushing plant in the Reserve . . . the woman once with a dog in tow. Tonight Lisa tells me that the dog is dead . . . stoned by the man. What hurts me . . .? The bleeding head of the dog, and that of the man, merge.

Small spider in this room — first saw it when it was hanging about six inches above the floor, next to this table. Took me a few seconds to realise that it had dropped itself on a thread all the way from the ceiling. Watched it very intently for a few minutes as it went down further to within an inch of the floor, then down again and so on. Effortless mastery and very beautiful. Realised I was looking at what Huxley called 'animal grace' in a short essay on Zen Buddhism. (Also the story of the beetle asking the millipede: 'How do you manage to walk with so many legs?' 'It's easy!') But even more impressive than its technical mastery of that invisible thread from which it hung in space and semi-gloom, must have been the first moment, the first act — total and unquestioning — that sent it down, down, down through an infinity of time and space.

I am totally incapable of a parallel act in my life.

The spider went all the way back to the ceiling. I thought I understood what it was all about. It had spun out a particularly long thread for use in its web. Or had it in fact ingested in some way the thread (I don't know much about spiders). I waved an arm in the space where the thread would have been — sure enough, it was there. But as I tore it the spider fell all the way to the floor. It wasn't hurt. I watched for a few more seconds as it moved away to start somewhere else.

But somehow the fall caused by my rude and violent intrusion seemed to diminish the power and beauty of what I had seen. What was the ultimate point to this effortless animal grace? It hadn't reckoned with the catastrophe of my interference. Certainly the spider was still alive and would carry on, but there was something blind and futile in it all now. In any case, the catastrophe might have been one that killed it. And then? The spider seemed more a metaphor of absurdity than anything else — its value as a lesson to myself seemed limited.

Then I remembered that Huxley had passed from 'animal grace' — which man certainly needs — to 'spiritual grace' of which man alone is capable.

I think I understand a little bit more now.

The 'social' content of *Boesman and Lena*. Nagging doubts that I am opting out on this score, that I am not saying enough. At one level their predicament is an indictment of this society, which makes people 'rubbish'. Is this explicit enough?

Sartre: 'Marx says shame is a revolutionary sentiment.'

Also: Gandhi and the Pariahs = the cornerstone of a system he wanted to destroy.

Lena, reduced to a 'thing' in Boesman's life. Lena's rebellion is focused against Boesman. He represents, *is,* the source of abuse of herself. He is her world.

And she, then, must pay off with Outa. Her reason for wanting . . . for wanting someone. The integrity (truth) of her experience of herself. Swamped by Boesman's violence and *his* life. And, on his side — the shame of it all. And then his terrible fear and loneliness when she finds something — Outa.

Outa's part — the equivalent of an improvised Cadenza . . . to be completed one day when this society (and our theatre) is decent and black, white and coloured actors can work together.

The Group last night — discussion of an idea they have for an improvised one-act play: 'The Last Bus'. Four characters: Nightwatchman, old woman, two Ciras with a pushcart. (Cira = African trying to pass for the lowest of skollie-type coloured.) Explored what set the Cira apart from a poor African — what it was that exempted him from police interference, would let him into a coloured bar, etc. A few physical details (the coloured cap, worn at an angle, rather than a hat) — but most important of all, Johnnie and Winston tried to indicate a psychology, an attitude, the 'Ja, my baas' of the lowest coloured as opposed to the 'I am a man' dignity.

181

Marvellous lesson last night from the Group — first reading of the rough draft of 'The Last Bus'. Very exciting realisation of the two Ciras — in dialogue and detail. Language a bold, virile mixture of Afrikaans, English and Xhosa. The specifics of their situation — a little handcart, two bottles of 'Ship's Sherry' etc. Vivid and real.

April

In this morning's paper, photograph and story of the demolition of a squatters' camp at Missionvale. The picture — shacks demolished, a pile of twisted corrugated-iron, packing-case wood etc. etc. and the people standing 'staring at the pieces'.

Yesterday Daan came to me (he was working in the garden): 'Baas, kan ek net 'n stukkie brood kry?'[1] For a moment I thought he wanted it for himself, that he was hungry, then he explained that he had found a monkey in the bush where he was dumping weeds from the garden. That it looked thin and sick. I cut a slice of bread and Daan and I went over. The monkey was still there. A weird and moving (terrible) moment when Daan fed it, the monkey taking the bread from his hands almost in a caricature of Daan accepting (both hands — traditional way of expressing gratitude) something from a white man.

Tonight, Katie Grootboom — another disturbing presentiment of Lena: knife-wound in her head. Her husband, Willem Blau, is living in the bush with another woman. Katie went to him to try and get back the two-year-old child (hers and his) that he had virtually abducted. She came to us to ask for a lift to Fairview where her mother lived, looking after her two other children. 'Baas kan kyk,' showing me her knife wounds, 'Ek het nie eers 'n broek of 'n onderrok.'[2]

Cried a lot in the car.

The mother's going blind. Endless rambling stories about Baas so-and-so, two years there, one year there, etc. Aged about thirty.

A final, unrelieved Hell.

(And Daan had asked me to buy him 'Vicks' for a bad knife wound on his face. Assaulted by Salisbury Park skollies as he left the butcher shop on Saturday with his meat. 'Hotnots, baas. Miskien het hulle gedink dit [his parcel] was bier.'[3])

If only Yvonne could see, and love, Katie Grootboom. Her children — another variation, youth and innocence, on the theme of Hell.

In a small (not yet obsessive) way, Katie had the Ancient Mariner touch ... Lena ... Look — a story — three months in hospital —

182

God is good — Baas Steenkamp — Baas this and that . . . on and on. Increasing familiarity — nudging me, showing me her scars. Then another story . . . on and on.

December
I strive quite consciously and deliberately for ambiguity of expression because it is superior to singleness of meaning and reflects the nature of life. My whole temperament inclines me to be very unequivocal indeed. That is not difficult — but it would be at the cost of truth.

1970

May

John Berry with us three days last week to discuss *Boesman and Lena* — his Off-Broadway production goes into rehearsals today. Fascinating to see him once again analyse a script in depth. Ruthless unrelenting search for the truth in and behind the word. Particularly the latter. Realise now vividly, as I in fact once noted while writing the play, that more than ever before my 'statement' — the 'action' of the piece — is in the sub-text.

These ideas: *Robben Island* — six actors in space and silence. A rigid, crowded square when the warder is present; an explosion into inner space (implosion: a flower of violence, event or action, moving inward) when he leaves and they are alone. N. and the farewell party. The whole story — but disguised? It would be impossible to get the specifics onto a stage at this point.[1] No, not disguised, simply *unspecified*.

Notes for Advocate Strickland[2] — Marlene, just discharged from Fort England mental hospital, and the asthmatic boy in the Grahamstown hotel. Strickland arrives.

Man Without Scenery — Fairview.

Piet at Algoa Park — the 'informer'. His wife. His friend.

Three statements after an arrest under the Immorality Act.

The white woman — librarian. The coloured man — teacher. The police sergeant. A constable at the typewriter.

Police station. Late at night. Flash camera on table. Right at end, another policeman comes on with photographs. Sergeant studies them wordlessly, then puts them in a file with the three statements.

Total darkness — then the sudden, and repeated, flash of a camera . . . woman in her nightie, man with just his trousers on. Several positions.

June

Whole of Serpent Players session devoted to discussing informers (impimpi). Impossible to believe, but the Group suddenly find X. very suspect. Evidence from New Brighton suggests he is closely involved with Special Branch. Even seems his sudden reappearance about five weeks ago, and non-appearance the past two Monday nights, has got something to do with latest refusal by authorities to return my passport. All the talk about informers brought Piet very vividly to mind. Certain there is still a play in himself and Gladys in their Algoa Park home.

Boesman and Lena for Durban[3] — on stage all that the actors will need — props, the material for the pondok, clothing — dress for Lena, hat and old jacket for Boesman, balaclava and old overcoat for Outa. No curtains — black surround.

When the audience is in, without dimming house lights, actors come on — barefoot, rehearsal clothes — and in front of audience put on their 'character' clothes. Outa takes a box and sits at the back of stage, his back to audience. Boesman and Lena load up their bundles and walk — suggestion of the 'dwaal' (confused wandering) in the back streets after the demolition — round and round the stage. Lena falls behind.

Eventually Boesman arrives at mudflats. Lena follows a few seconds later.

At what point stage lights? House lights? When Lena sees Outa for the first time, the actor must turn to face audience. Lena calls him — he stands and walks into the action. Lena and Boesman never leave the stage. Houselights up just before final exit. Outa? His death?[4]

'Seal Island' — *The Island:* First image — the eight prisoners thrown violently into their 'space', protecting themselves futilely, marked by violence 'outside'. Barefoot, bloodied noses, prison uniforms dishevelled; a groaning, self-pitying heap of humanity. Then the chain of sympathy. Then the weather forecast and news bulletin.

Elements: 1. Norman — his release. The farewell party. The speech from the young boy. 'You will forget.' 2. Bioscope (in the cell) and Concert (for the warders). 3. Solitary (a fly in the cell). 4. Work. (Meaningless activity. Emptying the sea into a hole. Five men trying to push over a tree.) 5. Let's all hang ourselves.

A chance to examine the myths, clichés, lies — the reality of this society, this time.

There is nothing sacred left! Beware! (Wild laughter.)

One of the prisoners after a macabre alienation from some sacred myth: 'What do we take seriously?'

Open with a man in a suit, alone on stage. After his release: 'I'll tell you.'

185

Last image . . .? Some lunatic, pointless movement (repetitive) of the remaining group of prisoners around the stage. Intermittent despairing cries, noises as they circle endlessly.

Counterpoint between the energy and violence of their movement (the warders are chasing them) and the despair in their souls.

Two uses to the 'space' — the four-sided reality, the cell, and the 'inner' space. Thus moments (wild and frenzied) when somebody or all, can't escape the former and find the latter.

Space, silence, and the eight actors in an ugly costume.

Actresses for some of the 'men'. Never revealed, only suspected, never explained.

Eight blankets — cloaks, held end-to-end a curtain, a roof. Ground plan defining space. Also walls for 'solitary'.

For the Group. We have reached an impasse, a reality which has only got the two-dimensions of an 'idea', of the intellect. The reality of a truly living moment in theatre (actors in front of an audience) must involve the *whole* actor, be a whole act in order to involve them wholly. Not just what we think, also what we feel — and the latter involving a confrontation with self, happens on the basis of memories, associations, fears, sins, hopes. Thus Zwelinzima (in *Friday's Bread on Monday*) has too many words now, and more important still, *only* words.

Possibly landed ourselves in this cul-de-sac because we fell back on an old formula — *The Coat*. We played safe, or lazy, didn't ask enough questions. It worked then because it was fresh and gave us our chance and method to explore. Now it is stale — our efforts lack magic, lack real searching. Our solutions are trite little exercises of the mind. Zwelinzima deserves a method of his own.

We have been illustrating an idea — not creating a new, uniquely theatrical reality. Actors are looking for words, rather than actions. Let's try to throw some of the words away.

Exercises: anger. Hunger. A long walk. Resignation. Helplessness.

Addressing the audience — arrogance? Pride. How, sincerely, do we want to 'talk' to them.

'Three Statements' — the apprehension of the man and woman; fear, shame, hiding, guilt . . . an embarrassing image of vulgarity and stupidity. Movement and sound — noise rather than words. Then the words — cold, remote — statement from the three actors, individually. The sound of a typewriter — the bell as the carriage is pushed back.

Sound 'score' for two noises — typewriter and its bell, and human voices protesting, jabbering, crying, talking gibberish.

'Our father' — the sound of a typewriter typing the Lord's Prayer.

Sometimes seems that the real purpose of this notebook is to give me a chance to make as many mistakes as possible before the real commitment to blank paper.

The De Aar immorality case — outsiders. Violation of a social taboo: incest, homosexuality, adultery. Impossible (absurd), because doomed, love. The essence of love = absurdity. Possession and loss.

The reason I have not been able to complete the Fairview play, or commit myself to the Piet (Algoa Park) idea, is that, as conceived so far, the characters are too 'helplessly innocent', too passively victimised by the situations I've created. No 'action' as, for example, in *Boesman and Lena* who, even though 'victimised' (Milly too — and all the others) manage a hell of a lot of 'doing'. No possibility of ambivalence in audience reaction to Fairview characters; compare this with the challenge, the demand made by Boesman (Hester, Morrie) when the total anatomy of the man's experience of Life is revealed.

This occurred to me when I remembered a newspaper report of a man (white) charged under the Immorality Act. The coloured woman he had been living with was unable to give evidence because she was mentally retarded.

Stated baldly like that, the relationship suddenly has a potential density and darkness completely lacking in the Fairview relationship. Darkness is not just a reality of life as we experience it, but an essential halo to the truly poetic image — a final region of paradox and an enigma of truths which defy statement (words) and can only be intuitively apprehended.

August

The Oresteian Trilogy as one of the projects for next year. Two questions: Clytemnestra? What is Justice?

Madness.

Clytemnestra and Orestes. Mother and son.

'. . . its full development from the first sin of the ancestor to the final release of Orestes from the load of guilt.'

September

Oresteian Trilogy — John Harris — the bomb in the railway station in Johannesburg. A cell? Madness?

A modern Oresteian Electra — an ancient Clytemnestra. How to live now?[5]

Orestes[6]

Sources: from Greek mythology — Aeschylus for Clytemnestra: Euripides for Orestes and Electra.

From our history, the image of John Harris and his suitcase.

From R.D. Laing (particularly *Politics of Experience* and *Bird of Paradise*) our compass bearings in terms of our exploration of 'inner space'. His influence reflected in our vocabulary = devastation; alienation (of experience from behaviour). His sense of desperate urgency. 'The bomb has fallen, we are only waiting for the sound to reach us.'

From self.

Very early on a sense that Harris stood in relation to his society as Orestes did to Clytemnestra. An intolerable burden of guilt for the crimes committed — the act of violence an attempt to escape the burden of guilt.

Actors: Yvonne = Aeschylus' Clytemnestra, and her *Iris* (news item in Jhb. paper: inquest into the death of one Pentz, stabbed to death by persons unknown . . . evidence of Rex, pedlar of shoelaces and razor blades . . . no fixed abode . . . Pentz and his stormy relationship with Iris. Pentz went to Palaborwa, returned after six months with a bankroll. Took up again with Iris — one night he was found stabbed to death. Iris not seen again.)

Val — Electra/Joan ('Patients' response to intensive psychotherapy' in American Journal of Psychiatry).

Wilson — Orestes/Harris (newspaper reports of Harris trial).

And for all the actors: Laing, Grotowski.

First real 'move' came out of talking to Y. We were discussing Grotowski's idea in *Towards a Poor Theatre* of the actor/spectator relationship in space being special and unique for each of his productions. We already had a station concourse bench in our imaginations and a devastated woman who was going to end up on it and be destroyed by the explosion from a large brown suitcase left beside the bench. Suddenly we stumbled on an image which energised our work virtually from that moment on until the last performance in Johannesburg. We saw our spectators seated (reduced first to a collection of strangers by making people sit next to strangers) on brown station benches (*Whites Only*) — one bench was to be unoccupied and reserved for the 'finalbeat'. The three actors were to be seated as the audience arrives. Slowly, hesitantly, barely audibly at first, Y. was to start talking as Iris — building up eventually to a long unbroken monologue compounded of the clichés, lies, hypocrisies, of our society (Clytemnestra as reflected in the cracked, tormented mirror

188

of our twentieth century awareness of self); the woman's (Iris) personal devastation — memories, regrets, half-recalled moment of horror (the killing of Pentz) — broken lyricism, terrible torrents of abuse, occasionally a splendid rage. While talking, rambling, she was to drift between the spectators, sitting down occasionally, but hardly noticing anybody or anything around her.

Simultaneously, there would be a series of small but calculated moves from the other two — Wilson and Val — particularly on Wilson's side, haunting the scene of his planned 'pivotal' act, rehearsing it, choosing his bench. We thought of the audience as initially almost bewildered, lost, in this seemingly haphazard series of actions and sounds, taking a bit from Iris — until the young man intruded, then going with Iris again — until the young woman was at your side, doing something and commanding your attention. Gradually a pattern was to emerge out of all this, a pattern made of a threatening sense of violence, there was to be a sense of terrible even if accidental convergence on the empty bench where the act of violence was eventually going to take place. Among many things, we wanted in this way to say to our audience of white South Africans: 'You could have been the person beside whom a young man left a large brown suitcase.'

Parallel with our exploration of the image detailed above, Y. and I embarked on a long dialogue as to why she as actress and myself as writer and director were turning our backs on the securities and orthodoxies of our past work. (*Boesman and Lena* in Durban excluded — for both of us a sense that that is really where we started to think about, and stumbled on, new directions.) There was also the provocation of Marshal McLuhan who, in talking about old and new media, helped me define exactly what my problems were in relation to the 'well-structured' 'plays on paper' of my past:

— to communicate what can't be expressed.
— an 'Existential' theatre in the sense that we confronted the Nothingness of space and silence with our Being.
— to take the desperation out of Silence, learn to live with it, let it happen if it must, and think of it as something real and positive — not 'nothing' or negative.

The issue on my side was simply this: Did the sort of play I had been writing with its central dependence on logical and chronological sequence (mechanical linkage) give me a chance of communicating my sense of self and the world as experienced by that self. Was I experiencing the world in the fashion and logic of an alphabet (A followed by B followed by C followed by D . . . followed by Z full stop) or was I experiencing self and the world rather like somebody spinning the dial on the short-wave band of a transistorised radio — the opposition in essence that = mechanical linkage or transistorised (instant) contact. Not just a question of efficiency either but of a new 'mode', a new 'way' of getting information across to someone else.

(In all this constantly haunted by — and at the same time frightened of — realisation that the time had come to 'turn a corner'; that if I didn't do it now, I would never do it.)

Y. and I talked endlessly around, into and out of this subject — both obviously recognising in the other's responses something long felt but only half-believed in the self — this confirmation that neither of us was alone in producing the courage we needed for our first tentative excursions into 'possibilities'.

In the first instance we looked at ourselves (me at Athol, she at Yvonne) and tried to find out, to discover or feel, if there were in fact regions of our experience of ourselves that had not been articulated or given a chance to communicate themselves in the work we had done in the past. We both felt that there were things to say, and ways of saying them that we had not yet encountered.

Our parallel exploration of Laing led Y. to her — or one of her — first statements. 'The shrinking of self' = inner space and her sense that if she was not careful she could travel so far into it ('sink into it' is possibly more accurate in terms of the 'colour' of her emotions which had no 'adventures' but rather seemed a premonition of loss of contact, of death finally) that she would not be able to come out. I must be specific here since this recognition and what she did with it relates so finally to the shape and content of her Iris, who was I suppose Y.'s projection of her own possible devastation (based on this experience of herself as in danger of losing all contact with another).

190

1971

June

London:[1] Progressively more uneasy about a naturalistic or 'documentary' production of *Boesman and Lena* in the Theatre Upstairs. Problem — from the metaphor of the 'rubbish' to arrive at the geographical specifics of the play — *mud flats?* Also to make the opening metaphor (rubbish) efficient and functional — to build into it some of the content of the play.

From Bloke Modisane, who is playing Outa: 'Speciality of the poor is they have no privacy.'

To the actors I said: 'Boesman and Lena have seen how they are going to die . . . they are going to die among the dustbins. Will there be a witness?' And: 'Boesman expresses himself in doing. Lena gives consciousness to his actions. Enough.'

First day of rehearsals.

Two hours in the morning picking my way through a colossal pile of rubbish in Camden Town near the Roundhouse. Staggered by what London was discarding, and the quantity of it.

Three hours of work in our small space 12' x 18'. Two realisations, the first — via Y. — a real sense that the 'space' is right, that having our audience around us on *four* sides is what we must take on here. In the space, a pile of authentic London rubbish — the three actors come to it, pick their way through it, find what they need, put it on, load it up. Boesman and Lena — the stupid walk round and round, 'Looking for a way out of your life.'

The second realisation — that the rubbish informs them, possesses them to the extent that they need nothing else, neither make-up nor total costumes — just themselves and the pieces of rubbish they choose to encumber themselves with.

Y. does not yet relate to Zakes as Boesman and vice versa. Both are playing to the performances of another actor — Y. to me and Zakes, to Ruby Dee.

November

Ahmed Timol — his suicide from the 10th floor of police headquarters in Johannesburg.

As reported in the Inquest into his death:

    Mrs Timol: When can I see my son again?

    Police: You won't see your son again.

    Mrs T.: Why won't I see my son again?

    Police: He needs a hiding.

    Mrs T.: I've never hurt my son so you must not hit him.

    Police: Because you didn't hit him, we will hit him.

He was thirty years old, school teacher, been to Mecca. He jumped at 4 p.m. on Wednesday, October 27.

S'kop. In talking to Brian Astbury[2] at the weekend, I told him about my ideas and central images for *The Island* and then, as an after-thought, resurrected my ideas for *Statements after an arrest under the Immorality Act*.

Yet again a vivid sense of the validity of the former and, surprisingly, also the latter. Why do I hesitate? Arrived back last night determined to start working on them. I feel the same way this morning. Feel urged to put a file down on this table marked *Play* and to get on with it. Would like to start with three statements and see what happens: The Policeman. The Man (teacher). The Woman (librarian).

Loneliness and guilt — both for the woman as a white and for both of them in the tabooed relationship. The Karroo — summer heat and light. The woman about forty, the man younger.

Two policemen enter, one sits down at a desk with typewriter and types as the other talks. First statement. The teacher is brought in — second statement. Teacher taken out, woman brought in — third statement. Man brought back — both charged. Taken to cells to await appearance before Magistrate in the morning.

Photographs.

Simple device of the typewriter stopping and the two policemen freezing when the teacher and librarian move into interior monologues.

Guilts on the woman's side develop a vein of cruelty in her relationship with the man.

His name — Errol. Writes poetry, interior monologues:

    'If black is beautiful

    and being beautiful white is ugly,

    What is brown

    I do not know what I am.'

'Brown is for butcher's paper
I am wrapped up,
wrapped up in myself.'

'Last night she lay with me again.'

'Why can I not speak except like
this,
say what I feel except like
this,
on white, white paper
to myself.'

The woman's crushing and final realisation at the end of what has happened — that it is over, finished . . . that the love, with its heaven and hell, is irretrievably lost.

A small Karroo town.

The barking of dogs in the location.

Both of them know the relationship is doomed — out of this their desperation, his pessimism, her cruelty.

Having apprehended them the policeman would reveal his intention to arrest them for a contravention of the Act. He would then ask them if they wish to make a statement, warning them at the same time that anything said would be taken down in writing and could be used as evidence against them. Then they would be taken to the police station where technically the arrest takes place with the entering of names etc. (Age, Sex, Race) and charge in the Charge Book, and the opening of a docket (brown). Then either into cells to await first appearance before a magistrate the next day (bail) or if there is somebody at the police station with the necessary authority, to be released on bail there and then. The policeman would then in his own time most probably get down a statement of the circumstances leading up to the arrest and a description of what he found when he apprehended the accused. In the event of either making an admission of guilt they would be asked to repeat the statement before a magistrate, and this would be arranged immediately.

Three Statements. The man sitting, waiting. Table and second chair. Library? Room in her house? Woman enters with a pile of books. Late afternoon of a hot and long Karroo day. A scene between them from this moment, through the fading light, into darkness and their

193

final communion; a scene revealing their respective loneliness, guilt, pessimism, cruelty, love ... the climax being both *their* climax and the arrival of the police.

They talk more as adulterers — no blatant reference to Immorality Act.

After 'apprehension' brief scene between them and the policemen.

Finally the policeman making his statement to a typewriter.

In a sense another version of Boesman's predicament: the constant emasculation of Manhood by the South African 'way of life' — guilt, prejudice and fear, all conspiring together finally to undermine the ability to love directly and forthrightly.

Yes! The man's predicament then not just the personal torment and guilt of the adulterer — the ultimate question is again articulated. What am I? It is not his heart and divided love that create his dilemma — but a system, a society.

The penalty is not just the loss of what he loves — but the negation of manhood. Therefore be very careful of the too easy and false parallel with adultery.

Also — is it not just too easy (for myself and audience) having as man and woman two sensitive, sympathetic characters and genuine love and need? What about a truly squalid relationship — the five rand fuck and a bottle of brandy in the back seat of a motor car parked in the bush along the Marine Drive.

Try to develop this line simultaneously.

At some point or the other in trying to start a new play always a moment of doubt, a loss of energy and the questions: Is this really not just the old theme in a different guise. The destructive habit of testing a new idea by comparison with an old one — worse still, the bones of a new one with the fleshed-out reality of one that went past being just an idea or an image. Try to create only one context for work — the present and its personal potential.

The point at which an image, or complex of images, ceases to be a 'personal fiction' and acquires a life of its own, a truth bigger than self. An unmistakable development, recognisable among other things for the new 'perspective' it gives to the 'self' that was living with them. A 'way' of seeing and responding to the world around me. Almost like a set of blinkers that focus my awareness on what relates directly to them, to the moments and incidents where they touch and correspond to the life around me. This experience still so vivid in my writing of *Boesman and Lena* where their Truth becomes bigger than self — where I moved from 'artifice' to 'witnessing' — with all the compulsion, urgency, moral imperative of that role.

What I am waiting for at the moment. My images still 'personal fictions'.

The 'life of their own' — a centre of pain, so that I 'feel' as well as 'think'.

Yet again from Camus's *Carnets* the story of Dimetos.

1972

May

Back at S'kop from doing *Statements* at the Space in Cape Town.

At many levels, possibly unavoidably because of circumstances, the most uncompleted, even careless, work I have yet done on a stage. Absolutely no doubt now that what I staged was *Notes for a Play*. The chance now, and the determination, to write the play.

An inviolate world — nothing strange could happen — and then it does. The textures of the two souls; yet again the seeming impossibility of finding each other, but they do. Loneliness.

The shape and texture of their consciousness, their sense of self.

Errol — his classroom, his people walking, himself walking, the notices BLANKES and NIE-BLANKES[1] — inner silence, the sounds he hears at night lying awake in bed.

Frieda — the sounds she hears lying awake in bed, her face in the mirror. Inner silence, other people seeing her, seeing them seeing her and so seeing herself, the sound of her voice.

For both — Fear.

As someone said on the last night in Cape Town, the play is a love story, the story of an impossible love. The policemen are just the external (as his wife and child might have been if Errol had been white) that makes the love impossible. This suggests to begin with two serious flaws in the production and text — the placing of equal emphasis on the policemen with their typewriter, and the relationship between the man and woman. Reduce the typewriter to the meaningless and stupid detail it is in *their* story. I did have a sense of this in saying repeatedly to Y. — I want *their* story to contain the policeman's statement, rather than have the *policeman's* statement contain their story. The second flaw — not as easy to define, but again a question of emphasis — of their fear and apology and explanation to the audience being equal, if not even greater, than their relationship to each other.

Their story needs an explanation and statement in depth and detail on a par with Boesman and Lena.

B & L = the hell of being together, of 'No escape'.

Frieda and Errol = the hell of not being together, of not being able to have the other.

196

The encounter between two totally different worlds — both experienced as a 'loneliness' — and the slow painful building of a 'no-man's land' where they are briefly together.

What moved Philander from the centre of his life, where he was living with a hollow sense of self, to its perimeter — because that is how as a lover, he finally faces Frieda, his back turned on all he really is, and why it cannot work (the relationship), why it progresses into a self-destructive sterility.

Frieda's sexual provocation (not by nature of anything done deliberately, simply by being what she is) as the relationship develops. The initial affirmation of 'self' in an affair.

Fear of strangers. Devious walks, walks cut short, walks not taken at all because of the possible encounter with a stranger — more specifically self (alone) and strangers.

The walk along the beach to Bushy Park the day before yesterday. Innocence and peace, a rambling interior monologue, imaginary conversations as I walked along the sand. Relief and liberation with the sense of being completely alone. I had even decided against taking Shauva. Rounding a corner I suddenly saw the first houses of Bushy Park and suddenly it was there again — unease, self-consciousness, the thought of a route that would skirt the possible encounter with a stranger as much as possible. Then, becoming conscious of all this, realising that if I'd had Lisa or Sheila or a friend with me, I would have felt secure and safe; would have walked boldly past the houses and the possible encounter with strangers.

Strangers 'demand' — never freely and easily 'myself' with them. Maybe not myself at all — the strain of being something they will like and leave alone, or of being 'Nothing', as nameless and faceless as possible.

Thus also my apparently incurable inability to say 'No'.

Inability to live quietly, (to be still) with the passage of time. The challenge I set myself yesterday to wait until the sun was on the horizon before I took my next cast (fishing for elf). Sun was already low — I only needed to wait about 10 minutes — but suddenly an acute spasm of desperation at the prospect of sitting and doing nothing. (I had deliberately left my pipe at home.) Once I realised this and faced up to the challenge of just squatting on a rock and watching the water while the time passed, it became a bit easier, then very easy and then finally even the beginning of a small hope.

The fear also of saying 'No', of choosing, because it involves losing. So instead of summoning up the courage needed for that act, balancing precariously on the tightrope between one possibility and the other, reducing life to a desperate eternity of inaction, courting the ultimate stupidity of 'falling' and so losing everything.

Errol Philander.

June

Starting about three months ago, the appearance of my father in my dreams. Last night again — long and sustained encounter with him. These encounters, giving as they do life to a relationship and centre of experience which I had long thought dead and finished, suggest Jung's 'eruption of the unconscious into the conscious' more tellingly than any of my other dream experiences.

My own judgment of my father — a gentle but *weak* man.

A sudden and clear realisation at this table of how, almost exclusively, 'woman' — a woman — has been the vehicle for what I have tried to say about survival and defiance — Milly, Hester, Lena . . . and even Frieda in a way; that, correspondingly, the man has played at best a passive, most times impotent, male. Image occurred to me of the large female spider and shrivelled, almost useless, male — there only for his sexual function. Thus Johnnie, Don, Boesman, Errol — all unable to 'act' significantly — the image of the castrated male culminating of course in Errol Philander's nightmare in *Statements*.

To go yet again into the equation Life = Loss = Death dangerously close now to a sterile, self-indulgent and false pessimism — 'false' because for a long time now I have been so close to realising a larger statement: Life = Death = Life = Death = Life . . . to infinity . . . but all of that in 'Brackets' because it is only one factor in a still larger equation and that I don't doubt contained by a still larger . . . and this in turn becomes an infinite and useless sequence until — what? The unnameable. The void.

Jung's *Memories, Dreams and Reflections* sustaining me a lot at the moment.

My living and writing still based on a vision which no longer expresses my sense of self, of 'being-in-the-world'. What could be more exciting than to have to start again . . . to have the chance, the need to start again?

July

Pursuing my problems with 'externals' — the police and Mrs Buys

198

who lives next-door to the library. I must incorporate in *Statements* the image of the two cobras that Emily saw copulating in the sunlight on the club grounds. Emily, Mrs Kelly, Daan, Mrs Harrison descending on them with spades and rakes — the two snakes too busy with each other to realise anything until it was too late. The splendour and magnificence of their love-making — and a few seconds later their smashed and writhing bodies. Those few seconds — the experience between the first photograph and the last. Six seconds in which men destroy something only God could make.

Errol: They can't interfere with God anymore.

Sacrilege and blasphemy.

The Immorality Act — at one level this country's unique contribution to the world of pornography.

A guilt-ridden inversion of the celebration of the erect penis and moist vagina.

In the secrecy of darkness, with one of the forbidden and therefore coveted women, the man has discovered his penis, fostered its erection, had intercourse and so affirmed himself in defiance of the white father-figure. But the latter discovers him and punishes him with castration.

Substitute symbols and activities — guns, police batons, sport, 'boys' and 'baas'.

The white man in Grahamstown who went mad and intended castrating himself and putting his testicles in a box addressed to the Prime Minister.

Sex provides the most primitive experience of 'self' — the double mystery/aspect of discovery and loss, both of 'self' and 'the other'.

August

I am now very near abandoning *Statements* as a flawed work which I will never get right. Shall put it aside for at least a month and if at the end of that time I still feel about it the way I do now, that will be the end of it.

How *do* I feel about it at this point? Totally confused — the literary acrobatics of the past few months have left me so giddy I can't even see clearly the little merit which I am sure it has. I just know that at the moment I have no faith at all in what is there already on paper — which is still what I brought back with me from Cape Town — and no faith at all in my ability to do anything about it. Then opposed to this is the undeniable fact that a lot of people — Sheila, Barney, Don, Ann O. and audiences — found the experience meaningful and powerful.

199

I came back from Cape Town convinced that what we had ended up with on the stage, and on paper, was 'notes' for a play and that all I needed was privacy and time to now 'write' the play. It is possible that I am fooling myself, but that is exactly what I have been trying very seriously to do for the past three months, without any success.

My first impulse was to examine the questions of form and structure – this ended with me being convinced that the two policemen as an 'actual' stage device were redundant if not actually confusing. The police statement was reduced to a programme note, or at the most, to a recording that the audience could sit and listen to if they wished, at the end of the play which was now going to concern only Errol and Frieda. This conviction that the policemen were not needed has remained fairly constant . . . though starting about a week ago I found myself exploring ideas which started to involve them again.

So . . . Errol and Frieda. Trying to focus just on them I started to live with what I've always regarded as the central image in their story – those six terrible photographs of Joubert and Philander scrambling around in the dark; twenty seconds of Hell which start with them together and end with them irrevocably apart; the twenty seconds that it takes to pass from an experience of life to an intimation of death. These photographs were, and remain for me, the essence of the experience I wanted to explore.

I have simply not been able to break the ice and drown in depth – I have not been able to escape sociology and sentiment, and live inside the terror and panic of those six instants – caught and frozen for all time by the camera.

My attempts to do so have ranged from a straight development of what we did in Cape Town to 'Orestes'-type experiments. At one stage I thought the answer lay in laughing at what was false in my thinking – my sociology – and going with what was 'real' – my responses to the photographs – and asking the audience to share both experiences. So I had Y. and myself presenting a 'slide show' – sending up my useless thinking about the Karroo, and being coloured, and being a frustrated spinster, but then suddenly coming to terms— now *personal* terms, with those six moments of horror. Every attempt has suffered the same fate . . . the only variation has been the time it took to die. At times my enthusiasm for the new 'idea' has lasted for a couple of days; at others it has withered and died within the hour.

Let me try to help my thinking along by listing, not in any order of priority, the sort of obstacle into which all these attempts have crashed and been ruined.

200

Reality and unreality. If it's a nightmare, who is dreaming it? Whose 'point of view' shapes the experience? How relate to each other two totally subjective experiences of self?

Themes — survival — Philander in the location, Frieda in her room — castration — loss of the other as an intimation of death; sex as an affirmation of self. Never felt that I ever satisfactorily fused these so that instead of separate ideas, they were facets of the one whole. As I tried to explain my problem to Y.: 'With Boesman and Lena a sharp focus on the specifics (Lena's bruises, the piece of bread, Outa, the dog, the bulldozer) did not stop me from making my statement about Man-Woman: in fact the specifics were my vocabulary and as simple and primitive as it was, I was nevertheless able to say my thing — all the more powerfully I suppose because my vocabulary was that simple and uncluttered.'

To what extent was I writing only for an occasion and to a deadline: the opening of The Space. Was I truly witnessing?

Paulus Olifant — the snake catcher. Jodphurs. His walk. Sack for the snakes and a forked stick.

September

After several weeks of doubts, I have committed myself to a total involvement with Winston and Johnny in their first 'professional' venture. First feeling was that the best way to launch the undertaking was to find an already written play suitable for the two of them — either a two-hander or something that could be adapted. While trying to find this I also outlined for them an idea which I felt could be developed along the lines of *The Coat* or *Friday's Bread on Monday,* but soon realised if something meaningful was to come out of working with them it was only going to happen if I turned the idea into a mandate and worked along the lines of *Orestes.* One rehearsal in this context behind us and no reason to think I'm mad to try to work like this with them, in the limited time at our disposal — around five weeks to a date at The Space, October 8.

Spent half the first rehearsal outlining, explaining and justifying the method. Told them something about Orestes — the holy actor as opposed to the courtesan actor — truth versus pretence — the 'poor' theatre as opposed to the 'rich' theatre, etc. They understood and responded with serious excitement to my rather jumbled exposition. Then applied ourselves to the 'idea'.

The image I presented to Johnny and Winston was three or four tables and chairs representing the lounge of a local hotel, crowded

201

with a type of arrogant and self-satisfied white student being served by two black waiters. Time — Saturday night; structure — the two of them, waiters, in the lounge before the arrival of the first customer, then the crescendo of activity and tensions to the climax of ' last orders please'; and finally, the two of them alone again, as they tidy up and come to terms with another day in their lives.

Stripped away externals — red-nosed characterisation, effects (hundreds of bottles and glasses), orders — in an effort to find our basic challenge. Decided that this consisted of one table, one chair and their relationship to it as 'the servant'. Obviously the table and chair (empty) is a symbol of whiteness; they are black. A white master symbol — black servant relationship.

First exploration: prepare and place the table and chair, and then wait. Just wait. Winston placed the table and chair, and waited. Johnny took over, and waited. Winston took over and waited. Johnny took over and waited — finally Johnny replaced the table and chair.

Then analysed sub-text experiences. Gratifyingly rich. Their individual relationships to the table and chair — subordinate, resentful, dependent.

The questions provoked in Johnny by this waiting — who am I? Where am I? Who is where? The mask and the face behind the mask. The ontological dilemma arising out of 'role' playing.[2]

October
Dimetos: a man back from a walk along the beach. Empties his pockets onto a small table — seed-pods and sea-shells washed up by the sea. A fragment of sand-rubbed blue glass.

The rotting carcase of a seal among the rocks.

The weed growing from a crack in the urinal of the boys' lavatory of the Moslem Institute. A Group Areas ruling had closed down the school so Johnny, Winston and I were able to rent a classroom to rehearse *Sizwe Banzi is Dead.* Appalling and depressing contrast with the building of five years ago when we rehearsed *Antigone* there in the Sub A classroom. This time we worked in the Standard 5 room. Then it had been well-kept and clean and bustling with activity. This time we encountered total dereliction — classroom floors strewn with abandoned textbooks, maps etc., the last lessons fading away on blackboards, windows and doors smashed, and on everything a thick layer of the ugly grey-blue dust of Korsten.

The first day of rehearsals we used the boys' lavatory. Then one

202

day the wind slammed the door closed. We couldn't open it, so started using the girls' lavatory. On about the last day of our rehearsal period I found the door of the boys' lavatory open again and went inside to pee. In the period it had been closed the seed of a common garden weed had lodged in a crack in the urinal, germinated and grown into a healthy young plant.

1973

January
Dawn on the mudflats after night filming *Boesman and Lena,* then
the drive past New Brighton beach along the freeway and back to
S'kop as the sun rose; the bay calm with ships at anchor. Moments of
real serenity. Similarly a few sunsets and early evenings as we packed
up after a day's filming. I was glad when we finally gave the mudflats,
and the Island in particular, back to itself. We never related to it other
than as an occupation force. The same at Missionvale.

The Island — a shrinking, dying world, with each spring-tide a few
more inches of the bank crumbling away. Its men, women and children, the young man I got talking to and who said, 'Ons geslag is
verkeerd.'[1]
    An oasis of privacy and safety — the only trouble that could ford
the spruit at high water, or struggle through the mud at lowtide, is
what they carry with them. But dying. A spirit of bitter and brooding resentment when the bottle of Golden Mustang or sherry is
half-way down. The outside world is not as far away as it used to be
— Mr Ackerman, the Nature Conservation Officer, has a boat; the
men who come there over weekends to fish are not allowed to dig for
prawn any more — spades and tackle are confiscated; the African
ranger on Ackerman's staff goes out on patrol with a pair of
binoculars.
    The connection between the slow death of the Island, the bull-
dozers and evictions at South End, Korsten, Salisbury Park, Missionvale, and the new housing schemes such as Salt Lake, on the other
side of the saltpan behind Missionvale. Five men were certified insane
last week in places like Salt Lake. In each case, after a period of ab-
normal behaviour — hearing voices, etc. — the men had erupted into
violence then been tied down to a chair or locked in an empty room
until the police came and took them away to the cells. Then an examination by two doctors and certification.
    And, always, for all of them, the dream of a big fish.
    Mr Ackerman, his uniform, binoculars and patrol boat, as totally
corrosive of that place and its meaning as the tides eating it away.
    A walk from Salt Lake to the Island in the lurid light of a sky fill-

ed with smoke from veldfires. Past the graveyard at Veeplaas. Past the saltpans with their 'ripening' red water. Salt Lake itself — the water seen as sweat.

The Island — 'This is our place, hey.' 'Ja . . . this is our place.'

The camaraderie of nameless strangers made brothers by a common fate. Yet again . . . a camaraderie of the damned. 'Ons geslag is verkeerd.'

Lena's song:

> Daar's 'n klokkie wat die waarheid vertel,[2]
> That Lena goes to heaven, and Boesman goes to hel.
> Daar's 'n klokkie wat die waarheid vertel.
> And it's too late to change de troef ou pel.

February

A long dry and now drought-stricken summer has culminated in an outbreak of bad veldfires in the Eastern Cape. Times during our filming at Missionvale when I couldn't look in any direction without seeing a tell-tale pall of smoke on the horizon. Heat and desperation. Euphorbias wilting in the veld; thorntrees dying. Starting about ten days ago a series of fires deep in the drift-sands area between S'kop and Summerstrand. Watched safely from a distance until the day before yesterday when a gale-force South-Easter suddenly swept one right up to the village.

Near-panic. The smoke was so thick outside you could barely see your hand; inside the house was grey with ash and smoke. At the height of the pandemonium buck were running around like mad-dogs; fire-engines, teams of African beaters, people evacuating houses in a catastrophic twilight.

Five African men spent the night sleeping on the sand in front of a neighbour's house, all with pangas, ready in case the fire swept down again — ashen-grey men, cold, utterly exhausted, hungry — while we slept in our houses. A fleeing buck was chased by a group of African men, armed with spades and pangas, and these followed by a motley collection of white children trying to save the buck from hungry New Brighton stomachs.

A summer that reminded me of the story from Piet: the terrible drought when he was a young man in the Alexandria district, trying to run the family farm. He tore down the half-completed milking shed to provide for a coffin for his African friend. Piet buried him . . . 'here lies a man . . .' then walked away into the veld and cried.

Fishing again. Twice into the Reserve in the past week. Caught no-

205

thing. Yesterday afternoon's spell — all of what fishing is about to me. Simple relationship between self, rocks and the sea. Warm sun, blue sea and the rocks black and wet as the tide went out. So active as compared with the stillness, the silent rhythm of the river. Dart as far down the rocks to a safe point, there to wait, thumb and forefinger of the left hand on the line, a small lump of expectation in the throat ... a small repetitive dance between the limits of Life and Death, Yin and Yang, the active and the passive ... black rock, white sea ... known and unknown ... the fishing line, with its baited barb unreeling from one into the other.

The Ashram suddenly and unexpectedly provides us with a small lesson in the harsh realities of Boesman and Lena and Sizwe Banzi. Melton's two pondoks in the bush on the Ashram have been 'discovered' by the Divisional Council. A notice from them the day before yesterday demanding the demolition of 'said illegal structures' within fourteen days. Melton?[3] God alone knows. On to the road with his wife and two children to look for somewhere else to stay, possibly back to the drought and poverty of the Alexandria district where he appears to come from.

'Sardinia Bay is rapidly becoming a much sought-after area. We are not going to let it become a slum.' — Secretary of the Divisional Council.

On the face of it there is absolutely nothing I can do to help Melton and prevent his eviction. I thought it was 'our land'!

And Daan in the garden, drinking himself to death ... two bottles of Lieberstein just about every day.

For the moment I can't see past the appalling wreckage of human lives that our society is creating. A dumb and despairing rage at what we are doing.

'We, all of us, *are* a mistake.'

Oscar Lewis's Sanchez family. Mexico City slum = Missionvale. What we most probably lack, and fatally so, is a real prophet of doom.

The fusing of Hopelessness (metaphysical predicament) and Hope (historical predicament) ... the reality, the Truth that is both, even as a coin is both heads and tails. Maybe that is what the Robben Island idea must be about. A dialogue, encounter, opposition and then resolution between Hopelessness (life sentence) and Hope (... 'my appeal has succeeded; I've only got six months to go').

Finally: When we run to the quarry tomorrow, and they chase us and the dogs snarl ...

Second chapter in the story of Melton's eviction from the Ashram —
Setting, the lounge, into which Melton has never before been invited
('Different now because of the suffering involved'). Present also,
John and Winston, an hour or so back in P.E. after another 'full-
house' run of *Sizwe Banzi* down in Cape Town. After discussing our
business I introduce them, with much embarrassment (because I
can't speak Xhosa), to the problem of Melton. Note the phrasing
. . . my sense, personal, was of 'the problem of Melton', not 'Melton's
problem'. I explain to Johnny my, the, abysmal lack of communication between us. I need somebody to 'translate', 'talk'. Winston wat-
ches; Johnny talks; I talk; Melton listens. And, as I say . . . Melton
sitting on the sofa in a room he has never before been invited into.
Melton playing nervously with an old eye-patch in his hands. Sore
eye, I think. A few drops of Eyegene when we've finished talking.
(Complacent sense of 'helping'.) Right at the end, Melton mentions
the sore eye himself and says something about being frightened of
losing it, of going blind. When I look, I see that an evil-looking film
(cataract?) has already almost covered the pupil. So much for Eyegene.

Anyway, the conversation proceeds something like this:
Self: Let's start right at the beginning. I'm not so sure how much he
understands. I have received a notice from the . . .
Johnny: (in Xhosa) . . . Melton listens. Nods.
Self: Tell him that I tried . . .
Johnny: (in Xhosa) . . . Melton listens.
Self: Explain to him . . .
Johnny: (in Xhosa) . . . Melton listens.
Etc. etc.

Melton is younger than me. Wife and three children. He was wearing a shirt, trousers, battered shoes, no socks. When I watched him
talk and listen to Johnny a most remarkable transformation took
place in a face that I have at times hated because of my inability to
reach it, communicate with it meaningfully. I can only describe
watching Melton's face as he communicated with Johnny on the
basis of total reciprocity — let me start again: I saw the beauty of
life, of value, of a sense of self infuse something that circumstances
had trapped me into relating to as 'dead'.

All he wants to do is live his life.

We dropped him off at the Ashram and he walked away from us
in a lull in the rain which had started last night and which promises,
if it continues a little longer, to break the terrible drought we are
now experiencing.

Grey sky.

Melton's courage.

And, a second later, Lisa on the side of the road on her horse, Seaweed, radiant, stunned with happiness.

March

Robben Island: the two men arrived on the Island handcuffed together. Their friendship forged in the long trip down, standing hand-cuffed together all the time, from the Rooi Hel[4] to the Cape Town docks.

Somewhere tonight, two men — shackled together — have started that journey. They will stand for all the 500 miles, pressed close together in the over-crowded prison van. There is a bucket in the dark suffocating cabin, but there are so many of them they cannot use it; they shit and piss as they stand, together. In the first grey light of tomorrow morning they will crawl out of the van at the Cape Town docks and be herded on board a tugboat and taken to Robben Island.

Somewhere tonight the same two men confront each other, shocked over the simple fact that one has had his sentence reduced through a legal appeal, and can start to count days, while the other . . .

Somehow and somewhere tonight B. is wiping his mouth after a good drink of beer . . . and A. is running to the quarry.

Who are they?

As always — was, is and will ever be — somebody must ask the question that can't be answered.

Dream images: a naked white pilot, standing strapped to his tiller in a harness, ferrying a load of people to their death by hanging — the images as remote and 'grainy' as old photographs. The people executed were survivors of a wreck; their 'crime' was never revealed. The photograph of the hanging bodies was too 'long' a shot for any details of pain and suffering.

A large, strange tree in the middle of a forest. Enormous bole. The impossibility of explaining or knowing anything about it because '. . . its branches start where the mists begin'. Not even climbing would have helped. The inevitable was not 'ignorance', but 'acceptance'. All categories of 'knowing' were defied.

The small shark — twenty to thirty pounds — on the rocks at Cape St. Francis; lying on its back, a heavy rock on its body just below the jaws, presumably so that it would suffocate to death. I had seen the angler catch it, recognised a shark, but had thought it one of the harmless sandsharks. When the angler packed up and left that parti-

208

cular rock, I took it over and found the shark. Far from being one of the harmless variety it had a mouthful of the most terrible-looking teeth — possibly ragged-tooth. Setting sun; rough white sea; strong South-Easter. The appalling intolerance and savagery of man when he encounters anything that does not fit into 'his' scheme of things. The vanity and vicious pride that is blind to the possibility of a pattern larger than 'his' needs and convenience. Out of the shark's terrible maws the voices of Jews in gas-ovens, the condemned in death cells, the thin spiral of 'time' on Robben Island.

Nothing is as deadly as ignorance combined with fear.

My thinking about the complex of Robben Island ideas and images reached a point yesterday where it suddenly occurred to me that they require a style and a form very different from the four plays of the past ten years. Words like 'distance', 'elevation', 'objectivity' occur to me. 'Classical' in the sense of a cool detachment, is another.

A large canvas as opposed to the intimate miniature.

At a distance of ten paces the pondok I built for Boesman at Swartkops looked like nothing. The only significant relationship to it was from inside . . . the room in Valley Road; the shack at Korsten.

Rain tonight — listening to it here in the shed where I'm writing. Like a firm and sure hand on something that is troubled. A mother's hand on her son's shoulder. And the wind like the neglected sister agitating — agitating in the dark. Still by herself — even though she touches so much.

One of those nights when the sea was giving bad advice.

The earth — Protestant. Sea — Catholic. Sky — Buddhist.

Daan: his walk from, and at the end of the day, back to Walmer location. Eight kilometres each way. Not the sort of man many stop to give a lift to. The weather of that walk — wind sun rain darkness.

The gardens he looks after here in the village.

Animals — the monkey he found in the bush, paralysed from the waist down. Fed it with his own bread. Tortoises. Snakes. The dogs of S'kop.

His friends — Sophie, Anna, Emily, John, Simon, Paulus Olifant, James at the pump station. The first time I ever heard Anna laugh was because of something Daan said. He was weeding, she was hanging up washing, they were talking.

His Reference Book — he deliberately lost it because it didn't have the right stamp.

His constant curiosity about people and what they were doing. Twisting his head off in the back seat of the car whenever I gave him a lift.

Dialogue:

Of Paulus Olifant, he says: Paulus catches snakes with his hands. You believe that? His hands. I seen him. Skaapsteker — just so . . . and in the bag. One bite and you're dead.

May

Vivid series of dreams involving guns and violence and torture and any number of incidents and images which involved other people, and myself feeling self-conscious and foolish. One seemed to suggest my inability to destroy evil in myself, another to warn against the potential to hurt what I love.

One dream of violence involved a gun. I was in Parliament and — during a lot of shooting, in the course of which two MPs were killed — I tried to assassinate the Prime Minister. I only succeeded in wounding him. I turned out to be a member of Vorster's staff. After the attempted assassination — he did not suspect my part in it — I continued in a disgusting, toadying relationship with him (almost as if I were parasitic and dependent on a powerful and hated 'father' figure). A second important relationship — I seemed to be looking after her — with a crippled woman — the State President's wife. Occasionally I spoke Afrikaans in the dream.

1. I am ineffective against what I know to be evil.
2. (because of this) I am a threat to what I love.
3. ? the reason for 1 and 2 . . . That I am still looking for the 'effective' father I never had as a child? Trying to destroy this undermining 'need'.

A powerful sense of the unconscious trying to talk . . . improvising, making a vocabulary of the externals that impinge on my life each day . . . re-assembled, loaded each night so as to convey meaning.

Then why was a knife not the central image — why repeatedly, a gun? To kill, destroy, *accidentally* with a knife is not really feasible. Guns, on the other hand, have got *triggers,* are loaded (unreleased — the dangerous potential). Also: I have got knives. I do not have a gun.

Dream: more important than 'what do they mean' is to let them really 'happen' to you . . . to live with them consciously as a decisive, formative experience.

Johnny's description of a shebeen scene with Norman: the latter drinking compulsively in a violent silence while a brash youngster

210

talked loosely about the need for militant action and courage. Norman finally erupted and, as Johnny put it, 'rubbed that kid's face in the shit'. What it amounted to was Norman just talking, talking about Robben Island: his arrival at the prison and being thrown into the corridor that led to his cell — the little window in one of the cell doors opened and the face of a well-known New Brighton man appeared there briefly, 'Norman! It is an honour to be here.' It was another six months before their paths crossed on the Island. 'It will be another six years before I see him here in New Brighton!'

The tree, a big one, which he and five others were told to uproot bare-handed. For six months, every day except weekends, they were led out to it. The six of them, their foreheads pressed against the bole, pushing, the whole day. Waking at night with a neck so sore it was impossible to find a comfortable position on his blanket on the floor. 'And let me tell you, little man, young man, with your big mouth, we uprooted it finally!'

The young man was a member of the Black People's Convention — highly critical of what seemed to him to be the prevailing spirit of acceptance and resignation in the township.

The informers that gave evidence against him in his trial in Cradock. He named them, their addresses . . . he sees them every day. They look the other way. What drives him mad is not that they were weak, and broke under pressure and told what they knew, but that they told *lies*.

Johnny went on to describe the scene at the Labour Bureau — the large cement-floored room full of work-seekers and the white man behind the counter. The men wait, reference books ready; the white man waits . . . short, aggressive little Afrikaner who, as Johnny puts it, had learnt the 'bad-half of the Xhosa language'. The telephone rings, the Afrikaner answers. Somebody wants a 'good boy'. Then a scene so awful, so degrading it is almost unbelievable: the white man stands on a chair and addresses the desperate throng '. . . Baas who wants a good boy.' The crowd goes mad. Eighty to a hundred men jumping around like monkeys waving their 'clean' books in the air. The white man drags it out; he knows a lot of the men by sight: 'You! I know you . . . sent you to a job last week. Why you back here? Unreliable kaffir, hey. Go to hell! . . . (to another one) you too old . . . (another one) . . . I told you not to come back . . .'

While the men, ravenous for work, continue to prance around like idiots, waving their reference books in an attempt to attract his attention.

He finally selects one from the forest. Again a drawn-out game . . .

211

examines the reference book to see where the man worked, how long in each job, etc. etc. Decides the man is a thief, throws the book down. While the owner is down on the floor trying to retrieve his book, the crowd goes mad again. Four or five games like this before somebody finally gets the job. White man closes the hatch, sits down and waits for the next telephone call. The crowd settles down and waits for the next chance. The man who was rolling a zol just before the pandemonium broke loose tries to scrape together the shreds of tobacco he spilt on the floor, etc. Most of them standing, leaning against the wall; a few bring along apple-boxes and sit on these.

Even the opening of the gate into the yard of the Labour Bureau at the start of the day is a game. Two or three hundred people — men, women and children — pressing against it. The white man almost opens, then closes, almost opens, then closes . . . finally throws it open and then the mad scramble to form the two queues — men one side, women the other.

The Island
1. *Space:* Restricted.
   The Island itself.
   The straight line from the prison to the quarry.
   The cell
   and — most savage of all — the solitary confinement cell.
   Locked doors.
2. *Time:* The taking away of a portion, or all of a man's life. Sentenced to so many 'years' of nothing.
   Experienced as a loss of Life, as a Living Death. You are no more.
   The grave of the Living.
3. *Meaningless Absurd Labour:* Punishment. Sisyphus.
   The loss of Freedom that imprisonment involves. What is 'Freedom'?
   Two men in a cell on the Island.
   Two men in New Brighton.
   What is the difference?

July
Shells of demolished houses and shacks at Salisbury Park — the coloured area which has been bulldozed as a result of Group Areas ruling. Roofs torn off, gaping, blind holes that were doors and windows, graffiti on the walls. In some cases all that remains is the bakoond and chimney, the house itself was made of corrugated iron

and was torn down in a few minutes by the demolition gang. The mission school likewise — all that remains is a derelict waste space with weeds already slowly obliterating the groundplan of classrooms. The unbelievable sacrilege of taking the destruction of a thing just so far (tearing off the roof and ripping out windows and doors) so that it cannot be used again. A world of ghosts — windswept and unbearably lonely. Exactly what I had tried to imagine, and understand in trying to write the Fairview play: 'A man without scenery'.

The splendid *Aloe ciliaris* I admired every time I drove past it when taking Lisa to school, is in bloom again.

Faces I shall never see again: the school principal — middle-aged, dapper little man; his pipe in his mouth. The young school teachers, trudging up the hill with their loads of exercise books. The four poor-white children who slunk out of the location every morning to go to the white school in Green Shields Park. Little Trevor, waiting for a lift from the pump station to the mission school.[5]

1974

February

Returned from London (the South African Season at the Royal Court Theatre: *Sizwe Banzi is Dead, The Island* and *Statements after an arrest under the Immorality Act*) to find Denis building on the Ashram. So, on the face of it, our days here at S'kop are numbered. One night last week, just before sleep, I realised what this meant. We are leaving S'kop. A spasm of the loneliness and pain that accompanies a conscious experience of loss.[1]

1975

January

Lisa in the back of the bakkie with Shauva and Isadora, on the way to Sardinia Bay for a late afternoon swim. I watched her in the rear-view mirror — she didn't know I was watching — and saw a Lisa I had never seen before. Eyes pensive, mouth exquisitely but quietly alive as she lived with herself — a face that subtly changed expressions in the way a landscape does its moods when broken clouds drift across the sun. An astounding maturity, a coherent centred 'self'. Why had I not seen it before?

The private self — the public self.

Daan: this, from yesterday's thinking about him: a man's world is threatened. In trying to defend it, he is finally forced to realise that it no longer has any coherence. We watch him as it falls apart and as he tries to find new or substitute dimensions in which to live. Does he realise that they aren't to be 'found' but 'created'? Our world is never a 'given' reality, but a 'made' one. To suggest in the questions addressed to yourself the dimensions of the experience you wish to create.

How does Melton's initial threat to Daan — trouble with the police — escalate into a challenge to his whole world and sense of self in it?

February

Dimetos — accepted a commission from the Edinburgh Festival to present a new work there and decided finally to take up the idea of Dimetos from the notebooks of Albert Camus.

Dimetos — a personal myth in three acts. Also Sophia, Lydia and Danilo.

February ends with the work very intact — in fact more than that: it has now become compulsive, any intrusion on my time in the shed is resented and even out of the shed a part of me lives constantly with the images already defined, the challenges to which I have not yet responded. The major challenge at this point is the dreams of Act III — still so unexplained that it is impossible for me to define my 'problem', though I have a sense that it is going to lie in finding,

215

creating 'action' in the total 'inner dimension' which they represent.

The most encouraging single fact is that I *know* I have already on paper complete and valid dramatic images, and all of them at critical definitive moments in the story. To define the Dramatic Image again: the coincidence of action and word at a point where neither alone is adequate — a coincidence marked by the 'instantaneous release' of Pound's definition.

Just as encouraging: the now constant experience that every idea creates resonances, consequences, both backward and forward in terms of the whole.

March

Dimetos — Act III: two levels, Reality and the Dream, Conscious and Sub-conscious. Dimetos and Sophia many years later. A sense that their lives have been arrested. Two things then happen. Some animal (dead) is washed up on to the rock near their isolated cottage beside the sea. The same night Dimetos has a dream . . .

The external, objective reality: Dimetos and Sophia many years after Lydia's suicide. They left the village after her death for an even more remote area and now live in a little house beside the sea — the only other human beings are occasional fishermen and even with these they avoid all contact. A sense of their lives having been 'arrested' — both of them in a cul-de-sac — of a past, too heavy and oppressive to allow for a future — even the present is a seemingly thin and transparent reality.

Dimetos has become a solitary scavenger of bones, shells, etc. left by the tides. Sophia lives with the past. Both are guilty.

Then one day some sort of animal, dead, is washed up on an inaccessible rock very near their house. It starts to decay and the prevailing south-westerly wind carries the stench into the house. Dimetos tries, without success, to reach the rock. The stench gets worse and at the same time aberrant elements begin to inform Dimetos's behaviour — so much so that even Sophia eventually registers them.

At this point Danilo suddenly appears. He and Dimetos confront each other over the hopeless tangle of motives and actions that led to Lydia's suicide.

Danilo leaves.

For Sophia the stench from the decomposing carcase and Dimetos's behaviour — he is frightened of sleep and his dreams, he is obviously going mad — become intolerable.

She leaves.

Dimetos is left mad and alone.

216

Finally Death commissions his hands in the way that Life did. Newton's Laws: Gravity = Love.

$$\text{Motion} = \text{Karma}$$

— and so splendid for being passionless, cold as stone.

'Every particle of matter in the universe attracts every other particle'.

'Every action produces an equal and opposite re-action . . .'

September

In what lies ahead for Dimetos — to divorce myself from the splendid and stark visual images of what we did in Edinburgh.[1] Go into the word.

Impossible at this moment to assess how far I have travelled along the road to what will be the final work. Do not need well-meaning friends to tell me about the obvious flaws — the result of haste, panic and a lack of clarity in the 'vision'. Was, and still am, provoked and bewildered by the positive and 'total' responses of strangers to so obviously still flawed and unfinished a work.

My faith in the complex of central images is totally intact.

Script, reflecting the stage *Dimetos* reached in Edinburgh, posted off to Paul Scofield yesterday. Four days fishing and then to work on the Eugène Marais film which Ross[2] is confident will happen as scheduled.

October

Stones and secrets. Because you can pick them up, hold them, you think they are accessible, are 'public' . . . they are the most secretive of things . . . their submissiveness is the most singular act of defiance in all of Creation.

The therapy of manual labour — reintegration of head and hands. A quiet time — the garden, fishing, reading and easy silences at this table. Letting Dimetos drop down, down, down: turning slowly to the Marais film.

Last night a dream in which laughter — mine — was the dominant element. I was watching something that seemed a combination of film and actual event and which involved exaggerating current fashions to the point of total absurdity. I have never laughed so much in all my life. First time I can remember laughing in a dream.

Call from Oscar Lewenstein in London to tell me that Paul Sco-

217

field had come up with a very positive response to *Dimetos*. Oscar (who will produce) read me the letter from Scofield: '... disturbed, moved and bewildered by the script ... I can't imagine what the rewriting on Athol Fugard's side could involve ...'

November
Marais's *Soul of the White Ant:* E.M. talking to Doorsie.
　His *Soul of the Ape:* E.M. talking to Visser.[3]
　Title of the film — *The Guest.* Sub-title — *An episode in the life of Eugène Nielen Marais.*

December
The Marais film, for the time being at least, shelved. Ross has again been unable to raise the money here in South Africa. Free now to concentrate on *Dimetos.*

1976

February

Dimetos: rough draft of reworked Act I posted off to Oscar. Feel certain the play is now finally on its way to being the one I wanted to write. My attempts before to work creatively, as a writer, with the actors, was a bad mistake and resulted in my getting lost and losing all faith in my vision. Over the past few months I've rediscovered it and moved towards its statement on paper.

Danilo is stronger and darker. Lydia more provocative and Sophia, more exposed.

In every sense a more 'accessible' experience than we had on the stage at Edinburgh. So much of what I myself didn't understand with my first attempts, now clear. Above all though, the emergence of pain and desperation as the dominant shaping force.

Something that helped enormously was to give Dimetos two specific settings in my imagination. Act I — New Bethesda[1] and Act II — Gaukamma Beach,[2] I also stopped thinking about a distant past, but again without letting any specifics creep onto the page. The play now reads (and could be so staged) as either present or past. I must also not forget my enormous debt to Roszak's *Where the Wasteland Ends,* and how that book helped me understand what I was trying to say. The strange coincidence of his Blake-Newton juxtaposition.

The sense of each character having a specific energy, and that the writing really consisted of plotting the patterns of the energy field and their charges, as they encountered each other. Also the lack of any 'play' in what we did on the stage at Edinburgh = Brecht's 'ease'.

The only truth any man can tell is his own. In all my reworking, the original complex of central images retained their authority and power.

A man must have a Secret, and as a result of that, an Act which takes others by surprise.

A night four days from the solstice: windless, still; nearly full moon; dogs barking . . . crickets and in the distance a Dikkop whistling. The night no more than a brief interlude between sunset and sunrise, uneasy sleep. (For Dimetos or Sophia?)

Dimetos — alienation. Loss of transcendence.

219

A human dilemma, but specifically that of man in the urban-indus-
trial world of the West, a result of 'single vision', of a technology and
science that alienated man from a sacramental relationship to the
world around and within him . . . a dilemma as unique to man in the
twentieth century as is the artificial environment created by his
science and technology.

Newton – 1662-1727. Discovered law of gravity in his 23-24th
years. 'We are not the first people in history to suffer the psychic
corrosion of alienation'. Roszak.[3]

Dimetos and Lydia in scene VIII – a sense on Lydia's side that there
is a third, a stranger, present, but whenever she looks for him all she
finds is her uncle's smiling face.

Lydia and Dimetos and their response to the horse galloping away
after its rescue from the well into which it had fallen. For Lydia a
transcendant symbol, a vision of freedom; for Dimetos, 'a stupid
animal'. Dimetos's dilemma, spiritual illness, defined in this – a
world of 'dense' 'things'.

Aquinas – 'Man has both reason and hands.'

Dimetos – 'Caring . . . the alchemist's stone. The heart.'

Head, hands and heart.

The remarkable coincidence that the very laws (Newtonian physics)
which have led to man's alienation in the twentieth century, can
also be read as the spiritual laws (Karma, Love) that can lead him
back to wholeness.

Dimetos – a political play in the sense that Roszak's *Where the
Wasteland Ends* is a political book.

London – prior to opening in Nottingham:

First day of rehearsals – A Chinese proverb from Paul: If a man
puts his hand to a machine, let him be careful that his heart does not
become one.

Y.'s sense that the only one of the four of them who had any sense
of the pain in store for all, was Celia.[4]

Second day – Actors on their legs.

Strong sense that I must think along the lines of the simple and
unified staging I had at Edinburgh. One space – the stage, and each
scene and the actors involved to possess and claim it with immediate
and total authority.

June
Back from London and *Dimetos* — the flight from Johannesburg to
P.E. The Karroo below. Reflections of the sun in the farm dams
and vleis — dull and muddy pockets of water turned into gold, silver
and pewter for a few seconds.

So, Dimetos. Now Marais.

Pretoria, and a week with Ross finalising our script for *The Guest.*
Background to our work — the horror of the Soweto Riots.

Driving back to Pretoria at night through a landscape of violence
and destruction — veld fires in every direction. Newspaper posters
and headlines as violent as the acts they were reporting — photographs more terrible than those that came out of Sharpeville. Might
not have been possible to work at all were it not for Marais's pain
and ultimately the summing up and transcendence of that, and what
was happening in the townships, in his *Lied van Suid Afrika.*[5]

September
Home after seven weeks in Pretoria and completion of the principal
filming of *The Guest.* An important experience and possibly the
most demanding and challenging role I have ever attempted. I have
returned with a love and understanding of that little portion of the
Highveld where we worked, that will stay with me for the rest of my
life. Oh God — South Africa! Inside me silence and stillness — like
that dormant, waiting, wide landscape, harbouring its small and secret life.

Hard to believe my life is my own again. Not a single commitment.

A terrible yearning to 'tell a story' once more — to set out, discover
and live in an imagined world, the way I did with *Blood Knot, Boesman and Lena.* Daan?

Visit from Barney — joyous and enriching. I said nothing more than
that I wanted to start writing again but he guessed that Daan was my
subject. Initially I felt jealous and angry that my secret had been discovered, but now, indifferent. It either is or isn't my appointment.
But such a strong, deep, stirring sense that it is. Notes about the veldfires at S'kop suggest the violent, elemental setting that could make
Daan my next appointment, the 'story' I want to tell.

Rain this spring such as I cannot remember in the time since our first
move to S'kop ten years ago. The bush unbelievably green, trees

221

flourishing and the tanks brimful. We should get through this summer without buying water.

Just as I try to steady myself and return to what I think is the centre of my life, assaults from outside — an appeal from the Royal Court Theatre to John and Winston to return with *Sizwe*. An 'assault' only because I wondered about the return of *Sizwe* with which we are all three now very tired — and the thought that maybe this chance should be grabbed to make something new. Every instinct however tells me that those days of 'making' are past. They hijacked my life and energies for three years. I won't let that happen again. That sort of 'making' would not in the slightest way alleviate the yearning to tell a story which still possesses me.

If I can't say 'No' now, I will never. And I need to.

On a sudden impulse I shouldered a rod and spent the morning in the Maitland surf. A perfect three hours — a light South-Wester, warm sun. Returned with the sense of a moment of peace, solitude and the waiting that is really my reason for fishing. No-one, nothing. One sweet and apparently barren cast after another. Virgin sand, black rocks and the careless energy of the sea — and, waiting for its return at the high water-mark, its artifacts — smooth, beautiful, 'nearly perfect', beach-rolled stones.

Realised that here on the Ashram a 'work or sin' morality has been slowly taking over my life. My Calvinism! It is with great difficulty that I hand myself over to simple sensual pleasure. Yes. That is the essence of my few hours on that rock this morning. Work was minimal — baiting the hook, casting — after which I held out my hands and waited. The emptiness I returned with is now more splendid than the expectations that had my heart racing when I positioned myself for my first cast.

Not quite alone — the silhouette of another fisherman on the rocks, about a mile away at the end of a gently curving little bay, and — more immediately — the pair I passed on the way to my rock. Our exchange: 'What is the tide?' 'Just on low water.' A coloured man about my age and, I suppose, his son, a boy of about ten. A wild, almost destitute aspect to the man, though his tackle was by any standards reasonable. The boy was silent and shy. Once again, either in terms of them or myself, I am acutely aware of the innocence which comes with that space and silence.

Rich and affirmative dream-life these past few weeks since completion of the Marais film. Lived with, dreams have an alchemic quality of turning life into an adventure — the most prosaic details of an experience become very mysterious.

My last thought at this table last night: *Dimetos* is not yet completed.

A letter from Fatima.[6] Desperately affirmative tone. It is very difficult writing back to her — so much I want to say and would like to talk about but if I did the letter might not reach her. Have torn up one attempt already because in my effort to avoid the prison censorship I ended up with pretentious and incoherent trivialities.

One paragraph in her letter however suggests the possibility of a dialogue between us that might get past the censors. Fatima has heard about the Marais film and with characteristic honesty asks how, after plays like *Sizwe* and *The Island,* I could involve myself in a film like that. She sees it as being totally without political commitment and therefore valueless in terms of the urgent and violent realities of our time.

What can I say in reply?

The old dilemma — can there be an action (the telling of a story) which, if informed with love and an attempt at the truth, is without significant consequences? (Accepting now finally that writing is a form of action.) Is the story of one man's hell — generated as it was mostly in the case of Marais by factors within himself, in the year 1926, on a remote farm in the Transvaal — of no significance today in South Africa with the Soweto uprising only a few months behind us?

The Marais poem — *Die Lied van Suid Afrika* — with which we end the film:

> She says: I claim as my sacred right
> The fruit of endless pain.

What writer today has answered the blind patriotism of our existing national anthem with a more withering and final recognition of the truth.

Two categories of action for the writer?
1. The one which will produce immediate returns (political pamphlet).
2. The long-term investment (story telling).

Possibly an even more important question: Does an action run out of consequences?

Having difficulty in finding a significant level of commitment to Daan and the complex of images associated with his name.

Daan: garrulous and innocent by turns. One moment argumentative, the next awed and naive acceptance.

Am I being impatient with him? He is, after all, like Dimetos and Marais, a man finally alone — and just as Dimetos had his Danilo, Daan has got Melton to reckon with.

Silences very rich. Even music an intrusion. The daily act of homage remains water for the birds and plants, all the more significant a ritual as we settle down for our summer drought. This pen — one of Lisa's discards — invites me to think and write differently from the one I normally use. A strident assertive nib where the other is self-effacing.

Frogs very loud now — the remote possibility of rain from the west.

The shed — the two dogs on the floor at night. Shauva dreams constantly whereas I've never yet seen Isadora do so. A dog without dreams.

For Daan, from Tomas Tronströmer:[7] 'Two truths draw nearer each other. One comes from inside, one comes from outside, and where they meet we have a chance to see ourselves.'

Daan's definitive 'act'? Which raises the question of his biography — what lies behind him? What angers — like Melton's — what failures . . . if any? How close had he already come to 'seeing himself'. What had taught him how to live as we find him?

Today's planting — *Aloe arborescens*. I'll never forget the one in Salisbury Park, its magnificent presence in winter, in full bloom; and the fire-blackened hearths and chimneys of demolished houses.

A real sense of drought again — the holes for the Aloes were dug in bone-dry sand. God! It would be so marvellous if they rooted.

The wind has turned. A moderate easterly all day, calm sunset and twilight and then, about half-an-hour ago, the westerly moved in. For me it remains a spine-tingling mystery how that wind brings with it a world so uniquely its own — soft, moist . . . yes! above all else, the possibility of Rain. How can I keep any company other than *Daan*.

In among all the wind rattlings and buffetings at the door, just occasionally a very clear and simple double knock. I answer: Come in. So far nothing.

1977

January

London — with John and Winston. Behind us a week of quiet rehearsals for the revival of *Sizwe* at the Royal Court. Came over with thoughts and ideas for the play so that it would catch up with the history of the past two or three years and, more immediately, the six months since the Soweto uprising last June. This has not happened — and not for want of any agonising or self-questioning on our side. The play has a life, now, of its own. If anything, the experience has been worth it just to discover that. I've always rated *Sizwe* fairly low, a play which walked the tightrope between poetry and propaganda. Maybe I'm wrong.

That first amble through the text on a bare Royal Court stage was very moving. Its structure and style remain clever — its essential honesty and humility still radiant — and, miraculously, John and Winston hand themselves over to it, are taken over by it, with the same spontaneity of four years ago. I am as confident of the integrity and honesty of its 'witness' now as I was then and, equivalently, am just as sustained by it.

The Ashram — fifth day back home. Strong and unsettling easterly today.

Digging a small dam with Tembile. Bought another spade which Mandla is using to manure our vegetable patch.[1]

Simple project: the hole. Tembile and myself. The beginnings of an honesty (all but withered in my life) — share the labour of another person.

Bought a load of nearly useless manure today. 'Useless' in Mandla's opinion — he crumbled it between his fingers, smelt it . . . all but ate it . . . then: 'Not very good, baas.' We have that in common: we both want to grow good vegetables. Food. The main problem is water . . . and my attempt to solve that is a small reservoir at the end of our drive which slopes gently along its entire length and which could be a marvellous catchment area — around 54 000 litres.

After one day's digging Tembile has had nothing to cope with except sand. Hope to God we don't hit rock.

Still digging with Tembile. Two days in a row I've spent a couple of hours in the hole with a spade and wheelbarrow. Realised my work rhythm was a macabre re-enactment of the opening of *The Island.*

Dry! My God! I understand now why the trees wilt. Three feet down and not a vestige of moisture. At the best of times the soil is very poor; now it is sand. You could put it into hour-glasses.

February

Behind us the driest January since records were first kept in 1926. Now desperately dry in the garden and water-tanks critically low. Work on the little dam proceeds: with any luck we should start cementing bottom and sides towards the middle of next week.

After a week of really hot and hard weather, the wind turned late this afternoon and the softest of drizzles is now falling — barely audible as a murmur from the metal ceiling of this room. Have a need to hear Mozart's 'Requiem' tonight, but the thought that I might miss even a second of real rain, the reality of a few gallons of water in the tanks, is too much. I'll wait.

Just had my ear pressed against the warm asbestos of the tank that collects water from the garage roof. Because it is only a drizzle, only a few drops at a time are finding their way along the gutter and into the tank — but such a sound. Echoed by all the space of the empty tank, those individual drops of water were a 'trip' into the sound of water. So deliberate! So measured. Truly a sound to spell out the mystery we try to encompass with four letters: Life.

One night when I had paused between sentences, a small insect crawled onto the vast expanse of white paper and wandered about. An impulse made me reach for my watchmaker's eye-glass; I slipped it into one eye and zoomed in on the little gogga . . . I forget the word it was crawling over but I will never forget the astonishment, the mystery, the awe of that encounter. It was no bigger than a match-head, but under the eye-glass I saw a symmetry, a complexity that took my breath away. For the rest of my life it will leave me stumbling over cobwebs as if they had been made of fencing wire.

And now as a result one of the special pleasures at this table at night — one like this; warm, sultry, recent rain and an unending stream of life from the darkness through the open window and to my light — is to put on my watchmaker's eye-glass and zoom in on a seeming fragment of life which turns out to be as awesome and complete as the night-sky above Bethesda.

227

29 mm of rain last night. Started again this morning and has been coming down light but steady ever since. All of 15 mm in the gauge already and no sign of a let-up tonight. Asbestos tank overflowing and the underground tank three-quarters full.

March

Tembile sentenced to fifteen months' imprisonment for stabbing a man in a fight about two months ago. We all thought there would be an option of a fine and had marshalled our resources to cope with that. Instead . . . I don't know anything about the actual incident though I did see the man Tembile had stabbed when the police came around to arrest him. The knife-wounds were very bad — four in all — and about six stitches in each.

So Gladys with her two children, the youngest a three-month-old baby, is without a husband and bread-winner for the next year.

Tembile and I virtually completed the little dam yesterday. His last few hours on the job, working alone, were so characteristic and so beautiful in the way he cared about what he was doing.

A good man.

April

For the second time, a dream of remarkable detail and precision involving a clock. (The first warned me of my failure with 'Statements' the first time I attempted to realise that idea.)

Last night's dream had the same 'feel' to it — a diagnosis of self by self. And again involved the making of a clock; but 'clock' almost belittles the scope of what was really involved. Time as such was only the centre-piece of a very complex structure — the writer's dream of a perfect piece of furniture: it had drawers, folding tables — everything. The significant element in this dream is that the 'clock' didn't involve simply the assembly of a set of pieces, the kit was of unbelievable complexity: screws by the hundred, nuts, bolts, shelving, pendulum. One dominant thought or realisation: 'It is going to take years.'

Now that I think back on it, another thought: my 'making' of the clock was a second-best; it would only be a mechanical model of the organic reality . . . a reality not 'made' in the sense that mine would be. 'Real time' as opposed to 'made time'. And: my assembly of the clock, the time I needed to do it, was threatened by an environment of social unrest. I might be forced to pack it all away before I'd even properly started.

All through the dream there were objects of great beauty — mostly of glass — beauty and hope were in fact the dominant modes of the experience.

Chasing each other at this table tonight are images for *Daan*. God! how can I not keep my appointment with that man.

Daan and a garden rake. Melton. Paulus Olifant.

My inability so far to resolve, and so write, Daan's story is quite simply a reflection of my confusion as to where to go, how to end.

Melton, in a flash, so real! So frightened but, equivalently, so desperate that the impossible, the definitive act is in his hands.

My dialogue with Daan — two questions: What is your truth? What is mine?

Talking to monkeys that aren't there in trees that aren't there is not going to satisfy me any more.[2]

May

These past months I have been trying to live through one of the most intensely experienced crises of my life. If Sheila and Lisa were to read that sentence they would stare at me in amazement, so effective has been the disguise of my inner agony, my death in life. As I write this I still see no light. But maybe tomorrow . . . Who knows.

The 'crisis' is, quite simply, the total extinction of my creativity. Without it I find living a pain I can only describe as intolerable. I have feared for my sanity.

November

Suddenly and inexplicably the story of Piet, Gladys and Steve (who like others, suspects Piet of being an informer and who in fact if he is an informer, is his victim) has come back to me. The complex of images and desperation which provide the energy for the piece, are intact. Those early attempts aborted because then I saw Piet at the centre of my story. Now I see that it is Gladys's play. Piet's monolithic goodness, the enormous assault made on it by him having been sent to Coventry by the comrades; the further assault of his having witnessed his wife's breakdown: then the yet further assault on his important friendship with Steve — despite all those assaults — it is not enough to sustain a piece. There are no ambiguities in Piet's experience, none of the dark ambiguities which I think make an energising central image in a play in the sense that Boesman has enormous ambiguities — he is unquestionably at one level the villain, but at the end he exposes a sense of self-disgust when he spills out his experience of himself and their life. This creates a necessarily ambigu-

229

ous image.

Now I see that Gladys has those dark ambiguities — her whole relationship to South Africa. More pertinently and succinctly — Piet and Steve are victims of a system, of a social and political order which they have tried to resist, but they are victims of something man-made, whereas Gladys is God's victim.

Notes

1960

1   Tsotsis — township hoodlums. For all further South African slang and Afrikaans words, see Glossary, p. 238.

2   These notes, made during the course of the voyage, and several that follow, made when back in South Africa, were the basis of a novel, *Tsotsi*, that was not published until 1980.

3   Sophiatown was a black suburb of Johannesburg from which the inhabitants were forcibly removed to make way for a new white suburb.

4   Glenda — Fugard's sister.

1961

1   *The Soul of the White Ant* by Eugène Marais was an important book in Fugard's life and in 1976 he made a film about Marais, *The Guest*, in which he himself played the part of Marais.

2   Dr M. — Sheila Fugard's father, Dr Meiring.

3   Oupa — Sheila Fugard's grandfather.

4   'I have buried three wives' — Sheila's grandfather had two wives and one companion.

5   Ossewa Brandwag — a pro-Nazi society of Afrikaners. His father, a leader of the society, had been imprisoned during World War II.

6   Nee, Oom, ons speel nie soo nie — No, Uncle, we don't play that way.

7   S.A.C.P.O. — South African Coloured People's Organisation.

8   In 1982 Fugard's play *Master Harold . . . and the Boys* was first staged at Yale and in New York. The principal character in the play was based on Sam Semela.

9   The South African system restricting what jobs Africans may do.

10   My voete . . . my bors! — My feet . . . my chest!

11   Gee . . . dan gee ek — Give threepence for a drink master. And if I had it, I gave it.

12   South Africa was about to become a Republic: a white Boer Republic in the eyes of the Africans, and, in protest, nationwide stay-at-home strikes were planned for the end of May, under the leadership of Nelson Mandela.

13   Hy is klein — He is small.

1962

1   The boarding-house where Fugard, his wife and child were staying while he directed and acted in the first production of *The Blood Knot*.

2   Zakes Mokae: Zach in the production.

3   Dorkay House — a factory building in Johannesburg where the African Music and Drama School was based, and where the first production of *The Blood Knot* took place in the Rehearsal Room.

4   Strachan, an artist, was awaiting trial, charged with sabotage.

5   Jack — former member of the outlawed African National Congress; Mbeki — representative of a radical newspaper in Port Elizabeth, later one of the accused in the Rivonia Trial.

6   The play, then called *The Silk Worms*, became *People are Living There*.

7   Both men had been found not guilty in their trial.

8   *Contact* — a liberal journal.

9   *Sponono* was an adaptation of a short story by Alan Paton. The musical later went to New York.

10   Ismail Meer, a lawyer, had been one of the leaders of the Indian passive resistance of 1946 and one of the accused in the Treason Trial of 1956-61; since then he had been banned from political activity. Fatima Meer was a lecturer in Sociology at Natal University.

11   They became the characters in the TV/Film script: *The Occupation*.

1963

1   Lionel Abrahams was then the editor of *The Purple Renoster*, a S.A. literary magazine.

2   Kirkwood — the home of Sheila's father, Dr. Meiring.

3   Ek praat . . . is — I speak before I'm a corpse.

4   Following the outbreaks of sabotage in 1961, that continued into 1962, many blacks had been arrested and brought to trial, as well as a handful of white students.

5   Union Artists — a black theatre organisation in Johannesburg.

6   Anders . . . weghardloop — Otherwise, old brother, I fart so much that I want to run away from myself.

7   As die man . . . dat dit bars . . . Hulle is ook maar mens — As the husband goes out the front door to work, then the neighbour creeps in by the back door to fuck the wife. Even the young daughters, man — sixteen-year-olds — they whore till they burst . . . They're only human.

8   rooi-kombers kaffirs . . . Môre Baas — . . . red blanket kaffirs (Xhosa). Genuine kaffirs. There in the Transkei when you're walking along the pavement, they get out of your way, raise their hats and say: Morning, Boss.

9   Hy sê . . . hand vol sand — He was always saying 'Africa!' God! One day I was the hell in. He said 'Africa!' again! I grabbed a handful of sand.

10   Alwyn heuning — aloe honey; Not 'n fok — not a fuck.

11   Die mens . . . poephol — People are clever — making assholes in mountains like that.

12   Daar's . . . dorp — There's a whore in every village.

13   Four years later *The Blood Knot* was filmed by BBC TV and the director, Robin Midgley, encouraged Fugard to complete *Mille Miglia*, which was done as a play on BBC TV in 1968. It was to be five years before *People Are Living There* was produced, and then in Glasgow, directed by Robin Midgley.

14   Not until 1969 was a Milly found in South Africa: Yvonne Bryceland.

15   Leon Gluckman, first producer of *The Blood Knot*, who played an important part in the emergence of black theatre with such productions as *King Kong* and *Emperor Jones*.

16   *Mille Miglia* was later written —commissioned by the BBC.

17 Barend — a character in *The Occupation.*

18 Dennis Brutus — a coloured schoolmaster and poet who had organised a committee against apartheid in sport, and been banned; then he had been
arrested for breaking his ban by attending a committee meeting, after which
he had managed to escape to Swaziland.

19 Strandlopers were one of the aboriginal Khoisan peoples of southern Africa;
they were flint-makers who lived by gathering shellfish.

1964

1 Govan Mbeki was one of the accused in the Rivonia Trial of 1964, and is
now serving a term of life imprisonment on Robben Island.

2 Pofadder . . . getrap — Puff-adder — Yes — Dangerous — What if somebody
had trodden on it!'

3 Directed by John Berry, with James Earl Jones and J.D. Cannon. Jones
went on to create the definitive American performances in Fugard plays:
as Boesman, in *Boesman and Lena,* and Steve in *A Lesson from Aloes.*

4 Kenneth Tynan had been very critical of the play in London.

5 Schoenmakerskop — a move from his mother's flat in Bird Street to a
cottage at 'shoemaker's head': in a letter he described it: '. . . seven miles
along the coast from P.E. The sea is at our doorstep, there is enough land
and need for the highly moral activity of tree planting and the beginning of
a vegetable patch to keep us in lettuce, carrots and spinach. I've never
realised fully how much of an Afrikaner I really am, until this moment
when I kicked off my shoes and stood barefoot on the earth. I keep looking
at my toes to see if roots haven't appeared.'

6 90 day detainees: Under the 90 day detention law, detainees could be held
incommunicado for 90 days, renewable for extended periods, while under-
going interrogation.

7 After difficulties in casting, Schneider abandoned the play, which had to
wait another 3 years before it was produced in Glasgow, by Robin Midgley.

1965

1 Congress of Democrats — an organisation of whites allied to the African
National Congress.

2 Junior Certificate, Standard 6 — (usually) third and first years of high
school.

3 Norman Ntshinga, one of the Serpent Players, was accused of furthering the
aims of the banned African National Congress. His wife, May Magada, was
also in Serpent Players. Between 1963 and 1966 hundreds of men and
women in the Eastern Cape were arrested, tried and sentenced to imprisonment for supporting the outlawed African National Congress or Pan-African
Congress.

4 Barney Simon, a close personal friend of Fugard's, and collaborator in
theatre, directed the play. Fugard was playing Johnny.

5 Vergewe my, pappie — Forgive me, Daddy.

6 The Government had recently legislated for segregated audiences.

1966

1   Fugard had been invited to London by Robert Loder (who had been one of the important backers of his work in the Rehearsal Room, Dorkay House) and Denis Duerdan.
2   Fugard directed the company in Soyinka's play and also directed and acted in *The Blood Knot*, with Zakes Mokae. Despite the initial success, financially it proved impossible to sustain the company.
3   Hy't 'n kaffer doodgery — He ran down and killed a kaffir.
4   The play was eventually written in 1978 — *A Lesson from Aloes* — with three characters; Piet and Gladys Bezuidenhout, and Steve Daniels.
5   Welcome Duru (who had been arrested on the day of the Serpent Players' first performance of *The Caucasian Chalk Circle*, in which he was to play the lead, Azdak) had served three years' hard labour on Robben Island.
6   Nog 'n . . . vrot mens — Another rotten old shack for the rotten people.

1967

1   PACT — Performing Arts Council of the Transvaal.
2   Productions cost around R50.
3   *Antigone* — Fugard had been refused a permit to enter New Brighton for the dress rehearsal and Serpent Players had been refused permission to perform before whites in P.E.
4   Not mentioned in the Notebooks was the South African authorities' withdrawal of Fugard's passport in June. In letters he wrote: 'Apart from a small initial shock when they called around for my passport we are none the worse for the experience. We'll no doubt feel the pinch later — when a chance comes my way and we can't get out . . .' And, a few weeks later: 'I have been very moved by the protests on my behalf.'
5   In the *Evening Post* it was reported that parents would break the law and go to jail if necessary, rather than allow their children to continue to go to school with the Dickson children. Yet some admitted they had never known or seen the Dickson family.
6   My God . . . Kyk net — My God, come and look! The little ones. Dear Lord! Just look.
7   Harold Strachan, after his term in prison, had given facts about prison conditions to the *Rand Daily Mail;* as a result he was sentenced to a further term of imprisonment and the editor and journalist working on the articles were brought to trial and eventually fined.
8   Bioscope — movies.

1968

1   Barney Simon and Ian Bernhardt of Union Artists.
2   Fugard had been auditioning actresses for Milly in *People* and had failed to find anyone suitable. Barney Simon persuaded him to go to Cape Town and see Yvonne Bryceland whom Fugard remembered vaguely from a past production and, on meeting her, he knew she was 'Milly'. The 'Lena' mentioned here is not from *Boesman and Lena* but the *Fairview* play, which he later abandoned.

234

3   Fairview — A man without scenery: Fugard had spent months on this which was now finally abandoned.
4   Loop skool — go to school.
    Die lewe . . . iets anders — Life is hard, isn't it, Daan! Lord, sir, each day there's something else . . .
5   Daan would become one of the three characters in the movie, *Marigolds in August*, written ten years later.
6   Luister . . . daai ding — Listen to me, boy. The Government's going to put a stop to that.
7   Notes 2 and 3 would become part of Kani's opening monologue in *Sizwe Banzi is Dead*.
8   From 'Variations done for Gerald van de Wiele' in *The Distances* by Charles Olson (Grove Press, 1960).
9   This is an extract from a letter. The matter was not referred to in the notebooks. Helen Suzman is a Progressive Federal Party M.P.
10 Hospital for blacks in Port Elizabeth.

1969

1   Baas . . . brood kry? — Boss, could I have a piece of bread?
2   Baas kan kyk . . . onderrok — Boss can look . . . I haven't even got a pair of pants or a petticoat.
3   Hotnots, baas . . . bier — Hottentots, boss. Perhaps they thought it was beer.
4   Yvonne Bryceland, who was to play Lena.

1970

1   '. . . impossible to get the specifics onto a stage . . . ' — because of the laws concerning prisons, and also censorship.
2   *Notes for Advocate Strickland* and *Man Without Scenery:* these did not become plays.
3   Earlier in the year, Fugard and Yvonne Bryceland had made a fifteen week tour with this play and *People are Living There* but had not gone to Durban because no performances had been arranged for blacks. During the tour, *Boesman and Lena* had played for two weeks in townships. Meanwhile, *No-Good Friday* was being revived by the Rehearsal Room in Johannesburg, and *Nongogo* by Serpent Players. Now a private and therefore non-segregated performance of *Boesman and Lena* was to be done in Durban.
4   *Boesman and Lena* had first been performed in Grahamstown and Fugard had written of Yvonne Bryceland's Lena that her performance was 'awesome in its range and authenticity, in the blunted bewilderment which she used as the dominant tone.' At this time in mid-1970 there were renewed attempts to get his passport returned for him to advise Berry on the production in New York. The request was again refused.
5   These notes were made during a week in September and again early in December. John Harris had been a member of the 'African Resistance Movement' which consisted mainly of young white liberals. In protest against apartheid, he had placed a bomb in the station concourse; an old woman had been killed and a child maimed; he was hanged.
6   Though the production was not evolved until early 1971, these notes on *Orestes* are appropriate here.

1971

1   Fugard had been invited to direct *Boesman and Lena* at the Royal Court Theatre in London, with Yvonne Bryceland and Zakes Mokae. Repeated protests in Britain and the U.S., as well as in South Africa, succeeded, and he was granted a passport.
2   Astbury and his wife, Yvonne Bryceland, had discussed with Fugard their intention of opening an alternative theatre in Cape Town which would be multiracial. It was called The Space and the opening production was the first version of *Statements*.

1972

1   Blankes, Nie-Blankes — Whites, Non-Whites.
2   After about a week that idea aborted and the next idea they took on led to *Sizwe Banzi is Dead*.

1973

1   Ons geslag is verkeerd — Our race is wrong / a mistake.
2   There's a clock/bell that tells the truth . . .
3   Melton — an illegal squatter on land Fugard had bought at Sardinia Bay, who provided the basis for a character in *Marigolds in August*.
4   Rooi Hel — Red Hell, the prison in P.E., originally 'royal'.
5   Inserted under August in the notebooks is a flyer/leaflet announcing performances of *Sizwe Banzi is Dead* in St. Stephen's Hall, New Brighton, on August 23 and 24. '*Sizwe Banzi* is going to London! Don't miss your chance to see the play that has taken South Africa by storm with John Kani and Winston Ntshona. Directed by Athol Fugard.'

1974

1   The Fugards had already named the piece of land in the bush 'The Ashram' and Denis Scarr, fishing friend, had designed the house.

1975

1   After preliminary performances in The Space in Cape Town and also in Johannesburg, the production was taken to the Edinburgh Festival.
2   Ross Devenish, who had directed the movie of *Boesman and Lena*.
     Fugard and Devenish had long wanted to make a film about the Afrikaner poet and naturalist, Eugène Marais, but the project had been delayed for lack of funds.
3   Doorsie — a character in *The Guest;* Dr A. G. Visser — Marais's friend, also a poet.

1976

1   Bethesda — a remote village in the Karroo where the Fugards have a small house.
2   Gaukamma Beach — a desolate stretch of beach near Mossel Bay.

3   Roszak, *Where the Wasteland Ends* p. 418.
4   The cast: Paul Scofield, Yvonne Bryceland, Ben Kingsley and Celia Quick.
5   *Lied van Suid Afrika* — Marais's poem 'Song of South Africa'.
6   Fatima Meer — lecturer in Sociology at Natal University and one of the leaders of the Black Women's Federation, who was among those detained after the Soweto uprising.
7   Tomas Tronströmer — a Norwegian poet.

1977

1   Mandla Neni looks after the Ashram land; Tembile is his friend.
2   Soon after this Fugard wrote the film script *Marigolds in August*, with Daan, Paulus Olifant and Melton the three main characters.

Glossary

agterryer	mounted attendant, henchman
bakkie	small light truck or van with open back
bakoond	brick oven
bloubek	'blue-mouth' — vulgar term of abuse
braaivleis	barbecue
broer	brother
bywoner	share-cropper, squatter
dagga	cannabis, marijuana
doek	head scarf
gogga	insect
Here	Lord
kafferboetie	abusive term for white person considered to be a negrophile, 'nigger lover'
koppie	hillock
lappie	rag or cloth
loodgieter	plumber
moer	murder, beat up
oom	uncle
pruim twak	a 'chew' of tobacco
skaapsteker	mildly poisonous snake of genus *Psammophylax*
skollie	coloured street hoodlum
smous	itinerant pedlar
suster	sister
swartgat	'black-arse'
tsotsi	township hoodlum, thug, gangster
voetsak/voetsek	rough demand to push off, go away
zol	hand-rolled cigarette